LETTERS ON SLAVERY

FROM THE

OLD WORLD:

WRITTEN DURING THE CANVASS FOR THE PRESIDENCY OF THE UNITED STATES IN 1860.

TO WHICH ARE ADDED

A LETTER TO LORD BROUGHAM

ON THE JOHN BROWN RAID;

AND

A BRIEF REFERENCE TO THE RESULT OF THE PRESIDENTIAL CONTEST, AND ITS CONSEQUENCES.

BY JAMES WILLIAMS,

LATE UNITED STATES MINISTER TO TURKEY.

Nashville, Tenn.:
SOUTHERN METHODIST PUBLISHING HOUSE.
1861.

CONTENTS.

Preface.. Page vii

LETTER I.

Introduction—Slavery established in North America by Great Britain —Slavery denounced by England only after the American Revolution—The New Republics obliged to adopt the existing Institution —Causes of Antagonism between the White and Black Races—M. De Tocqueville on Slavery in America..........................Page 9

LETTER II.

Reasons why Slavery could not be Abolished, and proofs that it should not have been Abolished—Emancipation would make the condition of the Slaves worse—The Abolitionists cannot accomplish their purposes even with the assent of the Slaveholders—Slavery was abolished in the North by selling the Slaves to the South 30

LETTER III.

Classification of the Adversaries of Slavery in the Southern States—The London Times on the causes of English Opposition to Slavery —What position would England occupy towards the Belligerents, if the Republican party should attempt to carry its measures into effect? —Would the South hesitate about defending herself to the last extremity?.. 44

LETTER IV.

Opposition to abstract Slavery resolved into opposition to Slavery in America, without considering the circumstances of its existence—Slavery Romances have misled the Public Mind—The manifest injustice of crediting them as History—The attitude of the present adversaries of Slavery in times past—Achievements of Slavery... 61

LETTER V

Labor, the Foundation of the Wealth of Nations—Duties of Government—Declaration of Independence, and its correct interpretation—Classification of Rulers, and the Governed—Names do not express the Qualities of Objects. ....Page 73

LETTER VI.

Different systems of Labor considered—Free Labor more or less dependent upon Capital—Southey on English Labor System—Unhappy Condition of the Factory Operatives—Products of Slave and Free Labor Compared........ 86

LETTER VII.

Unfavorable results of Emancipation by England—Beneficial results of Slave Labor in the United States—Comparison of the condition of the Slave and Free States of the American Continent—Great importance attached by England to tropical productions—The interests of England and the Planting States identical........ 103

LETTER VIII.

Opposing interests combined in the Anti-Slavery Party—Causes of disaster to Republics—Tendency of Slavery to produce equality in the dominant race—Causes of opposition to Slavery by aristocratic bodies—Morals of Slave and Free States—Capital and Labor united in Slave States........ 118

LETTER IX.

Influence of Public Opinion—Origin of the Anti-Slavery Sentiment in England—Failure of schemes to destroy the value of Slave Labor in America—Revolting Inhumanity of the systems instituted to supersede Slave Labor—Comparison of the Slavery System with those proposed as Substitutes—Subjugation of India by England—A trial by the Moral Law........ 136

LETTER X.

Summary of the relative advantages of different systems of Labor—Results of the Comparison—Characteristics of Great Britain—An Anti-Slavery Poem—Does not fairly illustrate John Bull—Reflections of a Philanthropist upon subjects suggested by the Poem—The Institution of Slavery more humane now than formerly....p 156

LETTER XI.

Great Britain—Her interests in American Affairs—Public mind of Europe excited by misrepresentations against the South—The London Times on Sumner's last Speech—"Republican" party of America—Its purposes hostile to the South........................ 175

LETTER XII.

Influence of Anti-Slavery Fanaticism upon Religion—Bible Authority on Slavery—Increase of Infidelity—Influence of the Clergy for Good and Evil.. 189

LETTER XIII.

Present Attitude of Parties in the United States—Success of the Republican Party will accomplish Disunion—Its Measures Examined, etc.. 200

LETTER XIV.

A Confederacy could never be established which did not recognize the equality of the States—Position of Parties illustrated—Aggressions of the South and North considered..................... 213

LETTER XV.

Duty of Citizens—Republican Measures are the results of unfriendly feeling; not the cause—Spirit of the Republican Party inconsistent with a desire to maintain the Union in its integrity...... 225

LETTER XVI.

The madness of the hour—In Europe the Dissolution of the Union is expected—A few words to Northern Enemies of the South—Conclusion ....Page 234

LETTER TO LORD BROUGHAM on the John Brown raid...... 249

THE RESULT AND ITS CONSEQUENCES.

Interest excited abroad by the last canvass for the Presidency, and its results—Amazement at the consequences—The South tranquilly living under the same laws as before, while the North is in a state of Revolution—Atrocities of the invaders—Fremont's Proclamation—Spectacle presented to mankind—Nature of the late compact of Union—Reserved rights of the States—While the Monarchies of Europe are upholding, the Lincoln Government is denying the rights of the people to self-government—The Union of South and North is opposed to the freedom of the former, and the happiness of the latter, and can never be restored—Characteristic differences between them—"Puritans," "Cavaliers"—The South will stand higher in the estimation of the civilized world after separation—The only issue is subjection or independence—Providence smiles upon the Southern people—Through the murky clouds the sunlight is already visible—President Lincoln's declaration that the States derived their powers from the General Government disproved, Note to page 288—The nature and terms of the compact of union between the States considered, Note to page 293......................... 277

PREFACE.

THE following letters upon slavery in the Southern States of the late American Union, were written at Constantinople during the canvass for the Presidency of the United States in 1860, and forwarded at the time for publication in a political journal. In deference to the desire of a number of intelligent gentlemen, they are now issued in their present form, as a single atom in the history of that great struggle which terminated in the election of a President by the united votes of the Northern States, to be speedily followed by the dismemberment of the Confederacy.

It will be necessary that the reader should bear constantly in mind that the letters were written before, not after the occurrence of these events. Although the anticipations of the author have been strikingly verified, both in Europe and in America, he does not pretend to have furnished new facts, or to have thrown new light upon the interesting and important subjects upon which he has written. But his position abroad afforded him opportunities, which were possessed by but few of his fellow-countrymen, for acquiring an insight into the real opinions, and feelings, and general public sentiment of Europe, in regard to the contest which was then in active progress between the North and the South; and also of the designs of those statesmen and politicians of the Old World, between whom and the active leaders of the anti-slavery party in America there existed a coincidence and agreement of sentiment and purpose.

In Europe, moreover, there was no attempt to conceal the ultimate objects which the leading "Republicans" of the North and their European allies proposed to accomplish, if the former should succeed in obtaining the undivided control of the General Government.

In Great Britain, as in America, the anti-slavery party was divided into two general classes: the one comprising the prominent statesmen, together with their less distinguished adherents, who looked to the political, and personal, and national advantages which might follow a gradual but sure process of emancipation in the Southern planting States; the other comprising the fanatics of one idea, and the extreme advocates of prompt action. Between the former and the leaders of the "Republican party," there was understood to be a perfect accord. Both agreed that the process of abolitionizing the South should be so gradual as not to produce any convulsion in the commercial world, by a sudden diminution in the products of slave labor; while it should be so cautious in its development as not to awaken any serious alarm among the great body of the Southern people.

Under whatever vail the anti-slavery leaders in the North may have attempted to conceal their real purpose in America, there was no effort to disguise the fact in Europe that "the mission of the Republican party was to effect the extinction of slavery in the American Confederacy." This opinion was so thoroughly implanted in the public mind, that any intimation of a doubt in regard thereto would have been received with incredulity by the public at large, and repelled by their European friends as an imputation against the personal integrity of their American allies.

It is a remarkable fact that the only intelligent observers

of the events which were transpiring in the United States, who were surprised at the immediate effects of the success of the "Republicans," were those who were themselves the instigators or actors in that great political crusade against the South. These seem, in their calculation of consequences, to have ignored alike the existence of that great body of earnest fanatics whose passions they had aroused to madness, while invoking their necessary aid, and of that natural instinct of self-preservation which would teach the freemen of the South, while fathoming the hostile intent of their enemies, that although it might be swift destruction to resist, it would be but an ignoble life and a lingering death to submit! They alone seemed blind to the consequences which would follow, as a necessary sequence, upon the heels of their victory. They alone seem not to have considered, that whilst the multitude of their mad followers would not be content to postpone gathering the fruits of their victory, and would press forward at once to reach the promised goal, the SOUTH would, AS ONE MAN, gird on its armor for defence, and by accepting the challenge to immediate combat, make "gradual emancipation" for ever impossible.

While it was universally understood throughout Europe that the only question at issue in the struggle for the presidency was that of slavery in the Southern States, and that the result would involve the destruction of that institution, or the dissolution of the Confederacy, in the event of the success of the "Republican party," the greater number believed that the only result would be the ultimate emancipation of the slaves. So active and successful have been the enemies of the South, in misrepresenting the character and qualities of the Southern people, there were but few who supposed that they could offer any serious resistance to the encroachments of their powerful neighbor. The events of the last few months have not only dispelled this delusion from the public mind, but they have created a revulsion in the sentiment and opinion of the civilized world, as startling in its magnitude as it is just in its conclusions. Europe is at length beginning to discover, as passing events are developing with a rapid movement, the true merits of this life-and-death struggle for supremacy over the soil of the South; how egregiously it has been deceived by the persistent misrepresentations of the Southern people by their unscrupulous enemies.

That the war in which the gallant sons of the South are now engaged will end in securing their independence, cannot be questioned; that its prosecution may be attended with heavy sacrifices, is equally true. But amidst all the evils which may accompany it, or the blessings which will succeed its successful close, not the least gratifying of the results achieved will be the vindication of the character of the Southern people before the civilized world, against the aspersions and misrepresentations which have been so unjustly and so profusely heaped upon them by those who claimed to be their fellow-countrymen.

Letters on Slavery.

LETTER I

Introduction—Slavery established in North America by Great Britain —Slavery denounced by England only after the American Revolution—The New Republic obliged to adopt the existing Institution —Causes of Antagonism between the White and Black Races—M. De Tocqueville on Slavery in America.

THE American-born citizen, who has been called to reside for a time in a distant country, may, after the lapse of a few years, cease to feel any great personal solicitude in regard to the mere material out of which a Presidential ticket is composed; yet he is all the more deeply concerned in observing and noting the popular impulses, the sentiments, and the purposes which animate the electors, and which are supposed to be represented by their respective candidates. However intense may have been his feelings when at home, touching the local, sectional, or personal controversies, which are often turned to account by ambitious men as auxiliaries to their personal aggrandizement, they are softened by continued absence, and soon become merged into that broad American sentiment, which embraces every foot of territory over which floats the flag of the Union! Not that he loves less the home and the friends which he has left behind him, or that the local attachments which have had their origin in education or association are less strong or active, for on the contrary these feelings which spring from and encircle the heart, are only intensified by absence. But the expanded vision discovers more clearly the magnificence of that great confederacy, of which each particular part forms an essential element; and in the contemplation of which the geographical lines which define these minute divisions, become fainter and more faint, until they are lost in the outline—the form—the dimensions—the aspect of that grand unit, which represents to the nations of the world the single sovereignty of the Great Republic.

I am sure that if these letters ever meet the eye of those for whom they are intended, they will not find therein the expression of a thought, or a sentiment, or a feeling, or an impulse, which is not reconcilable with that broad and comprehensive Americanism which embraces each and every member of the federal Union.

That the writer is a Southerner by birth and education, may be readily inferred. That he feels in every fibre of his heart an earnest and unchangeable attachment for the political institutions of the State in which he was born, which no time can eradicate, and which neither obloquy nor misfortune can abate, he is proud to declare; yet he trusts that this frank avowal will not close the eyes and ears of those who may have different local attachments, against the truths which he may enunciate. However unsuccessful he may be in implanting his own convictions in the minds of others, he only asks that they be considered with the same frankness, and under the influence of the same American feeling which animates him in their utterance.

In order to arrive at just conclusions in regard to the merits of a question, which enlists, to a greater or less extent, the passions and prejudices, as well as the interests of those who are arrayed upon one side or the other, it is well to understand the relative positions of the parties to the controversy. A knowledge of the motives of human actions is essential to an understanding of the merits of these actions themselves, and we may reasonably distrust the arguments of those who have a great personal, selfish interest behind the ostensible object which they propose to accomplish. The passions, the prejudices, the interest, or the ignorance of men often impel them to act unjustly towards their fellow-men; and no injustice is more common than that of condemning others for apparent or real faults—as tested by the standard of abstract right—without considering the circumstances of those against whom such censures are directed. In order to comprehend fully the true merits of the subject of controversy between the North and the South, upon which the respective sections have arrayed themselves in the now pending contest for the Presidency, it is necessary to begin at the beginning—to commence at the foundation, and to trace step by step the origin and progress of the causes that have produced a conflict within the heart of the Confederacy, which may end in disaster to one or both. Many statesmen and wise men in the old world, both of the friends and enemies of the Republic, declare unreservedly their belief, that the Chief Magistrate now in the occupancy of the Executive Chair is the last of the line of American Presidents who will rule over the present confederacy of States. At home and abroad the danger is apparent, and as the writer of these letters cannot participate personally and actively in the conflict, he adopts this as the only means by which he may communicate with his countrymen. For this he offers no other apology or explanation, than that he is an American citizen.

The first African slaves who were introduced into what now constitutes the United States of America, but which at that time formed the larger part of the North American provinces of Great Britain, were transported thither in British ships, under the sanction and by the authority of the British Government. The speculation was pecuniarily successful, and under the special patronage of this Power, slaves were imported in such large numbers as to alarm the European inhabitants for their personal safety. The colonists thereupon urged the British Government to abandon, or at least to suspend, the farther introduction of these barbarians, and seconded their request by a detailed statement of the evils which they believed that they had reason to apprehend, if the system should be continued.

But the Government of Great Britain was deaf to their representations and to their complaints, and the traffic in slaves was prosecuted with increased activity and effect. The trade was valuable to England in a double sense. First, the price paid for the slaves enriched the British subjects, who were either directly or indirectly interested in the traffic, while at the same time it gave profitable employment to her ships, and added to her power upon the ocean; and secondly, the productions of the colonies rapidly increased, stimulated by this augmentation in the number of her operatives.

The treatment of these captives was necessarily harsh and cruel; for besides being savages but just subjected to the galling and unaccustomed restraints of servitude under civilized masters, with no other feeling towards those by whom they had been enslaved and held in bondage but that of hatred, they were formidable in numbers; and when added to the strength of the native races who were at enmity with the colonists, it will readily be seen that a lack of due circumspection or vigilance might have been attended with fatal consequences to the sparse population of European blood.

From that period up to the very moment when, after a long and sanguinary and cruel war, the American colonies achieved their independence and became one of the family of nations, the Government of Great Britain never ceased to encourage the importation of slaves. It constituted, up to that epoch, a most important branch of her commerce, and the great value which she attached thereto may be estimated by the fact, that at the end of a long and bloody European war, in which she figured as one of the chief combatants, she only claimed as her portion of the spoils of victory, *the exclusive privilege of prosecuting the slave trade.* This dearly-bought concession she exercised and enforced with as much energy and zeal as she employed after the American Revolution, in constituting her navy into a police of the seas for the suppression of the traffic.

It may with truth be said, that of all the nations of the earth, Great Britain has contributed most—first, towards the establishment of African slavery in America, and afterwards towards exciting against it the prejudices of the civilized world. Having forced the human chattels upon her reluctant subjects, that she might reap the rich harvest of their labors in the fertile fields of the new world, she never repented herself of the "sin of slavery"—she never felt the bowels of her compassion yearning towards the "miserable captives" of her own cupidity, until by a successful revolution these colonies threw off their allegiance and erected themselves into one of the independent family of nations. The sceptre of the slave power thus and then passed into the hands of a rival, and from that period dates the conversion of Great Britain to the doctrine of universal emancipation.

Scarcely had the American Revolution brought

about this unanticipated and disastrous phase in the immediate and probable future condition of slavery, and the slave trade, than the British Government changed its tactics with most indecent haste, and caused her navy to institute a rigorous search after all vessels which were engaged in what she then denominated the "infamous traffic in human flesh." These, when found, were captured—carried into British ports—condemned as lawful prizes—the proceeds thereof placed in the pockets of the captors—and the *liberated* Africans were sent to work for a term of years, as involuntary "free laborers," upon the plantations of British subjects. This is a curious but characteristic illustration of the facility with which English philanthropy adapts itself to the exigencies of British pecuniary interests.*

An enlightened and unprejudiced judgment would decide that her sudden conversion, and her ostentatious horror of the institution of slavery, occurred at an epoch well calculated to create doubts in regard to the genuineness of that philanthropy, which, however noisy in its demonstration, was painfully at variance with her practice, as long as

---

* The reader is referred to the case of the American brig Fortuna —Dodson's Adm. Reports: vol. 1, page 95—and of the American ship Arcadia—reported in Acton's Adm. Reports: vol. 1, page 24. The capture of the former occurred in 1807, and of the latter at a period somewhat later. In both instances the American vessels were condemned as lawful prizes by the Lords of Appeal, and the products thereof divided among the crews of the vessels which had seized them.

she retained a controlling interest in the traffic in slaves, and in the fruits of their labor. And we have a right to assume that a strongly-impelling incentive to her present active intervention in the anti-slavery movement is, that by impairing or destroying, by a gradual but sure process, the institution of slavery in America, she may without a rival become the great producer of cotton for the consumption of the world, by means of her vast possessions in India. It is for this, among other causes, that her leading anti-slavery statesmen have misrepresented the institution of slavery, which she erected in the territory of the United States, and have endeavored to excite against that country the prejudices of the civilized world. Unable to achieve this result so readily by any other means at their command, they have adopted the subtle method of building up a powerful party within the Confederacy itself, and thus throwing upon American citizens the burden of working out their policy and purposes. They have leagued themselves in America with every abominable heresy which, under the license of unrestricted liberty, has obtained a partial success in certain parts of the Republic. They are in intimate alliance with impracticable foreign-born Red Republicans—Fourierites—Agrarians—the advocates of "Free Love" and "Woman's Rights"—Deists, and Atheists—all leagued together under the designation of the "Anti-slavery Party."

These are your American allies, O haughty England! They are the leaders of these, who are feasted and honored in your Baronial Halls, when, after an assault of more than usual virulence against the institutions of their native land, they visit the shores of the father-land to receive the wages of their treachery!*

There may arrive a period when England may regret that, in giving aid and comfort to these, she has repulsed those who certainly are not least noble, chivalrous, or generous among the descendants of English ancestry in the New World.

Upon the establishment of the independence of the United States, about one-fifth of the population, in round numbers, were slaves, many of whom had been but recently brought from the shores of Africa. Thoroughly barbarous—without even the instincts of civilization—they still formed a considerable portion of the population; and in the formation of the new Government, it was necessary to assign for them a position. The questions arose: What shall be done with these wild and uncultivated savages? What rank shall they occupy in the State?

If these slaves had been at the time congregated together upon the neighboring tropical islands, or if they had been isolated from the body of the European inhabitants in provinces more or less remote, there would have been allowed a much wider latitude in determining what should be their future condition. Their emancipation, either immediate or prospective, would have been a mere question of expediency, involving only a certain sum of money, as a remuneration to the owners. Great Britain, under like circumstances, abolished slavery in her distant possessions, doubtless under the conviction that she could thus assail with greater advantage the institution of slavery in the United States, and in the end substitute for both, the labor of her millions of conquered Asiatics in India. Whether her measures were well taken, or whether the speculation has proven to be a profitable one, it is not my present purpose to investigate.

But the revolted colonists found themselves in no position in which such an alternative was presented to them, even if it would have seemed the part of wisdom to have adopted it. By the policy of Great Britain in establishing these slaves upon the American Continent, they were intermingled with the white inhabitants in the greater part of the States of the new Confederacy. They were established as domestics or farm laborers at almost every domestic threshold, and hence the questions involved in deciding upon their future position were of much graver significance, and their choice of means was much more limited.

The new Government being a Republic, founded upon the principle of equality of rights, was bound in the beginning to confer *upon all whom she recognized as citizens* the same equality of rights under the Constitution. From this position there was no escape. To have conferred upon one class of citizens certain rights, which should be withheld from another, would have been not only absurd, but in a

Republic, impossible. The primary—the essential condition of a Republic is the absolute political equality of the individual members composing it.

It certainly requires no argument to prove that these African slaves were totally unfit, by nature, habit, and education, to enter upon the discharge of the responsible duties of free citizens. To have created them such would, in the very act of inaugurating the Republic, have sounded its death-knell! Every instinct, every impulse, every feeling of the white race would have revolted against the contaminating association, while the friends of the infant Republic would have had the mortification of witnessing its destruction, even before the erection of the corner-stone of that edifice, which now stands in all its magnificent and complete proportions, the pride of every American and the wonder of mankind.

Wiser counsels prevailed. The African, unsuited to be a citizen, was continued in his condition of slavery, and the product of his labor and that of his descendants has enriched the world—has contributed largely towards bringing within the reach of the great masses of mankind the essential products of the warm latitudes; and last, though not least, it has been a principal element in developing the resources and increasing the power of the Great Republic.

Soon after the establishment of the new Government, the Congress enacted a law fixing upon a period, not remote, after which no slaves should be introduced from abroad into any State or Territory of the Republic. Of the nearly four millions of slaves now held as such in the United States, not five hundred have been introduced in contravention of that enactment.

It is, in this connection, worthy of special remark, that for the ancestors of the great body of Africans at this day held as slaves, within the limits of the American Republic, the estimated value thereof, was paid, under the sanction and approval of the British Government, to British subjects! *For nearly every drop of blood* which flows in the veins of the slaves of the United States, *England has received the price in gold!* And yet this England shakes her gory locks at *us*, and says "the sin" is *ours!!* She points to her desolated islands, with their famishing freed slaves, and tells us that her "skirts are clear."

Judas Iscariot betrayed his Lord and Master for the paltry bribe of thirty pieces of silver; but after the act of guilt and shame was past recall, reflection came, and with it came remorse. He cast away the guilty wages of his sin, and prayed for pardon, but his crime was too great for forgiveness. England, in what she now denominates the "unholy traffic in human flesh," also received the wages of her sin. She never reflected upon the "enormity of the crime against humanity," until "the great market for human blood and sinews" was closed against her. Then came her tardy repentance; but worse even than Judas, she has never cast away from her, nor offered to restore the wages of her sin; and shall she be forgiven?

If the institution of slavery in the New World has proven to be a curse to mankind, if as is alleged by modern philanthropy, its existence is a crime against humanity, then, of all the nations of the globe, Great Britain is the most to be condemned for its establishment and its perpetuation. If on the other hand, it is a system of labor, which while conferring blessings upon the slave, and elevating him to a rank above that which any of his race have ever before occupied, has at the same time contributed materially to the happiness, the prosperity, and the civilization of the world, impartial justice would not assign to England, any portion of merit, for her instrumentality in the benefits which have resulted from its establishment.

But to return again to the subject from which I have for a moment digressed. The separate States which had secured their independence, although exercising sovereignty, each within its defined limits, delegated certain powers to a government, erected by themselves, which should be the representative of all. They established the Federal Union, but the sovereignty of each State remained entire, except wherein a limited power was surrendered specifically to the General Government, having reference almost exclusively to their foreign relations and to their mutual intercourse.

The free inhabitants of the slave States, consituting a large majority of the whole, being desirous rather to establish a firm, and lasting, and prosperous government, than to test in practice the merits of a doubtful theory, adapted their form of government to the exigencies of the circumstances by which they were surrounded. As before stated, they recognized in their Constitutions the political equality of all the European races. This was but the admission of an existing fact. But they denied to the African slaves the rights of citizenship. These were wisely left in the same relative position to the white races which they had occupied while the country was under the dominion of Great Britain. The change, therefore, in the form of the government was not attended by any violent changes in the habits or conditions of the people. Had different counsels prevailed, and had the governments of these States sought to engraft upon their Constitutions the theoretical idea of universal equality, it must be admitted that the governments thus established would have failed to secure the end proposed, and would in all human probability have resulted disastrously to the interests and the happiness of all. There would have been a perpetual conflict between the two races, or there would have been an amalgamation of them. Either would have been alike fatal.

This departure from the theoretical doctrines of visionary enthusiasts, who would change even the laws of Heaven itself, to make what they conceive to be a perfect government, has from that period to the present, afforded for the adherents of this system a theme for unceasing denunciation.

It may here be said that the adversaries of slavery, beyond the boundaries of the slave States, ask that something be done which is revolting to every feeling, or sentiment, or thought, or impulse of the dominant race. They demand that the free white citizens should not only disregard the prejudices of education, and the instincts of nature, but even set at defiance the apparent will of Omnipotence, which has marked with signs so unmistakable the distinctions between the races.

We may readily imagine a physical force competent to the destruction of the liberties of the freemen of the Southern States. We may conceive of a concentration of power, adequate to the purpose of enchaining their limbs, and consigning the bodies of the refractory and unyielding to loathsome dungeons. But in view of the feelings with which the Africans are regarded by the European races in America, we cannot imagine any possible exercise of human tyranny potent enough to compel them to admit in their hearts a political equality, or an amalgamation with the degraded race. However theoretical philanthropists may refuse to recognize in their systems of government the distinctions of color, capacity and race, still the ineradicable prejudice exists, and the testimony of the past, as well as the promptings of common reason, teach us that in establishing laws for the government of mankind, we must not eschew the common and prevailing sentiments of the governed, except in the presence of an overwhelming force of bayonets.

In the case we are considering, the distinctions are so legible—the lines so ineradicable—the differences so indelibly stamped by nature itself, that the repugnance must be perpetual. Any withdrawal of the legal barriers which now keep the races asunder, would inevitably result in the destruction of one or both.

Let not the honest and well meaning opponents of slavery delude themselves or others into the belief that there can be any essential modification of the existing relations between the whites and the blacks, while they inhabit a common territory. Let them remember that an essential condition of a republic is, that all who are recognized as citizens must be invested, under any given state of circumstances, with an equality of rights. Whenever the States of the Confederacy or the General Government recognize, by their Constitutions and their laws, two sets or classes of citizens, invested with unequal privileges, and with different sets of laws for each, they violate the fundamental principle upon which a purely republican government is founded. In making laws therefore to be applied to the great mass of Africans, they must be regarded as either slaves or citizens. If as citizens, then must they be placed upon a political equality with the European races.

Even assuming however, that in a Republic there could exist recognized classes of citizens, with different and unequal political rights, is it not plain that a change which would involve only a partial degree of liberty would render the condition of the African worse than his present state of servitude? Accomplish this change and it could only be perpetuated by an overwhelming power from without; and upon the instant when the external pressure should be removed, that instant would the conflict between the races commence—the one to free itself from all political inferiority, the other to reduce the African to his former condition of servitude—without considering the cost during its progress, this could only result in the complete subjection of one or the other.

Whatever may be the abstract merits of slavery—whatever its evils or advantages, it is manifest that when Great Britain introduced Africans into her American Colonies, she designed that their enslavement should be perpetual. She never could have conceived it possible that they would occupy any other relation to the European races. No brazen collar around the neck of the slave, was necessary to distinguish him from his master. The hand of Omnipotence in characters broad, deep, and ineffaceable had marked him, as of a different and inferior race. The British slave dealer sought in the traffic *present gain*, but the British Government, looking to the future, and anticipating no change in the sovereignty of the country, sought to enlarge the productions of her colonies in all time to come by transplanting a race with characteristics so widely distinct from the Europeans, that whatever might be the desire of the dominant race, they could not occupy towards each other any other relation than that of *Master* and *Slave*. In establishing African slavery therefore, the British Government designed that it should be perpetual.

In regard to the existence of this natural repugnance, heightened by habit and education, even M.

De Tocqueville, notwithstanding his theoretical and cultivated hostility to slavery, bears ample testimony. Anxious as he was to discover arguments adverse to the institution of slavery, and eagerly as he sought for, and recorded the evils, real or imaginary, emenating therefrom, and indulging those prejudices as he did, to the great injustice of the American Slave States, he was constrained most reluctantly to admit, that any material change in the relative condition of the races would result disastrously to one or both.

M. De Tocqueville says:

The abstract and transient fact of slavery, is fatally united to the physical and permanent fact of color. The tradition of slavery dishonors the race, and the peculiarity of the race perpetuates the tradition of slavery.

That the negro transmits the eternal mark of his ignominy to all his descendants; and although the law may abolish slavery, God alone can obliterate the traces of its existence.

The modern slave differs from his master, not only in his condition, but in his origin. You may set the negro free, but you cannot make him otherwise than an alien to the European. Nor is this all; we scarcely acknowledge the common features of mankind in this child of debasement whom slavery has brought among us. His physiognomy is to our eyes hideous, his understanding weak, his tastes low; and we are almost inclined to look upon him as a being intermediate between man and the brutes.

If it be so difficult to root out an inequality which solely originates in the law, how are those distinctions to be destroyed which seem to be founded upon the immutable laws of nature herself. When I remember the extreme difficulty with which aristocratic bodies, of whatever nature they may be, are commingled with the mass of the people, and the exceeding care which they take to preserve the ideal boundaries of their caste inviolate, I despair of seeing an aristocracy disappear which is founded upon visible and indelible signs. Those who hope that the Europeans will ever mix with the negroes, appear to me to delude themselves.

Hitherto, whenever the whites have been the most powerful, they have maintained the blacks in a subordinate or servile position; wherever the negroes have been strongest they have destroyed the whites: such has been the only course of events which has ever taken place between the two races.

I see that in a certain portion of the territory of the United States at the present day, the legal barrier which separated the two races is tending to fall away; but not that which exists in the manners of the country: slavery recedes, but the prejudice to which it has given birth remains stationary. Whosoever has inhabited the United States, must have perceived that in those parts of the Union in which the negroes are no longer slaves, they have in no wise drawn near to the whites. On the contrary, the prejudice to the race appears to be stronger in the States which have abolished slavery than in those where it still exists; and nowhere is it so intolerant as in those States where servitude has never been known.

It is true that in the North of the Union, marriages may be legally contracted between negroes and whites, but public opinion would stigmatize a man who should connect himself with a negress, as infamous, and it would be difficult to meet with a single instance of such a union.

In the South, where slavery still exists, the negroes are less carefully kept apart; they sometimes share the labor and the recreations of the whites; the whites consent to intermix with them to a certain extent, and although the legislation treats them more harshly, the habits of the people are more tolerant and compassionate.

In the South, the master is not afraid to raise his slave to his own standing, because he knows that he can in a moment reduce him to the dust at pleasure. In the North, the white man no longer distinctly perceives the barrier which separates him from the degraded race, and he shuns the negroes with the more pertinacity, because he fears lest they should some day be confounded together. Thus it is in the United States, that the prejudice which repels the negroes seems to increase in proportion as they are emancipated, and inequality is sanctioned by the manners, while it is effaced by the laws, of the country.

I am obliged to confess that I do not regard the abolition of slavery as a means of warding off the struggle of the two races in the United States. The negroes may long remain slaves without complaining, but if they are once raised to the level of freemen, they will soon revolt at being deprived of their civil rights; and as they cannot become the equals of the whites, they will speedily declare themselves as enemies. In the North everything contributes to facilitate the emancipation of the slave; and slavery was abolished without placing the free negroes in a position which could become formidable, since their number was too small for them ever to claim the exercise of their rights. But such is not the case in the South. The question of slavery was a question of commerce and manufacture for the slave owners in the North; for those of the South it is a question of life and death.

When I contemplate the condition of the South, I can only discover two alternatives which may be adopted by the white inhabitants of those States, viz: *either to emancipate the negroes and to intermingle with them, or remaining isolated from them, to keep them in a state of slavery as long as possible. All intermediate measures seem to me likely to terminate, and that shortly, in the most horrible of civil wars, and perhaps in the extirpation of one or other of the two races.*

When the Europeans chose the slaves from a race differing from their own, which many of them considered as inferior to the other races of mankind, and which they all repelled with horror from any notion of intimate connection, they must have believed that slavery would last forever, since there is no intermediate state which can be desirable between the excessive inequality produced by servitude, and the complete equality which originates in independence. The Europeans did imperfectly feel this truth, but without acknowledging it even to themselves. Whenever they have had to do with negroes, their conduct has either been dictated by their interest and their pride, or by their compassion. They first violated every right of humanity by their treatment of the negro, and they afterwards informed him those rights were precious and inviolable. They affected to open their ranks to the slaves, but the negroes who attempted to penetrate into the community were driven back with scorn.

If it be impossible to anticipate a period at which the Americans of the South will mingle their blood with that of the negroes, can they allow their slaves to become free without compromising their own security? And if they are obliged to keep that race in bondage in order to save their own families, may they not be excused for availing themselves of the means best adapted to that end?—*Democracy in America*, page 388, American edition.

These must be received as the conclusions of one who entertaining strong prejudices against slavery, visited the Southern States with the view of finding proofs in corroboration of his theory. He permitted his enlightened and comprehensive mind to be biassed by a distorted conception of its evils, yet with all his undisguised hostility, he is constrained notwithstanding to express his conviction, founded upon facts, reason and observation, that any change in the relative condition of the European and African races in America would be fatal to both.

The prejudices of this distinguished author were *against slavery as a system of labor, not against the slave-holder*. Hence while his opinions in reference to the former were moulded in conformity with these prejudices, he was not indisposed to do justice to the latter. His inclination was *without crushing the slave holder to elevate the slave*—differing in this essential particular from modern abolition philanthropy which, without any special desire to *elevate the slave*, seeks only to *reduce the master* to that standard.

LETTER II.

Reasons why Slavery could not be Abolished and proofs that it should not have been Abolished—Emancipation would make the condition of the Slaves worse—The Abolitionists cannot accomplish their purposes even with the assent of the Slaveholders—Slavery was Abolished in the North by selling the Slaves to the South.

THE institution of slavery, as we have seen, was a legacy, whether for good or evil, left to the United States of America by their former sovereign. As slaves, the Africans were transferred from the kingdom of Great Britain to the new Republics, and as slaves they were thereafter held. Whether or not slavery is right or wrong in the abstract, the slave States found themselves in the presence of an existing contingency, which, as before said, left them no alternative but to adopt, and endeavor to make available to their interests, an institution which they might wisely direct, but which they could not abolish.

No one who desired to witness the successful establishment of the new Government could have regarded with any other feeling than distrust, any attempt to elevate these slaves to the condition of free citizens. The instinct of self-preservation, and a dawning perception of the sublime destiny which, in the not distant future, would attend the development of that great country, alike forbade such an unhallowed amalgamation. And the beginning of that dawn is now before the world. The wisdom of that decision, without even considering the necessity which left them no other alternative, is already apparent. Where there is so much to admire; so much for which, as a people, we have reason to be proud, how can the true friend of America seek to plunge into that vortex of abolitionism from which we could only hope to escape through disaster and a sea of blood?

Here the defender of American slavery might pause in the presence of that necessity which allowed no discretion or choice in regard to the continuance of slavery, and submit the question, without argument, to any unprejudiced umpire. Whatever might be the predilections of just men sitting in judgment, however their sensibilities may have been excited by works of fiction, by falsehood or by caricatured truth, the decision could not be otherwise than that slavery inaugurated in the United States by its former sovereign was perpetuated by the Republic under the ruling of an inexorable necessity.

But even this impregnable fortress of defence is weak in comparison with others which have been erected by the dominant race upon which the duty has devolved of directing and controlling the institution which they thus inherited.

Was slavery under British auspices a crime in its inception, and a curse in its perpetuation? America has converted it through the fruits of its labor into a blessing to mankind! Was slavery cruel? America has made it merciful! Did British cupidity drag the unhappy African from his native land, and consign him to eternal servitude? American practical philanthropy has given to the involuntary exile a home, better far than he or his ancestors had ever known. America found in the slave which she inherited a savage, and she has civilized him! She found him a heathen, and she has Christianized him! She found him naked and starving, and she has clothed and fed him! Slave though he be, yet in all that concerns his comfort, physical well-being, and contentment—in every thing save the name, the condition of the slaves of the United States, as admitted even by the enemies of the institution, is far in advance of that of any similar number of laborers following similar occupations, in any other land under the sun.

Before proceeding to refer more in detail to facts concerning the existing condition of the African race in America—or before making an exhibit of some of the chief benefits which have resulted to mankind through the immediate instrumentality of African slavery in America, let it, for a moment, be assumed as granted that the abolition party has so far achieved its purpose as to convince even the slaveholder that slavery should cease to exist. What measures shall be instituted to accomphish the result?

It will be an approximation sufficiently near, to estimate the slave population at about four millions.

The present money value of slaves in the prime of life would probably not fall short of eleven hundred dollars each. The average value may therefore be set down at about five hundred dollars each. This would make the grand total value of the entire slave population, *twenty hundred millions of dollars!*

It is not pretended that of this number five hundred have been placed in that position by the present owners, or I might say, by the present generation. They have been bought and paid for by the present possessors or their ancestors, under the operation and guarantee of the laws of the land. The slave owner of to-day had no more instrumentality in the enactment of these laws, than he had in the establishment of the institution of slavery. Both had their origin at a time when the country was under the exclusive dominion of Great Britain.

The slave-holder has thus become possessed of his property under all the solemn sanctions of the law. If a wrong has been done, it dates back to a period long anterior to his birth, and even before the existence of the Republic itself. He holds his slave by virtue of the same system of laws which entitles a citizen to the possession of any other description of property, and he cannot justly be deprived of its use without adequate compensation.

A single State in the vicinity of other slave-holding States, may enact laws fixing upon a stated period after which slavery shall not exist. In this manner, slavery has been already abolished in the Northern or colder latitudes of the American

Union. But in every case the slave-holder has been able to protect himself against pecuniary loss by transferring his slaves into States where the institution still existed. Although by this means the *institution* of slavery has been abolished in many of the States, yet *the slaves themselves were transferred to a different locality, and they and their descendants are at this day in bondage.*

The abolition of slavery therefore in the present free States of the Confederacy, involved no pecuniary loss to the citizens who were their owners; nor did it change, in the smallest degree, the position of those who were then and there held in bondage. They only *changed their masters and their homes.* But in considering the question of the abolition of slavery throughout the entire Confederacy, with a view to the emancipation of the slaves, it assumes proportions of much graver magnitude. Not a single State of the American Union which has enacted laws prohibiting slavery within its limits, ever contemplated that the act of emancipation would cost its citizens a single dollar, or give freedom to a single slave. The object of the change which it was deemed desirable to accomplish, had reference solely to what was regarded as the interests of the dominant race. The rhetorical and poetical effusions which attended the discussion of the question, were of course signalized by the usual protestations of philanthropy, humanity, and benevolence; but the arguments of controlling potency were, that slavery had ceased to be profitable in a pecuniary way—that the climate was not adapted to that description of labor—that the change could be effected without cost—and that an act of emancipation was in reality but the recognition of an existing fact; for the reason that the laws of trade had already transferred the mass of the slaves to the warmer latitude of the South. By the provisions of the law, ample time was allowed to effect the transportation of the slaves, *as slaves*, to a more congenial soil.

It may fairly be assumed that this measure did not have for its object any vindication of the "unalienable rights of man," or the eradication of the system of slave labor; else, instead of abolishing the institution in such manner as to afford time and opportunity to sell the slaves in a foreign market, steps would have been taken to secure their emancipation, even at the expense of a small tax upon the citizens. This could have been accomplished at a comparatively trifling cost, for the self-established laws of interest, more potent even in their moral influence that statutary enactments, had already, as before stated, caused the great body of the Africans to be transported from the colder latitudes of the North, to the more genial temperature of a Southern sun. Thus, only a comparatively small number of slaves remained to be affected by the act of emancipation. Cheaply as the Northern States might then have vindicated the doctrine of "equal rights," the cost, small as it would have been, was deemed too great. And happy as was the conjuncture, for practically testing upon a small scale the capacity of the African for self-government, and the mingling together of the two races in a common brotherhood, the opportunity and the occasion passed away forever.

The connection is not inopportune to ask from well meaning and honorable citizens of the North, an answer to some questions which here naturally suggest themselves.

If you would not expend hundreds of dollars, in giving freedom to your handful of slaves, how can you now ask that the South should expend millions, in giving freedom to her multitudes? If you dared not hazard the experiment of conferring equal political rights upon only thousands of Africans, how can you ask the Southern States to grant such privileges to four millions of slaves? If you could not fix upon any intermediate condition between absolute slavery and citizenship, for a number so small as scarcely to be estimated in the aggregate of your population, and thus allow of their remaining within your own States, how can you ask the South to place all her vital interests at hazard by the semi-enfranchisement of slaves, equal in number to one half of her free citizens? If by the operation of your laws the South became the purchasers of your slaves, how can you desire to compass her destruction for the sin of slavery? But above all, if you found slavery "a political evil and a sin," and by the transportation of your slaves to the Southern States relieved yourself of that "evil," and abandoned the practice of that "sin," how can you now require that *slavery in the South shall be perpetuated by refusing to it any outlet?* How can you claim that the descendants of the slaves you sold in the Southern markets shall remain in perpetuity where you have thus placed them? How can you deny to those who have purchased them, the same privilege which was accorded to you of abolishing, or rather banishing the institution of slavery from their midst, whenever *the laws of self-interest* teach them that *it is not philanthropic* to hold their fellow-creatures in bondage?

But to return from this digression. It is manifest that the abolition of slavery in the United States under existing circumstances, would involve the entire loss of the total value of the slaves. How and by whom is this immense sum to be expended? No undue proportion thereof could upon any principle of justice or morality be charged upon those who may happen at the moment of emancipation, to be in the legal possession of the slaves. It cannot therefore be compromised by permitting them to retain an estate for life, or for a limited term of years, in the services of the slaves or their descendants. The laws by virtue of which they hold them as property guarantee the possession of them and their posterity forever; and they might with equal justice be limited to the enjoyment of an estate for life in the land or the homestead purchased or inherited in fee simple from their ancestors, as to be deprived of any part of their interest in the slave.

The question then still reverts: how is the cost value of the slave to be remunerated to the owner?

Granting the interest of Great Britain, and seeing that she would be the greatest beneficiary from a slow but certain system of gradual emancipation, how much would her Government contribute to this achievement of humanity? How much would her factory operatives be willing to be taxed for the accomplishment of a work, one of the first effects of which would be to take from their own mouths the scanty fare which is the wages of their daily toil? How much would the anti-slavery aristocracy contribute to the accomplishment of an object which seems to fill so large a space in their bosoms?

An aristocracy which bestows the cheap tribute of its tears upon the African in the remote wilds of the New World, on the other side of the great Atlantic, but which fails to see, or seeing, fails to offer its sympathy to the suffering, half-clad, half-fed millions at home, to whom, in recompense for their daily toil, is eked out the miserable pittance which is barely sufficient to supply the commonest demands of nature.

But it would be unprofitable to occupy time in considering the means necessary to the accomplishment of that, which a single glance suffices to show is impossible. The loss could not be made up to the owner, nor any part thereof bearing any commensurate proportion to the entire value. It becomes necessary, therefore, in order to carry out our hypothesis, that the slave-owner, either by force or moral conviction, has agreed to surrender all his pecuniary interests, and submit to the ruin which would be entailed upon him by the destruction of all his property. Having consummated the act of emancipation by this enormous pecuniary sacrifice, we have but entered upon the threshold of the difficulties by which, to the eye of real philanthropy, the whole question is environed.

What must be done with these four millions of liberated African slaves?

Honest and well-meaning persons have said, without considering of the necessary means, "Transport them to the land from whence their ancestors were wrested by Great Britain!" This, however, would be physically impossible. But even if it could be accomplished, it would be an act of inhumanity, involving a thousand-fold more suffering than the worst form of slavery as now existing, to say nothing of the violence which it would be necessary to employ in order to force the freed man from the scenes of his former servitude.

This scheme failing, we are left without other alternative than to provide for their future abode in the land where their destiny has been cast. What, then, should be their political position in regard to their former masters? What privileges should be bestowed, and what withheld? Should they be admitted, either immediately or in the contemplation of the future, to a social or political equality with the European races?

As already declared, this could never be. The prejudices, the instincts of the latter, are all opposed to such an association. Nature itself revolts against the unnatural amalgamation, and education has rendered the antipathy ineradicable. Heaven itself has marked upon the brow of the African the seal of inferiority; and no laws, however stringent—no physical power, however great, could enforce upon the whites the recognition of such an equality. To believe that they could do so, is first to suppose them already degraded.

None but an enemy to the dominant race, or an impracticable dreamer, could wish to witness such a consummation. The theory of the universal equality of all the races of mankind is most beautiful and attractive to the merely speculative mind; but when it is attempted to enforce it in the practical affairs of life, it is found to be a fallacy and a delusion.

Rejecting, then, this adjustment as unwise, unnatural, unjust, and finally impossible, there remains but one other alternative, and that is, while conferring upon them personal freedom from the restraints of servitude, and of a master legally authorized to control them, and give direction to their labor, to withhold from them the political rights accorded to other citizens. We have already considered the manifest inconsistency and danger of recognizing two sets of citizens, with unequal privileges, by a government which has for its corner-stone the principle of entire equality for all who have a right to be called citizens.

But would not such an enfranchisement, in its practical results, prove to be a most cruel kindness?

As a slave, he would have at least the protection of one master interested in his welfare; as a freedman, almost beyond the pale of governmental protection, with no one to take care of him, of a despised and inferior race, a stranger in a land of strangers, how miserable would be his fate! Even if every obstacle to the consummation of such a result were removed, philanthropy might well pause before conferring the boon of freedom at such a hazard.

As a slave, he would have but one master, whose duty and whose interest it would be to clothe, to feed, and to protect him in youth and in old age, in sickness and in health. As a freed African, he would have many masters, but none who would feel any interest in his welfare. He would live miserably from the cradle to the grave, despised of all, and shunned by every one; and it is impossible for the practically benevolent mind to conceive how in any single respect his physical, moral, or social condition would be improved by this nominal change in his relations towards the more powerful race. On the contrary, the practical reasoner cannot resist the conclusion, that in all things his condition would be essentially worse.

It is thus discovered, by an investigation of the subject of slavery in America, and an analysis of its present condition, with a single eye to its abolition, that upon every hand we are met by obstacles beyond the power of man to obviate; and that no material change can be effected in the present *status* of the slave, without entailing far more deplorable evils than those which it would be proposed to remedy. Even after we have arrived at the point where all interests would acquiesce in any practicable scheme of emancipation, it is apparent that it would be impossible.

Whether for good or for evil, the institution of slavery exists, and will continue to exist, in some form or another, so long as the European and African races occupy together the same territory, or until some overruling power from without reduces both to a common subjection. Furthermore, whether or not it will be the fate of the white race, whose destiny has been cast with the transplanted Africans, to be held responsible for the existence of slavery, they will at least bear within them the consciousness, that for the offence, if it be one in reality, they are wholly free from a just responsibility.

But if slavery is a thing so detestable, why should not the friends of humanity utter their imprecations against those who entailed it upon mankind, rather than against the present generation of slaveowners, who have been obliged to adapt themselves to an existing reality, and who have only given direction to an institution which they had no agency in creating, and which they had not the power to eradicate? But, above all, how stupendous is the wrong of those who, from motives the most sordid, entailed slavery upon the Southern States of the American Union, now from motives even less commendable, thrust themselves forward as the great champions of human liberty and universal emancipation!

I have only adopted this train of argument, and have for the moment acquiesced in the extreme views of the Abolitionist, in order that we might, without disagreement, follow out his schemes of emancipation in any direction which his inclination or his judgment might direct; and we have seen that whatever path he follows, he encounters evils of far greater magnitude than those which he seeks to eradicate. But I would be doing injustice to the Southern slaveholder—injustice to the benefits which the system of slave labor has conferred upon mankind—injustice to that overruling Providence which ordains all the institutions of man, were I to rest the defence of the Southern States of America upon any other foundation than that of having worthily employed the means which have been placed in their hands for the purpose of promoting the welfare and happiness of mankind.

LETTER III.

Clasification of the Adversaries of Slavery in the Southern States—The London Times on the causes of English Opposition to Slavery—What position would England occupy towards the Belligerents, if the Republican Party should attempt to carry its measures into effect—Would the South hesitate about defending herself to the last extremity?

BEFORE instituting an inquiry into the advantages and disadvantages which have resulted to mankind from the judicious employment of slave labor in the Southern States of the American Union, it would be well to classify the different parties or interests, which are at the present day banded together in hostile array against the States of the South, and which are now combined in support of the Republican party, each with the hope of accomplishing its own special purpose. To know who are the parties to a controversy, often materially assists in directing the mind to correct conclusions in regard to the merits of the controversy itself. If a known adversary or rival urges me to perform an act, which he declares will result in great benefit to me, but which I perceive will be much more likely to yield advantages to him, I may be pardoned for at least postponing any action which would produce such result.

The anti-slavery party of Great Britain is conceded to be at the head of the hostile movement directed against the planting States of the South.

Its partisans in America say that in this, their allies of England are influenced solely by considerations of philanthropy, benevolence, and an inborn love of freedom.

The plain, out-spoken matter of fact index of British public sentiment, the London Times, furnishes in a late number, in brief but emphatic language the key which affords an insight into the real motives that are thus slightly veiled under the assumed garb of benevolence and philanthropy. In discussing the importance of tropical productions as an auxiliary to British wealth and power, the Times says:

> Now in England we say that the slave trade shall no longer be permitted to be carried on in any quarter of the globe, if by negotiation, or by arms it can be repressed. In the case of the United States, indeed, we are compelled to content ourselves with the assurance that the American cruisers will do the work. *Will any one, however, say that it is not mainly owing to the ceaseless exertions, to the philanthropic energy, to the entreaties, to the persuasions of this country, that the anti-slavery party in the States owes its strength. Blot out England, and English sympathies, and English power from the map of the world, and the battle between the North and the South would be fought on the other side of the Atlantic on very different terms.* Slavery shall not be in our own dominions, nor the slave trade anywhere if we can help it. Could we have gone a step farther and annihilated the peculiar institution in all other countries, as well as in our own, the problem would, in the main, have speedily received a satisfactory solution. This, however, was beyond our power, and consequently we find ourselves in this anomaly, that we without a slave population must compete in the markets of the world, with other countries which have slave populations, and that with respect to tropical productions.

This brief extract from the great London organ, discloses the foundation upon which rests the hostility of the Abolition party of England to slavery in America. The purpose they seek to accomplish for their already rich and powerful country is, more riches and more power for England, with a corresponding diminution of riches and power for the American Confederacy. They propose, under the broad banner of philanthropy, to strike a fatal blow at the advancing wealth and power of a nation, which, although yet in its infancy, is the rival in both, of the greatest among the great powers of the world. These objects are pursued with a persistency and a determination which never wearies nor falters.

There is no nation on earth whose inexorable policy is more sharply defined, or more thoroughly understood, than that of Great Britain. To subdue the world to her will, and to make herself the arbiter of the destinies of all; to dictate terms on which the existence of other nations will be tolerated; to assume a general surveillance of the whole, and to interpose obstacles to the greatness and power of those whom she may regard as rivals; all are embraced within that comprehensive policy which she has pursued with a success as marvellous, as her efforts have been persistent. The measure of her zeal in the support of any cause, is the measure of the interests she has involved in the issue, and any other nation may well pause and consider of the probable consequences, which are likely to result, before accomplishing changes in its internal policy which she may suggest.

It may with truth be said, that the Government

of Great Britain, while conferring upon the inhabitants of her own "fast anchored isle," the priceless boon of constitutional liberty has done as little voluntarily to promote the growth of free institutions in other lands, as any absolute despotism or sham republic that has existed during her whole career of greatness. With an aristocracy so enlightened, and so capable of performing from habit and education, the high functions it is called upon to exercise; with a population, which among the better classes, illustrates in an eminent degree, many of the virtues and noble qualities which adorn human nature, and which among the masses, is characterized by its industry in peace, and its sterling qualities in war; the Government itself, in its practical bearing and conduct towards the rest of the world, has seldom exhibited those characteristics of justice and magnanimity, which so eminently in private life distinguish her people. The obligations of treaties have been too often regarded as of binding force, only so long as they were subservient to her purposes. Countries have been conquered only to be plundered. She puts forth her strength to stifle the growing power of other nations, or to build up a weaker nation on the ruins or at the expense of a formidable rival, only that her own supremacy or relative greatness may be maintained. Her career of conquest has been too often marked by the tears and blood, and practical servitude of those whom she has subjected. And in all the catalogue of weaker powers which have fallen before her victorious arms, there is not an instance upon record, out of the millions whom she has subdued, in which she has permitted the enjoyment of that freedom and liberty of which she so proudly boasts herself to be the champion and exponent. The vices which a sound morality condems have been too often criminal in her eyes, only when they could not be made available to the accomplishment of her policy—oppression only a wrong when practiced by others—freedom and independence, boons which none but the inhabitants of her own favored isle were worthy to enjoy.

In considering the only political issue involved in the present life-and-death struggle of the geographical sections in America—the one for political supremacy—the other to retain the control of its own domestic institutions—it is impossible for us to lose sight of the ever-present reality, that the adversaries of the South are fighting the battle under the leadership of the political anti-slavery party of Great Britain. Although it is not to be supposed that the object of the great body of Americans who are enlisted in that conflict is primarily to achieve a triumph of British policy in the Republic, yet such would be the effect of a successful effort to impair by degrees and finally to destroy the institution of slavery in the Southern American States. But whatever may be the motives by which the great anti-slavery party of England may be governed, however inconsistent may be their present attitude with that which Great Britain has in times past occupied, we are met face to face with the undeniable truth, that this party is to-day the leader of the anti-slavery movement against the Southern States. It is a fact, that its immense moral and social influence has been and is still exercised with the view to create and to foster a public opinion throughout the civilized world adverse to the slave States of the Confederacy. And it is also true, that mainly through its instrumentality, and under its recognized leadership, a party has grown up hostile to the existing institution of American slavery and to the slaveholders, not only in Europe, but in the Northern States of the Confederacy, formidable in numbers, respectability, and influence. That this anti-slavery organization in England should succeed in attracting to its views, and in infusing prejudices into the minds of others, where they, the unrelenting assailants, are always present, and where those who are assailed have no available means of defence, should not be a matter of surprise. But they even penetrate into the Confederacy itself, and there, as elsewhere, infuse the poison of their principles into the hearts of native citizens of the Republic. At first glance this may seem strange and most unnatural; but a brief consideration of facts will exhibit the secret of that influence which preponderates over all the incentives of personal interest, as well as the promptings of patriotism.

The American Revolution, which destroyed the political supremacy of Great Britain over her revolted provinces, did not wholly obliterate that moral influence which she very naturally exercised over a portion of the citizens. It would be an error to suppose that the entire population of America desired to witness the successful accomplishment of the Revolution. There was during the entire war of independence a formidable party which still adhered to its allegiance to the mother country; and while they were forced to submit to a result which they could not prevent, they only acquiesced because they were powerless to resist. Their political allegiance was changed, but their attachment to the government from which they had been severed continued. The remnant and the descendants of this party, silent during the interval of peace which followed the close of the Revolutionary war, again made itself manifest in the last war between the Republic and Great Britain. They were still sufficiently numerous to paralyze the strength of the General Government in some of the New England States. That contest concluded, they have since been active in the effort to establish the policy of Great Britain in reference to slavery in the Southern States of the Confederacy.

This party may be regarded, for manifest reasons, the most formidable of all the internal enemies of the Southern States. It acts upon no convictions of abstract right, but merely as the exponent of British interests and British policy; therefore, no facts, no arguments, however conclusive, can divert it from its purpose. Its hostility is not founded upon fanaticism, and therefore does not thwart its own purposes by its madness. Its opposition to slavery does not grow out of any desire to establish universal political equality, or to bring about impracticable social reforms; and hence does not excite either ridicule or contempt by its folly or its wickedness. Guided and directed by the single purpose of conforming itself to the will of Great Britain, it cannot be overcome or diverted from its purpose by any of the ordinary methods which may be used to convince an adversary of error. Formidable not so much in numbers as intelligence, it artfully combines the various and incongruous elements of opposition and moulds them to its purposes. Embracing a large proportion of literary men—professors in colleges and other educational institutions—this party has not only the advantage of presenting the cause of England in its most attractive garb, but of instilling its unpatriotic principles in the minds of the rising generation.

In order to account for the fact that Great Britain has been able to enlist in her interest so large a proportion of the literary men of New England, it must be borne in mind, that from the nature of their pursuits, they look with a sort of reverence upon England as the great fountain of English literature. They read English books, adopt English ideas, become imbued with English prejudices, and hence regard with partial vision all which emanates from that source. As the votaries of Fashion throughout the world cut their apparel, shape their hats, adjust their hair, and tie their cravats, according to the dictum of the mantua-makers, milliners, and tailors of Paris, so does the class of literary men referred to, fashion its phrases and model its ideas according to the received standard in Great Britain.

When we consider the secret springs of human actions and the natural tendencies of the human mind, we cease to be surprised, if we have entertained such a feeling, that in a country whose political ties have been so recently severed from another, and where unrestricted liberty of opinion is allowed to all, there should linger an attachment, amongst at least a portion of its inhabitants, for the institutions, the policy, the ideas of the fatherland.

It is under the intelligent direction of this class that the crude and fanatical ideas of the ultra schools of social reformers, which spring up through the immunity afforded by free government, are diverted from their impracticable, general designs, to the special purpose of swelling the power of those who are adverse to the domestic institutions of the Southern States.

This last class constitutes the great body of those who desire, from perhaps honest and conscientious, though mistaken motives of philanthropy, to subvert the institution of southern slavery, because its existence conflicts with the Utopian principles upon which they think that mankind should be governed. Their ostensible aim and real purpose is the same. However much it may be regretted that the latter will permit themselves to be the blinded instruments of gain-seeking men—however we may lament that obliquity of mental vision which would risk the hazard of so much evil for the doubtful prospect of achieving a little of good—still it would be unjust to deny or to doubt the sincerity of their convictions.

There is still another class in the Northern States of the Federal Union who engage in the clamor against what they denominate the "slave power," whose seeming opposition scarcely needs to be commented upon in enumerating the real antagonists of the institution of slavery, because their design is not in reality to *destroy* slavery, but to *acquire a political supremacy* over the slave States, and to *share with the planters the profits* of slave labor. I refer, of course, to the great manufacturing interests of New England, and, I may add, Pennsylvania. Wealthy beyond any other class, and employing their wealth in such manner as to give them great political consideration, they exercise a powerful, and, I might say, a controlling influence in all local elections.

To a full understanding of the motives which impel this class of citizens to seem to seek what in reality they do not desire, a brief reference to the industrial pursuits of the different sections is necessary. The political power of the Confederacy may in general terms be said to be divided into two great classes, to wit: Manufacturers and Agriculturists. Upon any political question involving the interests of these, the other classes range themselves upon the one side or the other, as their interests, principles, or inclinations may suggest.

It has ever been the aim of the manufacturing interests to enforce, under various pretences, the payment of a portion of the earnings of the agriculturists into their coffers. Under the popular disguise of "protection to home productions," this system for a long time prevailed; and to this day our statute-books are disfigured by the relics of this most unjust system of forcing one class to contribute of their earnings to the wealth of another class. The doctrine of "protection" became unpopular with the agriculturists in proportion as its true merits were discussed and understood. However the sacrifice they were called upon to make might be urged by appeals to their patriotism, an enlightened understanding could not fail to perceive that the real effect of such a system was to take away from the gainings of their labor, in order to add to the wealth of those who were already much richer than themselves. The numerical strength in this contest was in favor of the agriculturist, and in process of time the system fell into disfavor and into partial disuse.

For the manufacturers to wage a contest against such superior numbers, upon the direct issue, would be fruitless, because the combined South and West—both alike interested in protecting agriculture from such an unjust burden of taxes—would be able at all times to offer a successful resistance. The crusade against slavery, on the part of New England manufacturers, was designed, therefore, *to detach the great agricultural interests of the free States in the West from their natural allies, the Southern States;* and thus, by dividing the adversaries of their favorite system, and creating between them an irreconcilable feud upon a collateral issue, conquer them in detail. Having wrought up the Western States to the proper pitch of enthusiasm against the existence of "the great sin," the manufacturers say "the best means of eradicating this evil is to build up the North at the expense of the South, by means of a protective tariff;" and they call upon the Western States to "submit to a small pecuniary sacrifice," for the attainment of so desirable a result. To the South they can say: "See arrayed against you the moral power of Great Britain, exerting its ramified influence throughout the civilized world. Add to this the overwhelming numerical and political strength of the North and the West. It is not our wish to destroy you; therefore, give us the protection we claim for our manufactures: that is, give us two bales of cotton of every ten you produce, and one-fifth of your annual products of wheat, and rice, and Indian corn, and we will find means to allay the storm which is ready to engulf you in irretrievable ruin."

The scheme has been, unhappily for the interests of agriculture, but too successful. The protectionists have succeeded in attracting to their standard a large support in the western free States, where once the doctrine of free trade had complete ascendency;

while the South, if she remains in the Union in the face of this overwhelmingly hostile array, which seems resolved to compass her destruction, is rapidly drifting to her only alternative of purchasing peace at the sacrifice demanded.

Considering the facts referred to, it would appear to be an error to suppose that the manufacturers, as a class, are in reality endeavoring to achieve the destruction of the institution of slavery. They only seek, through a protective tariff, to divide with the planters the earnings of slave labor; and they assail slavery with the view of making allies and instruments of the agricultural States of the West.*

Is there not danger that, in thus "sowing the wind, they may reap the whirlwind?" It is easy to stimulate, but difficult to allay, the angry passions of mankind. A child may kindle a conflagration in mere wantonness, which a host may not afterwards be able to suppress. The voice of one gifted demagogue may incite a listening and attentive

* Since the foregoing was written, there has occurred a striking verification of the opinion here expressed. Almost upon the instant of the withdrawal of a large number of Southern Representatives and Senators from the Congress, the anti-slavery party, being thus left in a majority, adopted the "Morrill Tariff Bill," which, for its violation of every principle of free trade, and for its highly protective character, is unparalleled in the history of modern legislation anywhere in the civilized world. The controlling purpose of the political anti-slavery party which now holds possession of the General Government appears to be, to deny to the South the privilege of commercial intercourse with any portion of the world beyond the limits of the Northern States, and thus to monopolize the lion's share of the profits of slave labor.

mob to deeds of violence and blood, which, once commenced, no eloquence could arrest. May it not be apprehended that, even in the hour of seeming success, they may reap a harvest of disappointment? Can the cautious, calculating leaders of the Anglo-Republican alliance restrain the impetuosity and the zeal of the fanatical masses who have been attracted to their support by an appeal to passions which, in the flush of victory, are only to be gratified by the immediate enfranchisement of the slave and the destruction of the master?

Upon the occurrence of any event which would leave no room for doubt in the southern mind that there existed a settled purpose on the part of the powerful free North to employ her political and numerical preponderance in destroying the institutions and the independence of the South, would the Southern States hesitate for a single instant longer in inaugurating prompt measures for their security and protection? Can it be expected that the South would delay until her enemies should have decided how and when the impending blow should fall?

Let not the peaceably disposed citizens of the North delude themselves with such a hope or expectation. Self-preservation is the strongest instinct of man's nature; and when the moment above indicated shall have arrived, if ever, it may fairly be assumed that the South will stand forth as a unit in defence of her rights, her interests, and her very existence as a political power in the State. All previously existing differences will disappear, and her united people will then and there demand that the battle shall be fought and decided. The issue of life or death will have been forced upon her, and the result will be the establishment of the independence of the South, or the immediate and unconditional liberation of the slaves. The conflict once inaugurated, what horrors may not fill up the interval to its bloody close!

Where, then, will stand the discordant parties and interests which have inaugurated this war upon the South? When the battle would be fiercest, and the issue the most doubtful, would England stretch forth her arm to aid the North in the accomplishment of a victory which would strike down at one blow that system of labor upon the products of which so many millions of her subjects are dependent for their daily bread? This interrogatory may not now be answered. She may hold herself in the position of an unfriendly neutrality towards both; but the England of to-day would not be the England of the past, if she permitted her sympathies or her sensibilities to divert her from the path of her interests.

As warmly as England has espoused the cause of the Republican party, it must not be supposed that she desires the immediate abolition of slavery in America, for such a consummation would find her unprepared to meet the crisis which would follow. Hence the British political abolitionists have thrown their powerful influence upon the side of the Republican party, under a tacit agreement and understanding among the leaders of each, that the process of abolitionizing the South shall be sure but slow; thus affording what they believe will be ample time for Indian tropical productions to be augmented, as those in the slave States of America diminish.

From this reference to the internal and external adversaries of the slave States of America, it will be observed that they differ essentially in the immediate objects which they hope to accomplish when their victory shall have been achieved; and that there exists amongst them but a single element or class which may be fairly presumed to be actuated exclusively by conscientious and philanthropic convictions. This, however, is made up of the radicals, socialists, agrarians, and fanatics, both in religion and politics, to whose madness no response of reason would be available, but whose folly would of itself defeat their purposes but for the direction given to them by other, and cooler, and wiser heads.

But of all these opposing influences, it cannot be questioned that the London Times is right in its boastful declaration, that if we were to "blot out England, and English sympathies, and English power from the map of the world, the battle between the North and South would be fought on very different terms." The indirect influence of the British anti-slavery party in moulding public opinion without, and its direct influence within, in giving consistency, point, and unity to the efforts of those who, whether ignorantly or advisedly, perform for it the services of friend and allies, render it apparent that if the Southern States of the American Union can defeat the purposes of that party, the battle against their enemies is already won.

I have thus hastily glanced at the different interests which are arrayed in hostile attitude against the slave States, and I have referred impartially to what may be fairly presumed to be the moving cause of the opposition of each. In making these general classifications, however, I do not mean to say that there are not many individual exceptions, who are actuated by motives different from those which I have assigned as common to the party which seeks the overthrow of slavery in the South. But it is to be noted that all the enemies of the existing institution of slavery in the Southern States are from without. The assaults thereon emanate from those who live under other governments—who are not themselves subject to the evils of which they complain, and who may perpetuate the exemption by remaining beyond the boundaries of its influence.

LETTER IV.

Opposition to abstract Slavery resolved into opposition to Slavery in America, without considering the circumstances of its existence—Slavery Romances have misled the Public Mind—The manifest injustice of crediting them as History—The attitude of the present adversaries of Slavery in times past—Achievements of Slavery.

It is a truth not to be disguised, that the predominating influence of the civilized world at the present day is adverse to the existence of slavery. The instincts of an enlightened humanity are undeniably opposed to that condition of society which is supposed to exist as a necessary concomitant of slavery, and hence many are found to condemn its existence without duly considering that when two races so different and so unequal as those which inhabit the Southern American States are thrown together, there cannot be established between them the relations which may and should exist between different classes of the same race.

Under the lead and direction of the anti-slavery party of Great Britain, this theoretical opposition to abstract slavery has been resolved most unjustly into a feeling of hostility to the institution known under that name, now existing in the United States. This feeling of hostility thus patronized by Great Britain has received from time to time fresh impulse from the slanderous publications of British tourists, who, like Dickens, have more intellect than honesty, and a more ardent desire to reap a harvest of gold by pandering to the prejudices and vices of their readers than the meagre rewards bestowed upon those who communicate unpalatable truths. Added to these are the productions which, with more or less of literary merit, emanate from native Americans who desire by this means to ingratiate themselves into the favor of the British anti-slavery party. It is worthy here of a passing notice that the Americans, the most honored by the hereditary governing classes of Europe, and those for whom the portals of their feudal mansions are always thrown wide open, are those who have merited that distinction solely by their virulent assaults upon their native land.

A discriminating mind in estimating the value of these productions, should remember that they emanate *only from those who are wholly unacquainted by practical knowledge with the system they pretend to explain.* They are those whose whole lives have been spent in an atmosphere of hostility and hatred to the institution, and who have visited for a brief period the locality where it existed, not to discover truth, but from exaggerated and isolated facts to find material for the support of their theory, out of which to fashion a "selling book."

Such have been the productions of the Dickenses of England and the Stowes of America. Professedly illustrating the workings of the institution of slavery, all who are familiar with the subject, know them to be slanders and libels and caricatures upon truth. Even as monstrous exceptions to the general condition of the slave and his master, every citizen of a slave State knows that they have no existence, except in the pernicious books referred to. Every unprejudiced intelligent man who has had occasion to travel through the Southern States of America, has had reason to be astonished at the gross deception practiced upon the public by these professional horror-mongers.

But even admitting for the moment, that the fictitious characters so happily illustrated in these romances, whose imaginary wrongs have caused so many tears to flow from sentimental maidens and British philanthropists, are the representatives of an existing reality; that they constitute exceptions to the general state of society may be inferred from the fact that a knowledge of their existence remained unknown to the oldest inhabitants of the slave States, up to the moment when they were enlightened by these productions, the authors of which had probably never passed six months in a slave State. How unjust to one's self, as well as to those who are thus wronged, to estimate the moral worth of the Southern States, or even the value of the institution of slavery, by these admittedly monstrous exceptions.

The gifted authoress of the most popular and most mischievous romance which has ever been published upon this subject, shortly after the public judgment pronounced her work a most brilliant success, visited England, to receive in person the reward to which all acknowledged she was justly entitled at the hands of British abolitionists. She was feasted and toasted in the aristocratic mansions of ennuied Duchesses and received the homage of the most distinguished British politicians. She returned after a season to her native land, and gave vent to her gratitude for the brilliant reception which had been accorded to her, by the publication of her "Sunny Memories." Suppose that she had entered England with the same feelings of hatred towards the aristocracy which she entertained towards the Southern citizens of her own country, and instead of taking up her abode in the palaces of the rich, she had entered the prisons where the vilest criminals were confined, and had promenaded the streets or penetrated into the dens of infamy and vice, which, in certain localities, contaminate that great city; and out of the materials thus furnished, and with heroes and heroines thus discovered, she had published, after the prototype of Uncle Tom's Cabin, her "Cloudy Memories" of London, as a true picture of English life, English habits, and English morals.

Unfortunately for the cause of justice, it is from materials even more meagre and less illustrative of truth, that the diatribes against slavery are composed, upon which even many good men have allowed their opinions to be formed and their prejudices to be excited.

The Southern States of the American Confederacy rest under the serious disadvantage of being the subject of assault emanating from those who entertain opinions upon the subject of Government the most widely variant, and unfortunately these extreme classes are those who act upon convictions of right without reference to any pecuniary interest which may be involved in the question.

The laws which recognize the existence of slavery, in their very nature, and upon their very face, deny the universal equality of the races of men. They assume that the African slave in America is not now, uever has been, and never will be a suitable companion or the equal of the white man, either socially or politically. Here then is a distinct issue, and an irreconcilable difference with, and an utter denial of one of the most cherished doctrines of agrarian or radical Democracy. Hence the Southern States are assailed by all the "isms" of the old and new world. They are a target not only for those who advocate specifically the doctrines of Abolitionism, but for those also who, upon the baseless fabric of an impossible equality, have erected theoretical Utopias in which the family of man, of every clime, religion, and complexion, may mingle together in a common brotherhood.

On the other hand, the Southern States and the institution of slavery are no less opposed by many of the leaders of that aristocracy in the old world which claims to govern *the masses of their own race*, by a right emanating directly from the Almighty!

In Great Britain, as well as in the more despotic governments of the old world, the special advocates and defenders of the "right divine," those most tenacious of maintaining intact the exclusive right to govern, which they say by the will of God has been transmitted to them from their ancestors, are leagued in a brotherhood of opposition to slavery in America, with all the fanatics of the new world, comprising the advocates of "free love," the "socialists," the Infidels the theoretical "Red Republicans," and "abolitionists," whose crude notions of liberty and impracticable conceptions of government have contributed far more towards bringing discredit upon 'free institutions' than in instilling into the minds of others the undeniable truths on which, to a certain extent, their pernicious theories are based. From those holding these extreme and apparently irreconcilable opinions in regard to the natural rights of man have emanated the most virulent assaults upon the institution of American slavery.

This seemingly incongruous combination of discordant materials would at a superficial glance appear most unnatural, and such a unity of purpose between them might be accounted as accidental. A more thorough investigation of the subject of slavery in the United States and of its practical bearing upon the social and political condition of the inhabitants, develops at once the natural causes which have produced this coincidence of feeling between those who are so widely asunder in their political principles. I will hereafter refer to these causes in detail. At present my purpose is simply to group together the elements and sources of that opposition against which the Southern States are called upon to defend themselves—while they have so many and such formidable adversaries who have no practical knowledge in regard to the workings of the institution which they unite in condemning, who, with the single exception of Great Britain, are in no manner responsible morally or politically for the sin, if it be one, of slavery, and whose motives even the most charitable will not ask us to admit, proceed wholly from a principle of benevolence or philanthropy—it is a truth, which should not be without due influence, that in every State of the Confederacy where slavery exists, there likewise exists a unity of opinion as remarkable for its undeviating and firm support of the existing relation between the two races as it is universal. The history of the world does not furnish an example of such unanimity upon any one subject, which has been so often and for so long a time a subject of active and thorough analysis and investigation. All conditions, all professions, all religions, agree that the institution of slavery in the Southern States, in consideration of all the circumstances under which it now exists, is right morally and politically, and that the present relations of the two races must be maintained at all hazards, so long as they occupy together the same territory.

When it is considered that of the European races resident in the slave States but a comparatively small number are slaveowners, this unity of sentiment and opinion should have some weight with those who have themselves no practical knowledge on the subject; and who derive their information chiefly from the distorted descriptions of its avowed enemies, or from romances written by ingenious authors to make selling books.

Before an impartial tribunal sitting in judgment to decide the question upon its merits, it would surely be regarded as a point worthy of consideration, that those who testify against slavery, as at present existing in the Southern States, are ignorant from personal observation of its practical effects, because they do not live within the sphere of its influence. Its great adversaries—those who are engaged jointly in the effort to crush it by every means within their reach—are Great Britain and the Northern States of the Confederacy. The first, as we have already said, established it upon the soil of the South, and afterwards secured from the European powers the exclusive right to the traffic in slaves; while the last, within the memory of those now living, sold to the Southerners the very slaves, or their immediate ancestors, to the very men from whom they would now rob them. What a curious spectacle to the eyes of disinterested observers! How strange that these should be the leaders in such a crusade! But we have to deal with facts. And these are they who assail the South for tolerating the enormous sin of slavery!

On the other hand, those who would testify in favor of the existing institution, and who will never consent that the relations at present subsisting between the African race and themselves shall be materially changed, are the citizens in mass, and, with scarcely an exception, who have passed their lives, and whose destiny has been cast, for good or for evil, where the institution has been established.

Such as I have described them are the adversaries and assailants—such the defenders of slavery in the Southern States of the American Union. To the success of the former, it is necessary that they should establish—first, their right to decide what shall be the political and domestic policy of the States of the South; second, they must show that the institution of slavery has made the condition of the slaves worse than it would have been if they had never been placed in servitude; third, they must establish that more good than evil will result from its abolition; and lastly, it will be conceded, in consideration of the peculiar attitude occupied by the chief assailants, that they must show in what manner they can remunerate the owners for the sacrifices they will be required to make, should their slave property be set at liberty.

It would be asking too much to require the defenders of the Southern States to prove that their peculiar system of labor has attained to that point of excellence from whence there can be no improvement. All human institutions are imperfect; and it is not pretended that this forms an exception. That there are evils incident thereto, is not to be questioned. It is sufficient, if it can be established, that more good than evil has resulted, and, in all human probability, will continue to flow from it. That the results achieved through its instrumentality have tended materially to promote the general welfare of mankind, and that these same benefits cannot be obtained under any other system of labor which has been devised—that incidental evils may spring out of the system—that cruelties may be inflicted by the master upon the slave—that instances of inhumanity have occurred, and will occur, is necessarily incident to the relations which subsist between master and slave, as well as between father and child, husband and wife, master and apprentice, power and weakness; but if it can be established that such instances are only exceptional, and that the slaves, whose condition we are considering, are provided with more of the physical comforts of life—that they are less often overworked, and that, as a class, they are happier and more exempt from the ordinary ills of life than any like number of laborers in the world, of whatever race, color, or nation, it would seem that those who are conscientiously opposed to slavery, upon the ground of its supposed inhumanity, should be satisfied to leave the matter where it stands.

Furthermore, although the public sentiment of the civilized world is averse to the existence of such a relation between man and man as master and slave, yet if, in addition to the manifold advantages to mankind which result from this institution, it can be established that the condition of the Africans, as slaves in America, is far better, in every essential particular than that of any of their race ever has been, from the commencement of recorded or traditional history—that from barbarians and cannibals they have attained to a moderate degree of civilization—that from heathens they have become Christians—that from a condition of wretchedness and misery they have become comparatively contented and happy—that having sprung from a race which has never achieved any thing for the good of mankind—whose entire history furnishes not one single name which is associated with any thing good—which has not in the past, in their native land, exhibited any qualities above the instincts of brutes—they have, nevertheless, through the instrumentality of the institution of slavery, been made to contribute, in an important degree, to the wants of the civilized world—it is not demanding too much of an enlightened public sentiment to abate somewhat of the natural feeling of repugnance to the existence of this relation between man and man, in view of results so advantageous to the human race, and which are attended, incidentally, by so many blessings to those in whose cause so much unnecessary sympathy has been expended.

That the results enumerated have followed, and that they have been consequences of the existence of African slavery, is susceptible of easy demonstration. Nor will they be denied by those who have investigated the subject without prejudice, and with the single purpose of discovering the truth. But, unhappily, public opinion has been forestalled, to a great extent, chiefly by those who have employed this instrument, not with a view to correct error and to propagate truth, but to gratify a feeling of unkindness and hatred towards those under whose auspices the products of slave labor have been made to contribute to the wants, the luxuries, and the comforts of the civilized world.

Instead, then, of requiring the Southern States to prove that their system of slave labor is without fault or blemish—instead of asking that it be tried by an ideal standard of abstract right, which will not allow the smallest evil with the greatest good—let us examine it simply as a human institution, with its good and its evil arrayed upon the one side and the other, "nothing extenuate nor set down aught in malice." When we have looked into the leading features of its history, from its origin to the present day, and have marked out its achievements, for good and for evil, before we resolve upon its destruction, or even make up our minds to impair its strength and influence, let us compare it with all the other systems of labor which have been adopted by mankind, with a view to the achievement of the same results. But, above all, let us institute a comparison between this system and the "factory system," the "African-apprentice system," the "Cooly system," and the "India system" of Great Britain, the greatest and most formidable of all the adversaries of slavery in America.

LETTER V.

Labor, the Foundation of the Wealth of Nations—Duties of Government—Declaration of Independence, and its correct interpretation—Classification of Rulers, and the Governed—Names do not express the Qualities of Objects.

THE foundation of the wealth and prosperity of civilized nations consists in labor. It is of all the subjects which engage the attention of Governments, the most important. The products of physical labor are essential to the greatness and power of any nation, whether it be the labor of her own subjects or citizens, or an appropriation of the labor of others for her aggrandizement.

Politically, there exists in every State two classes—those who govern, and those who are governed. When regarded in reference to all the relations which subsist between men towards each other, the latter class may be resolved into three, which are distinct and strongly defined in all the various relations of life.

There are in every civilized State —first the rulers, those upon whom are confered the right of establishing laws for the government of the great mass, who occupy the relation of subjects or citizens. In whatever manner this power is acquired, whether by inheritance, or the free choice of the governed, or by accidental circumstances, the duties of those who hold this important position are the same, however different in practice may be the performance. The foundation of these duties may, in general terms be defined to be, so to govern as to confer the greatest sum of happiness upon those whose rights and interests are confided to them; that is, to confer the greatest amount of good to the greatest number, without infringing upon the natural or legally defined rights of any portion of those who may properly claim to be citizens. There are sacrifices to which the minority must submit in deference to the general good of the whole; but such sacrifices must in all well regulated governments, be founded upon recognized general principles, and can never be demanded, upon an emergency not fully provided for, unless in obedience to the universally recognized law of nature—self-preservation.

In the erection of a free government, as well as in the progress of its existence, the citizens have a right to admit or to deny to aliens or foreigners, the full rights of citizenship. Even though the government be founded upon the principle, that "all men are by nature free and equal," yet in its practical application, it could only be intended to refer to those who were *specifically designated as citizens.* If such a principle in its broadest sense were accepted and adopted by a government, it would bear within itself the elements of a speedy dissolution. For the peace and well-being of society, there must be a degree of homogeneousness amongst its several members. Due regard must be had even to the prejudices of race, religion, and color, to habits and to customs. It must be conceded, that however broad and comprehensive may be the principles upon which a government may be founded, its laws are *local* in their operation *as to territory*, and *specific* in their application as *to persons*. The Constitution of a free government, or the general principles on which by express or tacit consent a nation is to be governed, whether or not founded upon the principle of equality, is simply the article of agreement by which the parties to the contract or arrangement are to be governed, and is not designed to confer the privileges of the partnership upon any other persons.

The history of the establishment of the Government of the United States of America, illustrates this general principle with perfect clearness. In the very inauguration of its independent existence, it is declared, that "*all men are created equal*, that they are endowed with certain *inalienable rights*," that among these are "*life*, *liberty* and the pursuit of happiness."

It would be a most manifest injustice to the intelligence, frankness, and common sense of the distinguished patriots who, in the name of the people, incorporated these declarations in their first act of independence, to suppose that they intended them to be understood in a literal sense. In the first place, it cannot be said that any two men are "created equal." One is born the inheritor of riches, another of poverty; one strong, another weak; one intellectual, another stupid; and from the cradle to the grave these inequalities are perpetuated. But if we give to the expression a common sense signification, namely: that all men who were then and there represented by them, and whose chosen agents they were, and in whose name they spoke, were desirous of establishing a Government *on the basis of a perfect equality of rights*, then it is the eloquent enunciation of a noble sentiment which the nations of the world might adopt with benefit to their subjects. Neither must we suppose that the authors of this famous declaration desired to express so absurd a sentiment, as that the rights of *life* and *liberty* conferred by the Creator, were literally and truly *inalienable*. For in all civilized nations there must be a power, not only to *alienate* or to *deprive* a citizen of his *liberty*, but even of his *life*.

But the best commentary upon this sublime declaration of the general principles upon which the revolted Colonies of Great Britain proposed to establish for *themselves* a new Government, and the surest means of arriving at a knowledge of the interpretation placed upon them by their authors, may be discovered in the specific laws and regulations which they founded in illustration of the principles thus announced.

Upon the establishment of the Constitution, those who were represented were the free citizens of European blood, who had been the subjects of Great Britain, or who had participated in securing their independence. The preamble to that instrument declares that,

We, the people of the United States, in order to form a more perfect Union, establish justice, insure domestic tranquillity, provide for the common defence, promote the general welfare, *and secure the blessings of liberty* TO OURSELVES AND OUR POSTERITY, *do ordain and establish this Constitution* for the United States of America.

It will thus be seen, that however general and comprehensive may have been the principles upon which the Government was based, yet in the very first act defining and applying these general principles, the *specific* purpose of the citizens in the formation of their Constitution is defined to be, *to secure the blessings of liberty*, not for mankind, *but for themselves and their posterity.*

So far from establishing in a literal sense, the inalienable right of all men to liberty, Section 2, Article IV. declares:

A person charged in any State with treason, felony, or other crime, who shall flee from justice, and be found in another State, shall on demand of the Executive authority of the State from which he fled, be delivered up to be removed to the State having jurisdiction of the crime.

No person held to service or labor in one State, under the laws thereof, escaping into another, shall in consequence of any law or regulation therein, be discharged from such service or labor, but shall be delivered up on claim of the party to whom such service or labor may be due.

Section 9, Article I, declares, that,

The migration or importation of such persons, as any of the States now existing shall think proper to admit, shall not be prohibited by the Congress prior to the year 1808, *but a tax or dutg may be imposed on sueh importation, not exeeeding ten dollars for such person.*

The two last paragraphs, refer to the Africans, who were, or might be held as slaves. From these it will be observed, that the authors of the Declaration of Independence, and the framers of the Constitution, not only recognized the existence of the institution of slavery, but authorized its expansion by permitting the importation of more Africans with the view of reducing them to slavery, and gave to it a legally and constitutionally recognized existence by claiming the right to derive a direct revenue from the traffic.

There is scarcely an article of the Constitution which is not at variance with a perfectly literal construction of the mere words promulgated in the Declaration of Independence. Not only was the servile condition of the African race fully recognized, but to Congress was reserved the right of declaring upon what terms foreigners, even of our own race, might be admitted to the rights of citizenship, with full authority to exclude them altogether from the exercise of those rights, or to dictate the terms upon which they might be permitted to reside in the country.

If Congress should to-morrow, in obedience to the clearly expressed will of the citizens, declare that no person born under a foreign government and not already a citizen, should be permitted to enjoy the rights of citizenship, who could say that the act would be in violation of any principle on which our Government is founded? The right to define the circumstances under which aliens may be made citizens, is an indispensable part of the sovereignty of a nation. This right of self-protection involves as a necessary sequence, the privilege of total or partial exclusion, as the interests of the citizens may require.

Those who assume that *the words* of the Declaration of Independence, should be construed literally, and in their application under the Constitution were intended to embrace all mankind, render a poor tribute to the sagacity or honesty of the fathers of the Republic, whose reason must have taught them that such a government would have been impossible; and who in effect gave their sanction to laws which in all their parts, from the first clause of the Constitution to the last act of their illustrious lives, did violence to such an interpretation of their meaning and intention!

But say the more reasonable advocates of a literal construction, "There must of course be understood to be exceptions to the general application of these principles." In announcing that all mankind were born free and equal, it was not meant thereby, that the rights secured to our own citizens were necessarily incident to foreigners or aliens who might come amongst us. Nor was it meant, that the rights of all men to "life" and "liberty" were, as therein declared, literally inalienable, because it is essential to the good of society, that there should exist a power in the State to take away the life or the liberty of a citizen who commits certain crimes.

This is certainly true, but if reason compels us in justice to the authors of that work, and in obedience to the dictates of common sense, to admit that there are some exceptions to the universal application in practice of the general principles therein enunciated, by what rule of interpretation is it declared, that the exceptions enumerated above are all that can be permitted? In effect we discover by investigation, that not only do the laws and customs of every government, admit of other exceptions than those referred to, but the constitutions and laws of every State of the Confederacy equally do violence to a literal construction of the rights of man as set forth in the instrument referred to—as an example, the universally recognized right of a parent to the services of his offspring up to the age of twenty-one years, and the similar right of the husband to the services of the wife during her entire life. Thus we find, that probably two-thirds of the citizens of America are, by the universally recognized laws of the land, and without the pretence of crime, held as "chattels" bound to service and labor, without any fixed compensation. Others virtually occupy towards them in the estimation of the law the relation of master.

But there are still other cases in which the Constitution and laws of the United States, as well as the laws of all other organized governments, deny even to free born citizens of mature age, unstained by any imputation of crime, the "inalienable right" to the enjoyment of life and liberty! The farmer may be taken from his plough, the mechanic from his tools, the merchant from his desk, and all be forced to leave family and friends, and march at a moment's notice to face death upon the battle-field, even though his judgment and inclinations may oppose the war in which his country may be engaged. Against his will, and in violation of his personal interests, and without having done a crime, his inalienable rights, according to the literal phraseology of the Declaration of Independence, are violated! Yet what sane man would not admit that this constitutes another proper occasion for the refusal to recognize the existence of the "inalienable right" to either "liberty" or "life."

Let us then do justice to common reason, to the signers of the Declaration of Independence, and to the framers of the Constitution. Let us consider that acting in the *name* and as *the representatives* of the revolted provinces of Great Britain, become free by their glorious deeds, the general principles which they enunciated were designed, in their practical application, *for those only whose agents they were, and in whose name they spoke*, namely: *the free white inhabitants* of the sovereign States they represented, *for* THEM *and for their* POSTERITY! Then there is found to be a sublime harmony in the principles they declared, and in the practical application of those noble principles, worthy, in all time to come, of the admiration of that posterity for whom were thus secured and consolidated the blessings of liberty.

But to resume the subject from which I have for a brief space digressed. The subjects or citizens of the State may be divided in general terms into three strongly defined classes.

First—Those who neither labor nor give direction

to labor; who are possessed of the means of support without being obliged to resort to the drudgeries of labor or trade, and who have come into the possession thereof by inheritance—by superior intellectual endowments, or by accidental circumstances.

Second—Those who give direction to labor; who do not actually produce by their own hands, but who make available the results of the labor of others. These occupy the station of intermediaries between the consumers and the producers—between those who labor and those who purchase the products of labor.

Thirdly—The great mass of mankind, who from necessity or choice, give sustenance to the world by the labor of their hands; who cause the earth to bring forth its fruits to feed the hungry; who produce the material to clothe the naked; who fashion the ships to transport the products of one country to another, and who in fine produce all that which is employed in ministering to the physical comforts, the convenience, and the luxuries of the human race. Upon this last class depend not only the greatness and wealth of empires, but the very existence of all the other classes who go to make up the aggregate of a nation. Production is necessary to the wealth of a nation. Wealth is an essential element of power, and power is indispensable to the protection of independence and liberty from external violence. Every dollar of value added to the productive industry of the State adds to the wealth and security of its citizens. The cotton bales produced upon the Southern plantations by slave labor, as well as the barrels of flour which repay the toil of the free laborers of the West, alike contribute to the wealth of New England. They are soldiers, fully armed for the defence of the Republic, but powerless for harm to its citizens.

That Government is therefore best, without reference to its form or name, which confers the greatest amount of happiness upon all its citizens, and which at the same time induces the greatest amount of production. The history of the world has exhibited that the benefits conferred by governments upon mankind are not always indicated by the name or the political form by which they have been known or designated.

The free republics of Southern America, regarded as a whole, have proven to be unworthy and incapable of fulfilling the legitimate ends of government. Anarchy, imbecility, and at times the most odious tyranny, have marked their downward progress from the date of their independent existence even up to the present moment of time, when some of them have almost ceased to be regarded as among the family of nations.

The laboring classes of France, under some of her most despotic rulers, have been left in the enjoyment of the greatest amount of real liberty and prosperity; while perhaps the most cruel despotism under which that beautiful country has ever groaned, was during the brief period of the first republic, when the very name of liberty was made odious by its excesses—when the blood and tears of millions of her citizens deluged the land; and when the civilized world stood aghast and horror stricken at the contemplation of scenes enacted in the name of freedom, as fiercely cruel and despotic as had ever in times past distinguished an epoch in the career of any other civilized nation.

In the United States of America, upon the other hand, there exists a confederated republic where according to theory and practice, up to the present period in its history, human liberty is happily blended with human progress, and where the two have marched hand in hand together. In all its acquisitions it has conferred upon the conquered the boon of its own freedom, and has made them equal participants in the benefits of its institutions and in the advantages of its growing power.

How can the anti-slavery American who contemplates the grand achievements of the infancy of the republic, attempt to destroy one of the chief elements of its greatness, for the doubtful prospect of accomplishing even all the good they hope for? Alas! that the madness of sectional hatred should close the eyes of so many worthy and patriotic citizens, to the danger of taking even one more step in the direction which their passions,—not their reason—is leading them.

The brief reference made to well known facts of history illustrates simply that neither the name nor the form of a government indicates, with positive distinctness, the degree of real liberty or prosperity enjoyed by its subjects. A despot even might confer upon his subjects all the liberty they desire, while the citizens of a republic, by a perversion of the principles of such a government, or an unwarrantable exercise of power on the part of a majority, or by the still more available despotism of a dominant section, may be made to endure the most odious tyranny.

While this is true in affairs of State, it is equally so in many of the affairs of life. Theorists are too apt to draw conclusions from *the names* of things, rather than *from the things themselves*—from the shadow rather than the substance. Even moralists are but too prone to direct their anathemas against theoretical, rather than real vices; against the garments which might seem to indicate the presence of vice, rather than against vice, which may clothe itself in the habiliments of virtue.

He who seeks to find truth, who aspires to arrive at just conclusions, without giving undue influence to his own mere prejudices or those of others, should remember that the names of things are not always even shadows of the objects they profess to describe; that the mere characters which designate a particular object, have nothing to do in making up the qualities of the object itself; and that theories, beautiful in themselves, and seemingly susceptible of the clearest demonstration, are often wofully at fault, when applied to the practical affairs of life.

LETTER VI.

Different systems of Labor considered—Free Labor more or less dependent upon Capital—Southey on English Labor System—Unhappy Condition of the Factory Operatives—Products of Slave and Free Labor Compared.

SINCE on the productions of labor rest the foundations of the wealth and power of nations, it is a question of controlling interest for governments to decide how, and under what form, the greatest amount of production can be obtained, consistently with the well-being and happiness of those who labor, and the general prosperity of all. Although each nation has a more direct interest in its own productions than in those of others, there is a community of reciprocal interests as well as obligations among the family of nations, which make the proceeds of the labor of each, important to the others. A State therefore should encourage and foster any particular branch of production in which it possesses natural advantages, not only for its own sake, but also for the promotion of the interests of mankind.

In general terms there may be said to be two classes or systems of labor, namely: that which is more or less voluntary, according to circumstances, and which is denominated "free labor," and that which is involuntary or forced, which is called "slave labor." That these titles or names afford no clear indication of the relative happiness, comfort, or even freedom of those who are ranked respectively under one or the other of the above designations, is susceptible of easy demonstration by reference to past and now existing facts.

Strictly speaking, there can scarcely be said to be such a thing as free labor, when applied to the great mass of mankind who are obliged to bestow their physical services for an employer in order to procure the bread necessary to sustain life. Take as an example the great body of the factory operatives of England. *They must work or starve!* They must perform certain tasks which are placed before them, or must submit to a deprivation of the common necessaries of life. Not only must they accomplish these tasks at the bidding of another, but having received the scanty wages which are said to be their due, and having purchased therewith the coarse fare which is necessary to appease the pangs of hunger, they have nothing left for the morrow; and so day by day the same alternative is presented to them,—*to do the task assigned them or to starve. The laborer has the physical power* to stay away from the workshop, but *the alternative* is ever present to him. Nature asserts its dominion, and again and again, until life's end, he voluntarily returns to his daily and never-ending toil. This is denominated free labor! The illustration will not be said to be an exaggeration. It does not even convey to the mind a picture so sad as the reality, in the case of more than a majority of the day laborers of Europe. I have referred only to strong men, not helpless women and children, whose necessities are all the greater for their weakness, and whose weakness makes them still more dependent and still oftener the subjects of injustice and wrong. All who have investigated the subject know that these are the alternatives and conditions upon which free labor is performed by a body of human beings, even in free and enlightened England, more numerous than the entire number of slaves in America.

I only refer to this state of things as a fact which none will deny. Not by way of complaint; for it may be an unavoidable evil attendant upon an overcrowded population. But it serves as a definition of what is meant by "free" in contradistinction to "slave labor."

It is not my purpose in these letters to adduce specific proofs in regard to all the facts which I assume to be true. I intend to deal with the subjects frankly, and in reference chiefly to general principles. In illustration of these principles I will adduce only such truths as will be readily admitted by the intelligent reader. To misstate, or even to exaggerate these facts would be only to weaken the cause which I defend; and to illustrate the operations of a general system of labor by its exceptions, would be to imitate the injustice which has been so much practiced by the writers as well as the readers of anti-slavery romances. I neither mean to deny the evils which are incident to the institution of slavery upon the one hand, nor the great benefits which have resulted to mankind from free labor upon the other. But I do mean to say and to prove that both systems, as mere human institutions, are attended in their practical developments by both good and evil. That neither one is adapted to all the wants of man, nor to all the productions of the earth. And that the institution of slavery in America has produced, under the intelligent guardianship of the present generation, more of good to mankind with less of evil to the African or of injustice to any, than either one of all the various systems of free labor which have been adopted as a substitute therefor, since the termination of the American war of Independence.

SOUTHEY fairly describes the condition of the free laborers of England when he says:

In no country can such riches be acquired by commerce, but it is the *one* who grows rich by the labor of the hundred. The hundred human beings like himself, as wonderfully fashioned by nature, gifted with the like capacities, and equally made for immortality, are sacrificed *body* and *soul*. Horrible as it must needs appear, the assertion is true to the very letter. They are deprived in childhood of all instruction and all enjoyment of the sports in which childhood instinctively indulges—of fresh air by day and of natural sleep by night. Their health, physical and moral, is alike destroyed; they die of diseases induced by unremitting task-work, by confinement in the impure air of crowded rooms, by the particles of metallic or vegetable dust which they are continually inhaling; or they live to grow up without decency, without comfort and without hope—without morals, without religion, and without shame, *and bring forth slaves like themselves to tread in the same path of misery.* . . .

The English boast of their liberty, but there is no liberty in England for the poor. . . . When the poor are incapable of contributing any longer to their own support they are removed to the workhouse. I cannot express the feelings of hopelessness and dread with which all decent people look on to this wretched termination of a life of labor. . . . To this society of wretchedness the laboring poor of England look as their last resting place on this side of the grave; and rather than enter abodes so miserable they endure the severest privations as long as it is possible to exist.

These are the unexaggerated words of an Englishman, who thoroughly understood the subject about which he wrote. But still it would be an error to suppose that there is no liberty, even for the poor in England. On the contrary, in many of the essential elements of freedom, our own Constitution and laws are founded upon the Constitution and laws of Great Britain. The evils to which reference is made grow naturally out of that system of free labor, which is a consequence of the present systems of civilized governments throughout the world; and though they exist to a greater extent in England, with its overcrowded population, than in America, still they follow, as an unavoidable sequence to laws which recognize the rights of property.

I have before me the voluminous reports of the Parliamentary Committee, which, a few years ago, investigated the condition of the laboring poor of England. Large as are the volumes which contain the results of this investigation, covering thousands of pages, each page is a record of misery, destitution, hardships, and crime, which can scarcely be contemplated without a shudder of horror. Is there any remedy for the evils thus detailed? Can laws be enacted by which they may be eradicated? Practical philanthropy must answer, that while they may be ameliorated, yet so long as one man is very rich, and five hundred are very poor, they cannot be eradicated. So long as the laws permit all men to accumulate wealth, there will be five hundred who are poor to one who is rich. What interest has *the one man* in the fate of the *five hundred?* First, to avail himself of their labor at the lowest possible remuneration; second, to obtain, in the shortest possible space of time, the greatest possible amount of labor. When the work is finished, or when the laborer is physically unable to work any more, the interest of the employer ceases. The estate of the rich man, in the sinews of the poor, terminates, and then the workhouse claims its prey!

But away with statistics and printed testimony. I appeal to the judgment and common sense of every intelligent reasoner. I appeal to the indelible record, written in ineffaceable characters upon the heart of every observant traveller in Europe and the more civilized portions of Asia, for the exact truth of what I am going to say.

One half of the free laborers of the so-called free States of the world, at this very moment of time, men, women, and children, are in a state of moral and physical destitution. One half of these earn a most scanty subsistence of dry bread, by performing the tasks which are set before them by a nominal employer, but a real master! The other half of this unhappy class, unable to work, or to obtain work, *are driven to the practice of the most loathsome vices*, not from choice, but from an inexorable necessity! One half of the free laborers, who are in a condition something better than these, are nevertheless obliged, by the greatest of all tyrants, necessity, to labor and toil at the bidding of a superior for their daily sustenance, with the ever-present cousciousness weighing upon their minds and spirits, that if sickness, for a single day, intervenes, their scanty wages will be stopped. If their disability is of long continuance, starvation, or the workhouse, are ever before them as alternatives.

This classification of the free laborers of the world assumes that one-fourth are in a position of independence, in which they may be, to a greater or less extent, discuss with their employers the terms upon which they will bestow the labor of their hands. Is there an intelligent, candid observer who will say that I have made too low an estimate of these, or that I have exaggerated the number of the dependent and destitute?

To the ignorant it is sometimes not well to tell the whole truth. A good cause is often weakened by endeavors to force too much knowledge upon those who are incapable of understanding. The mind naturally rejects all the testimony in favor of any proposition, if a portion thereof seems to be an exaggeration, a misapplication, or a misstatement. The savage chieftain of a tropical island listened attentively to the sublime truths which were taught to him by a Christian missionary; and believed! He credited without difficulty the miracles which had been performed by the Most High, as communicated in the sacred pages of the Holy Bible. But when the missionary informed him that by a law of nature, and without any direct interposition of the Almighty, there were some countries where, during a certain season, the water became hard like stone, he who had never known any other temperature than such as is produced by a tropical sun, refused to believe, and ended by rejecting all the truths which had before been taught to him.

But, just as surely as water becomes hard like stone in a certain temperature, do the inequalities recognized by the laws of all civilized nations of the present day, in the relative wealth of the different classes, produce that virtual slavery which, however disguised under attractive names, is *still the subjection of one man to the will of another.*

Great Britain, in many respects, stands foremost among the great powers of the world. Of all the governments of the old world, her Constitution and her laws embody the noblest principles. The press is free, and the complaints of any class of citizens may be spread before mankind without hindrance from any quarter. She stands foremost in the rapid march of improvement, which has signalized the present generation. I have already said that her governing classes, and her subjects, taken collectively or individually, are, in many respects, worthy of the highest respect of mankind. It is, therefore, fair to consider that the condition of her free laborers is at least equal to the average of the free laborers of the world. Now, when I declare that in the estimate I have made, if I have exaggerated at all, it has been in assuming the class of laborers which enjoys a partial freedom, as larger than the facts would warrant, I know that I am sustained by the documentary testimony published by Parliament, and I am sure that every enlightened and candid Englishman, who has made himself acquainted with the subject, will not hesitate to admit the truth of what I have said.

So far, then, as regards one half of the laborers of England, free labor may be defined to be the inalienable right of the subject to starve, rather than perform the tasks which are commanded by a master. It is certainly a glorious privilege; but alas for the weakness of poor human nature, few are found willing, by accepting voluntarily of the alternative, to prove themselves martyrs in the glorious cause of freedom! We may pity them for their weakness, we may weep over their sad fate, but we cannot blame them for preferring to obey the instincts of nature, rather than the promptings of manhood.

Far be it from me to say that it would be proper to take away from the English laborer this glorious birthright of liberty. Poor as it is, at a moment when infirmities and want are pressing upon him, it is probably the best inheritance which has been bequeathed to him by his ancestors. Nor do I mean to express the opinion that the introduction of a more humane system, such as that of the African slave labor of America, would on the whole be desirable.

But I do mean to say, that all the different systems of labor which are in operation throughout the world, are attended with evils. If each nation would therefore endeaver with an honest purpose to remove these from their midst, instead of seeking to reform their neighbors, true philanthropy and benevolence would be much the gainers.

Although it may be assumed that in certain latitudes and under certain circumstances, (both of which conditions are fulfilled in the Southern part of the continent of America,) African slave labor is the best, the mildest, and the most humane of all other systems, yet it is not pretended that the interests of mankind require that it should be universal. Common reason teaches that the same rule or system of labor cannot be applied to the overcrowded continent of Europe, and to the sparsely populated wilds of tropical America. Neither can the human race be generalized in such manner as to apply the same fixed rules of government to all. There must be an adaptation between them; laws sufficiently stringent to answer all the purposes of society, when applied to certain communities, would prove wholly insufficient under a different state of circumstances, for the protection of the weak, the peaceable, and the well-disposed, against the encroachments of the wicked and the strong.

Free labor in England may accomplish all that could be desired in regard to material development, because not to labor is to starve. But in tropical countries such an inducement to work is wanting, because a bountiful nature, almost spontaneously produces all that is necessary to the absolute physical wants of man. Therefore when the alternative is presented to a freeman to labor or not to labor, he chooses the latter, for the very sufficient reason that he can subsist without it. There is no fact more clearly established, by actual experiment, than that neither the European nor any race of freemen can or will labor successfully in tropical climates. Even in the more temperate latitudes of the Southern States of the American Union, the articles of tobacco, cotton, rice, and sugar have only been successfully produced in large quantities, through the instrumentality of slave labor.

Should, therefore, slave labor be abolished, and real free labor be substituted therefor, tropical productions must, to a great extent, cease to contribute to the necessities or to the luxuries of mankind; or they would at least, from their limited production, be attainable only by the wealthy classes.

The philanthropist should bear in mind that the greater part of that soothing beverage prepared from the coffee bean, which is alike the cheap luxury of the rich and the solace of the humble and the poor of every land, *is the product of slave labor*. The cane sugar and the syrups, which from their cheapness have become accessible to the poor, and which may be found in every laborer's cottage in America, and to a great extent throughout the world, are alone made accessible to them, through the instrumentality of slave labor! To these may be added the articles of rice and tobacco, the use of which has become almost universal among the great body of laborers throughout the world. Cotton, by means of which mankind is clothed, is the product of slave labor!

From the single slave State of Brazil alone, there is an annual importation of coffee into the United States, of about *one million of bags*, valued at fifteen millions of dollars. It is consumed by every family, and by almost every inhabitant of the Republic.

Of the cane sugar which is exported from the countries where it is produced, for foreign consumption, about seven hundred thousand tons are the result of slave labor! Less than five hundred thousand tons are the product of Asiatic and African races, subjected to the European powers, while the entire product of free laborers of the European races, sold in foreign markets, would not supply the necessities of the city of Boston alone!

Of cotton, the product of the world offered for sale in the European and American markets, is now about four and a half millions of bales; nearly four millions of which are produced by the Southern States of the American Confederacy, something more than half a million by subjugated Asiatics and Africans; while that produced and sold by free laborers of the European races, would not supply a manufacturing township of Massachusetts!

He whose heart throbs with a single generous or benevolent sentiment towards the laboring, toiling millions of poor, may well for an instant pause, and ask himself if it is the part of true philanthropy to strike off, at one blow, so many of the few comforts which their limited means permit them to enjoy? I know that it is difficult for him who has at command the ready means to purchase all that his appetite craves, without regard to cost, to imagine that the deprivation of one or two simple articles can amount to any great sacrifice. But such should remember, that while they may procure substitutes, the poor have no such resource. While they, by means of their wealth, may still supply themselves with the articles referred to, even at their enhanced value, they have only been made accessible to the poor by means of their cheapness, and their use must be abandoned when they become dear.

Upon a memorable occasion, a number of the inhabitants of Boston, in defiance of British power and British interests, heroically entered the English ships which lay in their harbor, and cast into the sea the tea of which their cargo consisted. The patriotic citizens refused to enjoy an article of luxury, which they conceived could only be procured by a submission to an unlawful act of tyranny on the part of their rulers. This noble sacrifice of their appetites to their patriotism was noised abroad in every land. It has been the fruitful theme of the poets' songs, and is the bright spot in the pages of her annals, over which the historian loves to linger. To this day, the Bostonian refers to the act of sacrifice, as the most brilliant and enduring testimony of the patriotic devotion of his ancestors to the cause of freedom. Although the deprivation was only to exist during a brief season, the world has not for this cause abated of its admiration for the heroic achievement over their appetites.

The anti-slavery party of to-day demands, that the toiling millions of mankind shall strike off for ever, from the list of their comforts and their necessaries, the products of slave labor. How vast the difference in the sacrifice made by the Bostonians and that which they this day require from the poor of the world!

Compare the products of slave labor, and the uses to which they are applied, with some of the more important achievements of so-called free labor, in the same field.

Look into the loathsome grogshops which contaminate the cities, the towns, the villages, the cross-roads, of almost every State of the American Union. Cross the Atlantic, and in every country of Europe, mark the spot from whence the reeling, bloated, beastly inebriate emerges: penetrate into Asia, and even into the benighted regions of Africa, and there may be seen, marked upon the barrel-heads, which are exposed to view as an advertisement to the consumer—both for the producer and the vender—in large and bold characters, which even a reeling drunkard may read—"*New England Rum!*" Alcohol never has been, and never will be a product of slave labor.

Pass over the Pacific ocean, and enter the densely populated territory of over-crowded CHINA. Mark there the terrible ravages of that trade in opium which England forced upon that unhappy country at the cannon's mouth. Read the remonstrance which was a few days ago transmitted by the Secretaries of the Church, the London, and the Wesleyan Missionary Societies, to the British Government.

The injuries inflicted upon the Chinese, (says the memorial,) by the immense quantities of opium, forced into the country against the laws of the Empire, are *appalling and incalculable;* exhausting the means, destroying the health, and debauching the morals of the people, to an extent that may well cause any Christian nation to shrink from the responsibility of being instrumental, in however remote and indirect a manner, in the production of results so deplorable and revolting. The trade, as it is now conducted between India and China, tends to lower the morality, and to degrade the character of British merchants; and for no other object than that of reaping for themselves *sordid and unhallowed gains,* from what may be truly described as *a traffic in debauchery, disease, and death.* It dishonors the English nation before God and man. It would entail lasting infamy upon the British name, if it became known that merely for selfish purposes of revenue and gain, we had compelled a foreign State, at the mouth of the cannon, to introduce among its subjects a poisonous drug, the introduction of which they have always steadily refused on the ground of its pernicious and demoralizing effects upon the people; thus exhibiting to the world *a professedly Christian nation* paying less regard to moral considerations than *the heathen rulers of China!*

Alas for the reputation of philanthrophic England, it is already known that she *has* forced this poisonous drug upon the Chinese nation, at the cannon's mouth!

Alas for the influence of the Christian faith! In contrast with this "act of infamy" by a great Christian power, the heathen Emperor of China, in response to the suggestion made to him, that he might derive a large revenue from the trade in opium, replied: "It is true I cannot prevent the introduction of the flowing poison; gain-seeking and corrupt men will, for profit and sensuality, defeat my wishes, but nothing will induce me to derive a revenue from the vice and misery of my people."

Old England develops the sublime system of free labor, by forcing this poisonous drug upon untold millions of the human race. The slave labor of the Southern States of the American Confederacy sends forth its four millions of cotton bales, to every quarter of the globe, to clothe the naked.

New England distributes, among other of the great productions of her free labor, throughout the world, that liquid fire which burns out the honor, the morals, the health, the lives of all who come under its pernicious influence; spreading crime, and misery, and degradation, in every land. Slave labor offers in lieu of this hellish draught, that mild, and soothing, and healthy beverage, which is alike the solace of the palace and the cottage.

Far be it from me even to desire to depreciate the magnificent results of free labor, both in England and America. In the development and expansion of the mechanic arts, and in their application to the wants of man; in the vast improvements which have been introduced into almost every employment of civilized nations, *both* are in advance of any other, and of every age, of which history affords us a knowledge. As an American and an Anglo-Saxon, I am proud of these great achievements; but as a

Southerner, born in a land to which slavery has been transmitted as an inheritance, for good or for evil, I am prouder still that the products of this slave labor have supplied raiment, and food, and other comforts for the rich and the poor of every land; *while no single commodity* which has been sent forth to the world *has contributed, in the smallest degree, to increase the vices or miseries of mankind.*

We have been taught in the holy Book to judge of the tree by its fruits—of men by their acts—and may we not be allowed to judge of systems by their results? Shall mankind be for ever fettered in its judgment by a reverence for mere names, or by respect for mere theories? Shall we reserve all our anathemas against vice, for the garments in which our fancy may clothe it? Or shall the wolf in sheep's clothing be suffered to enter among the flocks and herds, because we do not choose to look beneath the garb of innocence, which guilt assumes to hide its criminal intent? Before endeavoring to remove the mote that is in thy brother's eye, would it not be the part of wisdom to cast out the beam out of thine own eye?

LETTER VII.

Unfavorable results of Emancipation by England—Beneficial results of Slave Labor in the United States—Comparison of the condition of the Slave and Free States of the American Continent—Great importance attached by England to tropical productions—The interests of England and the Planting States identical.

I HAVE assumed as facts—that slave labor has supplied for the use of mankind the necessary articles of cotton, sugar, tobacco, rice, and coffee—that free labor never has succeeded in producing them; and I have inferred that if slave labor should be abolished, the great mass of those for whom the consumption thereof has become almost a necessity, would be obliged to abandon their use altogether.

If any practical proofs are desired to establish the want of adaptation of the European races, or of free labor, to the purposes of production in the tropics, it has been amply demonstrated by the results which have followed the abolition of slavery in the Colonies of England and France, and in the present condition of the Governments of the New World.

In all South America, the only Government which has attained to any great political importance is Brazil. It is the only nation which has kept pace in its improvements with the advancement of the world, and it is the only independent Government on the American Continent, except that of the United States, where slavery has not been abolished.

The institution of domestic slavery has existed in the United States of America from a period long anterior to its independent existence as a nation, up to the present moment of time. Never in recorded history is there evidence that any other country or any other people have made such rapid advances to greatness, wealth, and power. While it is not contended that this result has been wholly achieved through the instrumentality of the institution of slavery, none will deny that the productions of slave labor have contributed powerfully and materially to its accomplishment.

This fact is fully established by the exports of domestic produce to foreign countries. Although the population of the free States is as about two to one over that of the slave States, yet the exports from the slave States during the last year (1859) amounted in value to nearly two hundred millions of dollars, while the entire exports of the free States fell short of eighty millions. The value of the cotton alone, exceeded one hundred and sixty millions. Although these aggregate amounts will be doubtless increased the present year, (1860,) yet these exhibit the relative exports of the two sections. This immense sum goes to the enrichment of the entire nation, and, in some shape or other, finds its way into almost every county in every State in the Confederacy. Politicians may talk flippantly of sacrificing this great interest "upon the altar of freedom," and fanatics and vain theorists may be really ready for the sacrifice; but unless common sense be entirely banished from the land, or lost in the mad passions excited by sectional hatred, it is still to be hoped that enough of true Americanism is left to prevent even one more serious movement in that direction.

These productions of the Southern States have not only entered largely into the consumption of the inhabitants of the earth, but they have given employment to millions of laborers, whose daily bread is dependent upon the supply of cotton. These products of slave labor are necessary to the happiness, the prosperity, almost the very existence of society itself, as at present organized throughout the civilized world.

On the other hand, look at the picture of desolation, anarchy, and thriftless imbecility which have marked the history of the Governments of Mexico and Central America. A fairer or a more productive clime is scarcely to be found upon the earth. There, Nature has lavished her choicest, richest bounties. With a soil as productive as any in the world—a climate, which with such a soil, produces almost spontaneously the best fruits of the earth—from one extremity of this favored land to the other, the eye wanders in vain in search of a single spot which has been made to yield of its abundant capacities to the wants or the luxuries of civilized man.

These results cannot properly be attributed to their political institutions; for upon the one hand, we have the example of the Republic of the United States, with a form of government similar, in all essential particulars, to those of Central America and Mexico; and upon the other hand, we have the example of the Monarchy of Brazil, where, as previously stated, a comparatively rapid progress and development have been made. Neither can the result be ascribed to the alleged degeneracy of the Spanish-American race, for there is no evidence that they are inferior to the Portuguese inhabitants of Brazil. Moreover, such an assumption is proven to be unfounded by the present condition of the inhabitants of the Island of Cuba. These are of the same race and of the same religion, and they inhabit a country similar in climate, soil, and productions to that favored land occupied with such fruitless results by the inhabitants of Central America and Mexico. Under all the disadvantages of her political condition—governed as she is and has been for the benefit of a foreign master, with no special evidences of paternal fondness, the Island of Cuba has still contributed materially to the supply of mankind with those tropical productions, which, from being at one time luxuries attainable only by the rich, have become necessaries all over the civilized world, for all classes of society.

This brief reference to the relative condition of the governments of America, and the comparative prosperity of the inhabitants, exhibits the fact that in every portion of that great continent, where African slavery exists, without reference to the form of the government, prosperity prevails, and the lavish bounties of nature have been made available to the wants of man. While, upon the other hand, wherever the institution of slavery does not exist, in all that region where sugar, coffee, cotton, and rice, form the staple productions, or where slavery has been abolished, ruin, decay, and desolation have been the result. The fruits which a bountiful nature have placed within their grasp remain ungarnered—ungathered! So far as the rest of mankind are concerned, the very land itself might be blotted from existence without material loss or regret, except for the hope that something may be hereafter done to elevate it to that rank among the nations of the earth which nature seems to have designed that it should occupy.

But it is not alone among the independent governments of the new world where the existence of slave labor has been proven to be necessary in the development of tropical productions. England herself having abolished slavery in her provinces, with all her re-creative power, and with all the stimulants of pride and interest to urge her to its accomplishment, has been unable to restore life or animation to her stricken, palsied provinces! Desolation abounds where verdant fields once bloomed. Decay has followed where were once rife the evidences of prosperity; and ignorance, indolence, misery and vice, now reign supreme amongst that unhappy class, whom the cruel philanthropy of England has enfranchised.

These truths are scraps from history. They exist at present as undeniable facts, which all who choose may verify. They are spread before our eyes in characters which cannot be misunderstood, if the purpose be to judge fairly and frankly by results, in lieu of theories. Where African slave labor exists in the southern latitudes of America, prosperity abounds, and the world is furnished with the richness of the products of that favored clime. Where it does not exist, there has been comparatively no progress—no production—no prosperity! Where it has existed, but has been abolished, ruin, decay, and imbecility have followed!

It being then an undeniable truth, that hitherto the world has only been supplied with the productions of tropical climates through the instrumentality of slave labor, and that all attempts to secure this result by free labor have been unsuccessful, even supported by the mighty influence and power of Great Britain, should the institution of slavery in the Southern States be stricken down in deference to the real or affected philanthropy of those who created it. Of those who kidnapped and transported from Africa, as in the case of Great Britain, or sold for money in hand, as in the case of the now so-called "free States" of the North, all of these very slaves, or their ancestors, whom they would now emancipate, and whose tender sensibilities were never aroused in favor of the victims of their own cupidity until they had received the full wages of their sin, and had transported the "human chattels" to their possessors, to be held in bondage, they and their descendants, by them and their posterity, forever! In view of these facts, is it not fair to presume that there is some moving motive of self-interest, which has a deeper hold upon their hearts than the philanthropic considerations by which they profess to be governed? Whatever may be the sentiments and feelings of that portion of the civilized world, which is not actively engaged in this crusade against the South upon the abstract question of slavery, should they not hesitate long and ponder deeply before they say "God speed" to the enemies of the planting States of the Confederacy in their present struggle? Having satisfied themselves that the existing relations between the African and European races, living upon the same soil, cannot be changed without bringing ruin upon one or both, let them consider of the probable consequences to mankind, if unhappily this selfish assault should terminate in the success of the assailants.

I have a right to suggest these considerations, also, to those Americans who are laboring with so much energy and zeal, in conjunction with others from without, to stimulate the hatred of mankind against the Southern States, with the avowed or concealed purpose of reducing those States to the degraded condition of the British tropical possessions. There is all the greater propriety in making this appeal to Americans, because it is not claimed that the consummation they desire would add to the material interests of any other nation or people than those whose interests are adverse to theirs.

Let me not be misunderstood. I know that it is the theory of many of the wisest politicians of England, as indicated by the London Times in the article from which I have made a brief extract, that the British possessions in India can only be successfully developed by a gradual but sure process of emancipation in America, to be followed by the entire extinction of slavery. This may or may not be true, but if I might venture to avow a difference of opinion from those who ought to be more capable of deciding upon the true policy and interests of that country, I would say that the hopes which may be founded upon such a contingency would, in practice, prove to be a delusion. England is already great in herself, and powerful and rich in comparison with the other leading powers of the world. May she not, by grasping at all, lose all? Now, the prosperity of the slave States is the prosperity of England. A combination of circumstances, wisely directed by the indomitable energies and gallantry of her citizens, have made her one of the ruling nations of the world, in a military sense, as well as in commerce and manufactures. In regard to the latter, she stands almost without a rival—certainly without an equal. On the other hand, the Southern planting States, owing to the causes before referred to, are the greatest producers of that commodity which is manufactured at such an enormous profit by Great Britain. Would it not be better that each should go on in the career which they are now following, and acting upon that fundamental principle of political economy which commands nations to develop their own resources at home, to sell where they can realize the greatest profit, and to buy where they can buy the cheapest, content themselves with their present prosperity, rather than seek a doubtful advantage from the destruction of the prosperity of others? It may be an error of judgment, but I cannot resist the conclusion that England is greater and more powerful to-day than she would be if slavery should be abolished, by even the slow process which the leaders of the political anti-slavery party propose to inaugurate. And in this connection, let me add that, about which I may speak with the confidence of one who is familiar with the subject by a life-time experience and observation. The relations subsisting in America between the Africans and the inhabitants of European blood can never be materially changed by the consent of the latter: which consent would be essential to "*a gradual*" enfranchisement of the slaves. Slavery, under the circumstances there existing, can only be eradicated by violence, sudden and overwhelming! The first step taken by her enemies looking to emancipation, would arouse the entire South to an energetic and a bloody resistance, such as the world to this day has never witnessed! Let no one be deceived in regard to the results which would follow swiftly upon the heels of such a movement! The four millions of Africans, who are now inhabitants of the South, can only be emancipated and left upon the soil by the extermination or the entire subjection of eight millions of whites!

Many of the anti-slavery advocates profess to be governed only by a desire to eradicate what they are pleased to denominate "a great sin." Others insist that they only "follow the promptings of humanity," in seeking "to restore the African to his native freedom." Others again ignore the rights of the black man, but look with compassion upon the white race, who have been "born under the influence of the demoralizing institution." And these are all the more intent upon accomplishing their mission of mercy, because those for whom their sympathies are so much excited persistently refuse to see the horrors of their situation. Others, we are bound to believe, are stimulated only by their hatred of the Southern people. But of all the hostile elements which go to make up the aggregate of that party which in Europe and America seeks, either covertly or openly, to destroy the institution of slavery in the Southern States of the Confederacy, it is not pretended that any human being beyond the limits of those States will derive any—the smallest benefit therefrom, except by that class of politicians just referred to to. They desire to shake off their dependence upon that American slave-labor, which, by feeding their looms, gives bread to their millions of poor! They hope, upon the ruins of the American plantations, to make their own country the great producer of tropical commodities. And with all this frankness and candor, when addressing arguments to their own people, they have the temerity, in assuming the leadership of the political anti-slavery party in America, to aver upon the opposite side of the ocean, that their controlling purpose is to accomplish a work of philanthropy, with the scarcely less benevolent intent to aid in removing a stain which rests upon the reputation of their kinsmen, and upon the fair fame of their free institutions!

That this class of politicians do not over estimate the enormous augmentation of wealth and power which might come into the possession of Great Britain, if their schemes should be realized, may not be questioned against the judgment of such distinguished statesmen; but it is equally true that they underrate the obstacles to their accomplishment. Even though the entire northern section of the Confederacy should unite with them heartily in compassing their objects—even though they should secure the reins of power in the general government of the Confederacy, still the South would not consent to the self-sacrifice, and her opposition would be fatal. The States of the Confederacy are, in many essential respects sovereign, and the small State of Delaware alone, with her five hundred slaves, could not under the Constitution be coerced to emancipate them, even although the Federal

Government, and every other State in the Union, should unite in demanding it.

In illustration of the important influence which these productions exercise over the destinies of the civilized world, I will extract a few paragraphs from a late publication in which Mr. McQueen, a distinguished British politician, announces the policy of his country. The fearful struggle of Great Britain in the long series of wars to which Mr. McQueen refers, is worthy of a passing notice. Never before did any other nation meet and overcome so many and such powerful enemies. All Europe, as it were, was combined in solid phalanx against her. Some stimulated by a hereditary hatred; others by jealousy and envy of her power; others by fear; and others still by the necessities of their position, all entered upon the struggle with the single purpose of destroying the power of that nation whose navy was in every sea; whose flag floated over vast possessions in every quarter of the globe; whose armies were unsurpassed in bravery or skill; and whose purse seemed almost inexhaustible. Still the world in arms was arrayed against her, under the leadership of the greatest military chieftain of ancient or modern times. Napoleon the Great headed the hostile array! The result is before the world. The Government of Great Britain still stands amongst the foremost powers of the earth, illustrating still the same heroic determination, the same energy, the same skill in maintaining her supremacy, which has ever excited the admiration and respect even of her enemies; with the same inordinate and absorbing selfishness which has ever repelled the undoubting confidence or the love of mankind.

During that fearful struggle [said the author referred to] of a quarter of a century, for the existence of a nation against the power and resources of Europe, directed against her by the most intelligent but remorseless military ambition, *the command of the productions of the torrid zone*, and the advantageous commerce which that afforded, *gave to Great Britain the power and the resources which enabled her to meet, to combat, and to overcome her numerous and reckless enemies on every battle field, whether by sea or by land throughout the world.* In her, the world saw realized the fabled giant of antiquity. With her hundred hands she grasped her foes in every region under heaven, and crushed them with resistless energy. . . . The increased cultivation and prosperity of Foreign tropical possessions, is become so great, and *is advancing so rapidly the power and resources of other nations, that these are embarrassing [England] in all her commercial relations, in her pecuniary resources, and in all her political relations* and negotiations. . . . If *the cultivation of the tropical territories of other powers be not opposed and checked* by British tropical cultivation, then the INTERESTS and the POWER *of such States will rise into a preponderance over those of Great Britain,* and the power and the influence of the latter will cease to be felt, feared, and respected amongst the civilized and powerful nations of the world.

When we consider that mankind generally, but more especially the governments which are instituted by men, in the very nature of things, seek their own aggrandizement, even at the expense of doing an incidental injustice to others, the citizens of the great Republic should make some allowance for the zeal of British abolitionism in attempting to destroy an institution, which in its operations they conceive to be inimical to their interests. When England defended and upheld and propagated slavery in America, it must be remembered that the territory and the slaves were hers; now that a revolution has deprived her of that territory and those slaves, and the ownership thereof has passed into other hands, it could scarcely be expected that her policy in reference to the industrial pursuits of that country would not undergo a radical change. That the anti-slavery party of Great Britain in assuming the leadership of the emancipationists of New England, and in the announcement of its intentions, should be profuse in its protestations of a merely benevolent and philanthropic purpose, should not be a matter of surprise; but in deciding upon the weight to which their counsels are entitled, we should, as men, consider the magnitude of the interests involved, and as Americans, we should not suffer ourselves to be deceived in regard to their real sentiments and purposes, in our admiration of the outer garments with which they have enveloped them.

In order that I may not be misunderstood, I will here again state my own belief that the policy of this party in assuming a hostile attitude towards the development and the power of the planting States of America, and by their irritating assaults against them, perpetuating those feelings of unkindness which were enkindled by the wars in which we have been engaged, is neither in accordance with their own interests or those of mankind. That England should have emancipated the slaves that were left in her possession, after the revolution of her North American slave provinces, with a view to the ultimate destruction of that great element of future power and wealth in the revolted territory, may be regarded as but a natural ebulition of animosity consequent upon the irritations which such a struggle always engenders. But the speedy disappointment of such hopes, if they were in fact entertained, and the perpetual alienation of these Colonies having been long since established, England should shape her policy in accordance with the promptings of a more enlarged statesmanship. No other two nations of the world have so many inducements to cultivate a sincere and enduring friendship. Every additional bale of cotton which may be produced in the planting States, adds just in that proportion to the material power and wealth of Great Britain. Nay, more than this, there are political considerations and heart sympathies, which when left to their own free action, impel them towards each other, and which it were wise that England should consider and respect. But even though the British anti-slavery leaders give no heed to such considerations, they should remember, that the friendships they cultivate in the United States, having their foundations only in a common sentiment of hatred, are not to be relied upon in the hour of trial and danger; while the animosities thus engendered live to bear fruits long after the causes which produced them have disappeared.

LETTER VIII.

Opposing interests combined in the Anti-Slavery Party—Causes of disaster to Republics—Tendency of Slavery to produce equality in the dominant race—Causes of opposition to Slavery by aristocratic bodies—Morals of Slave and Free States—Capital and Labor united in Slave States.

THE superficial observer, in analyzing the component parts of the great anti-slavery party, is surprised at the apparently discordant materials of which it is composed. He discovers that the zeal of the fanatical advocates of the equal rights of all men, without regard to color, religion, qualifications, or education, scarcely keeps pace with that of the champions of the divine right of kings and nobles, in accomplishing the destruction of an institution which seems to be equally at war with the interests and opinions of both. The most uncompromising of all the enemies of slavery in the Old World, spring from the hereditary governing classes—the most fanatical and vindictive in the New World, are those who would be recognized in Europe under the designation of "Red Republicans." This coincidence of sentiment, however, grows out of the antagonism of slavery to the extreme doctrines of both.

The unsuccessful efforts which have been made in Europe to construct Republics upon the ruins of Monarchies, have had their origin in the ignorance of the masses of the populations. This ignorance has been made use of by more enlightened demagogues to subvert the very Governments which they professedly sought to establish. The ignorant people were led to believe that liberty and license were synonymous, and that freedom consisted in the absence of the restraints of law. The calamities which have generally followed upon the heels of every successful effort to overthrow Monarchical Despotisms, have been brought about by the excesses induced by such violations of the principle upon which a Republic should be founded. Moreover, these same ignorant classes were in turn equally the instruments by which Despots have been able to resume their lost power.

In the formation of the different Governments of the American Confederacy, if the negroes had been made citizens, they would have constituted the material out of which demagogues would soon have produced a state of affairs that would have caused a radical change in the form of the Government. Happily, such a policy was not adopted, and hence the slave States entered upon their career as Republics without being subjected to those dangers which originate in the ignorance and incompetency of its citizens. The material which has been successfully employed in the Old World to make Republics impossible did not exist. That class of the community which elsewhere led by wicked counsels produces revolution, was unknown in the slave States. The humblest white man felt that there were below him, socially and politically, a considerable portion of the population. He had all the incentives of pride to fulfil properly the duties which, as a free citizen, he was called upon to perform. No matter how humble his position, he never occupied that station in regard to the wealthier portion of the population which would impress upon him a feeling of inferiority. He performed none of those menial services for others which would degrade him in his own estimation, or which, from the nature of his relations to his employer, would make him but an instrument in the hands of his superior. All these services were rendered by slaves.

The existence of slavery thus rendered facile the establishment of free government by the dominant race. There was no hazard in conferring equal political privileges upon the whites, and the natural influence of slavery has been to create a feeling of personal independence among the superior race, which makes them more capable of performing the duties of free citizens. These States have by this means been exempted, in a great measure, from those popular tumults which have been the graves of the Republics of the Old World. In effect, while the free States of New England have been overrun by fanatics who display their absurd and pernicious principles under the forms of "Fourierism," "abolitionism," "atheism," "free love-ism," "womans' rights-ism," and many others equally detestable, they are absolutely unknown in the slave States, because the populations from which proselytes to such doctrines are usually obtained, do not there exist, and there are no materials out of which the intelligent, but vicious or fanatical leaders, can construct a party.

The abolitionists of England, as well as of the Northern States of the Union, without designing to do so, confirm the facts above stated. It is often with these a subject of mortification and complaint that the Southern States, as they aver, generally select their Representatives in the Congress from among their most intelligent citizens, and retain them for a long period in the management of their public affairs; while in the abolition districts, scarcely have they elected a man of ability, ere he is thrust aside by another, who, in his turn, is superseded almost before he has made himself familiar with the routine of his duties, by one more radical and more skilled in the subtle arts of demagoguery. This is the testimony furnished by the enemies of slavery. In truth, however, it may be readily inferred that, from the causes which exist, such results would naturally follow.

The effect of slavery has, therefore, been to establish free institutions for the dominant race, and upon a solid and durable foundation. That the existence of the institution of slavery has a powerful influence in establishing and preserving equality among the different classes of the governing races, may be readily conceived. For example—let us imagine that one-third of the entire population of

Great Britain, embracing the most ignorant of her population, were removed, and their places supplied by African slaves, how long would even the venerated institutions of that loyal population withstand the determined assertion of the right to equality on the part of the remaining Anglo-Saxons? The population whose ignorance and dependence would have been a perpetual bar to the establishment of equality, would no longer exist. The instruments which may now be used by the governing classes in maintaining their supremacy, would have passed away, and with them, would disappear those hereditary distinctions which are now recognized as natural and proper, and even necessary. In this tendency of the institution of slavery to Democratize the dominant race, by elevating all classes to the capacity of self-government, may be found one of the principal causes which have contributed to array against it hereditary governing classes. The judgment and the instincts of mankind generally lead them in the direction of their interests. Those who are in the possession of exclusive privileges, rarely give credit to the wisdom or morality of measures which have a tendency to curtail or to render unnecessary the exercise of such rights.

The governing class of the State is not only jealous of rivalry, but, apprehending no danger from itself, it is always endeavoring to perpetuate, and to increase its power. Whether it be the government of a monarchy, or an aristocracy, or of the people, the same principle of human nature is always at work—more power—and more and more. On the other hand, the governed, with more or less earnestness, desire the extension of their privileges. In every State, therefore, there is a perpetual contest. Though it may not find occasion for practical development, it exists in the mind, and only lies dormant for a season, awaiting a proper moment for its manifestation. The tendency of the institution of slavery being opposed to hereditary distinctions of rank among members of the dominant race, very naturally accounts for one of the causes which have impelled the supporters of despotism to unite with the advocates of the most extreme agrarianism, in opposition to the institution of slavery in America. Upon this hypothesis only can we account for the extreme zeal of many of the governing classes of Europe for the expulsion of slavery from the American continent, unless we attribute to them individually and collectively a loftier appreciation of human liberty than other classes can lay claim to.

It cannot be that they oppose slavery because this institution conflicts with the doctrine of the universal equality of the races of mankind; because they maintain for themselves the right to the exercise of exclusive privileges, which they have inherited from their ancestors, and which they also claim the right to transmit to their posterity. It cannot be on the score of humanity, pure and simple, for I presume it will scarcely be denied, that the system of slavery in the United States is not only the mildest system of labor which exists, but, by the admission of even the most persistent and uncompromising enemies of the slave States, the slaves are more kindly dealt with, are better fed and clothed, and more rarely overworked, than any similar number of free laborers in the world. It cannot be because of the demoralizing tendencies, or vices incident to slavery; for if they have eyes they must see that there is more vice and immorality, more human degradation, more unpitied misery, illustrated by the history of any one single day of the year, in the city of London, or Paris, or Vienna, or even New York and Boston, than a whole year would bring forth amongst all the slaves of America. It is true that among the slaves there is vice, for they are human; but they are never forced to the alternative of *vice* or *starvation*. They may yield to the temptations of a naturally wicked heart, but never are they induced by necessity to the commission of crime. The wicked imaginations of obscene men and women picture among the families of the Southern States, scenes of immorality and debauchery. Who does not know, that in any one of the cities I have named, as well as in hundreds of others which might be enumerated, the vices referred to are practised to a larger extent between master and servant, or "help," of the same race, in one month, than during half a generation in the slave States, between master and slave. In the one case there exists a natural repulsion, as well as the stimulant of pride. Even these barriers, however, are powerless to prevent altogether this species of vice. But let any one compare in his mind, the relative inducements, incentives, and opportunities for the commission of the vices referred to, between black slaves and their owners, and white hired servants and their masters, and he may decide the question for himself, without desiring further testimony than the existing relations of the two would furnish.

In this connection, let me refer, for an instant, to the revolting spectacle which meets the eye in all large cities, under the operation of what is denominated the system of free labor. Look, for example, any evening of the year, upon the crowded streets and avenues of London. There you behold—not hundreds—not thousands—but tens of thousands of human beings, fashioned after the model of the fairest of God's creatures, offering themselves in the highways and by-ways, body and soul, to any purchaser who will give them money to buy bread. They would even work for the pittance of ten cents or twenty cents a day—the scanty wages allowed to a free laborer of their class—but there are none to give them employment. There is no fire in the miserable apartment to give warmth to its inmates. There is no morsel of food to appease the pangs of hunger. The tempter is present pointing to the manner of obtaining both: the purchaser is without. Are the victims young and well-favored? they offer *themselves* in exchange for that which will support life, Are they old and without charms? they beg of those whom they may encounter, in the name of humanity, for something wherewithal to sustain a little longer their miserable existence. Perhaps the first person they encounter is a clergyman of the abolition school. He turns coldly away from the blandishments of the one, and the tears of the other, and entering his study, sits down to compose an appeal to mankind, in behalf of the suffering slaves of America! No sentiment of pity for the misery which exists around him; no horror of the crimes or vices which he cannot fail to see; no earnest effort to amend that system which is the fruitful parent of so much misery and vice, can move him to employ his great intellect, or exert his great influence where it might be availing. For him and for his class, there is but one great sin; and that is the sin of American slavery in a far distant land. There is but one object of compassion; but one which calls for the exercise of benevolence, and that is "the little negro baby."

This clergyman is unfortunately but the type of a class, which for the sake of humanity, it were to be wished, were less numerous. Unhappily, *Old* England is not the only land in which they are to be found. The example has not been without influence across the Atlantic, where it has assumed a form even more revolting.

We may make due allowance for the injustice done by the abolitionists of Great Britain to the planting States of America, because they believe that they have a great political interest in embarrassing first, and in overthrowing afterwards, at the proper moment, the institution of slavery. We may respect the convictions of the dreamer, who hopes to witness, with the disappearance of slavery, the realization of what is regarded by practical men, an impossible equality. We may pardon the politician who takes advantage of the popular excitement to secure his way to place and power. But for the professed teacher of God's Holy Word; for the man who claims to be a disciple of Christ, and a follower of his holy counsels, but who prostitutes the pulpit to the purpose of inciting hatred, instead of love; who preaches for blood and war instead of peace; who from the holy desk distributes "Sharp's rifles," and other instruments of murder, with instructions to go forth and slay; who, in effect, teaches his congregation that all the other sins of the world are as nothing compared to the sin of slavery—who can regard him in any other aspect, than as the enemy—whether innocently or otherwise, it is not my province to judge—of that meek and lowly Jesus, whom he professes to serve.

But to resume the consideration of the opposition made by hereditary governing classes, to American slavery. It cannot be because of the degradation it imposes upon the African, for no informed man will be found to assert that any of his race have ever, in any time past, occupied a position so elevated in the scale of humanity, as that of those who are now held as slaves within the slave States of America. Upon this point there exists no contrariety of opinion. The ultra abolitionist, and the extreme slavery propagandist, are in regard to this fact, in perfect accord.

Neither can it be that this opposition arises from any promptings of Christianity, because, though heathens in their native land, slavery has christianized them. Many of these philanthropists say that none can be saved who die without a knowledge of Christ, yet, but for the existence of African slavery, who can believe that fifty of these four millions of slaves, would ever according to this view have "fallen into the way of salvation?" Would they have consigned these people to the horrors of eternal punishment? If the doctrine to which I refer be true, such would have been their terrible fate but for their enslavement.

The philanthropic and benevolent, both of England and America, send forth their Christian missionaries to every benighted land, into which these self-exiled teachers of our sublime faith can procure ingress. They endure patiently hardships, dangers, and death, in their zeal to promote the cause in which they are engaged. Many of these I have known well. I have entered their dwellings in the far away mountains of Asia, and even in Africa I have witnessed the operations of their good work. They are a good providence and a treasure to the benighted lands to which they are sent. The influence of their example and their teachings spread blessings all around them, even though their doctrine be rejected. They live apart from the home-friends they love, they perform the duty which is set before them, they die in obscurity in a foreign land, and are forgotten; but the fruits of their good works live on forever! All honor then to the Christian missionary, who makes of himself a real martyr in the cause of true benevolence! Yet all the labors of all the missionaries who have been dispatched to heathen lands from England and America since the revolution, have not converted to Christianity one tenth of the number which slavery has brought into the fold of our Saviour.

While we cannot expect that the advocates of the Divine right of classes to govern, will, as a body, abate anything of their hostility to an institution which tends to eradicate the political inequalities of the dominant race upon which their system is founded, may we not hope for a different result, among true friends of freedom, who may have formed erroneous opinions in regard to practical results by following too closely the indications of their theory.

If the advocates of the universal equality of man are really desirous, as they undoubtedly are, to witness the establishment and perpetuation of free institutions, as now existing in the United States of America; partial though they admittedly are, and confined to the European races, why should they wish to place them at so much hazard, to subject them to so fearful on ordeal, as to insist upon the recognition of an equality between races so far removed from each other by education and habit, so dissimilar in all things? It they consider that the failure or success of "the experiment" of free government, now being made in the New World, will have an important bearing upon the fate of free institutions for centuries yet to come, why should they desire to stake all upon the cast of a single die? Why should they wish to deprive "the experiment" now in the morning of its success, of its surest bulwark—why should they desire to hazard the interests of millions of the white race, for the purpose of conferring a doubtful benefit upon but comparatively a handful of Africans?—and all for no probable good, except to test in practice the proof of a theory which the vast majority of mankind believe to be founded in error?

There exists still another class both large and formidable, who oppose slavery upon grounds altogether antagonistical to those we have been considering. They profess no sentimental philanthropy, no belief in the natural equality of the African, no sympathy for sufferings which they say do not exist, no disposition to elevate him for his own sake to political independence. They oppose slavery because they say slavery is inimical to free labor.

A little practical knowledge of the facts will convince any one who investigates the subject, that this assumption is wholly groundless. In free States there is a perpetual conflict between *capital* and *labor*. There may be a truce from necessity, but the war is renewed when that necessity ceases to exist. Capital is ever seeking to procure labor, at the minimum amount for which it may be purchased. Labor seeks to obtain from capital the highest reward for its services. This contest must be perpetual until all men become laborers or all capitalists.

The terms on which this perpetually recurring battle is fought, are most unequal. The decision is almost always in favor of capital. The issue may be held in abeyance for a season; a momentary success may even give heart and courage to the laborer; but in the end the crowning victory has always been secured to capital. Why? because capital may exist indefinitely as to time, *without eating*. The laborer *must have his daily bread! Bread* may only be had for *money*, and *capital* will only bestow that money for labor. Labor may fight bravely and hopefully for a day, but it goes to bed on an empty stomach. It may arise in the morning refreshed by its slumbers and courageously renew the battle, but it retires at night oppressed with the pangs of hunger! On the third day it may struggle against its sleepless, cautious, passionless, heartless foe with the desperation of despair. On the fourth day it yields itself as vanquished, or perishes. In either event capital is the victor.

In slave States, or at least to the extent to which slaves are held and the general influence which it naturally exercises, capital and labor form but a single interest—there cannot be a conflict, because capital is labor and labor is capital. The interests of capital and labor are one, because the two are identical. The capitalist seeks by every means in his power to enhance the value of labor, because labor is his only capital. If labor recedes his capital declines. If labor advances his capital is augmented.

In slave States therefore, labor is always comparatively high, and free labor, as well as capital, is the gainer thereby. There is not a country upon earth where the aggregate of labor, free and slave, commands so high a price as in the slave States of the American Union. And I appeal to the experience of every mechanic or laboring man, however humble he may be, who has resided in both free and slave States, to *pronounce* upon the correctness of what I am going to say; namely: that there is no other country under the sun in which labor is as much respected, or in which the laborer is accorded so high a social rank, as in the slave States. I know that this statement does not accord with Abolition theories, but I know that which I have said to be true, so far as my own observation extends, in every part of the world which I have visited. And I may add, that in no other country is there as much true contentment, happiness, and comfort, or as little destitution or want as exists among the laboring population of the slave States of the American Union, of whatever color, race, occupation, or condition. These are my sincere convictions founded upon experience and observation. They may be tinctured by my never disavowed love for the land of my birth; but I am thus far sustained by the unanimous testimony of all, who like myself, have had a life-experience on the subject about which I have thus presumed to differ with so many hundreds who have never placed foot upon the territory where slavery exists.

But there is still another important consideration, which is opposed to the enfranchisement of the slave, even if it were possible; that is, a due regard to the interests of the millions of the white race who now reside, and whose destiny has been cast in the slave States. What would be the condition of the free white laborers in the midst of these millions of freed Africans who, from being capital would be converted into competitors for the stinted pittance which capital would bestow for labor? The free-born mechanic and farm laborer would be reduced to the alternative of competing with the African upon equal terms. Suppose that which it is impossible to believe, that the free whites would submit tranquilly to the galling and revolting association, is there a philanthropic friend to the free laborers of his own race who would wish to reduce them to a condition so humiliating? The standard value of labor would be that which unscrupulous capital would stipulate with the ignorant and indolent African. Free white labor would be powerless to defend itself against injustice, because there would be an ever ready substitute of African labor, which capital could employ during the rare intervals in which intelligent labor might vainly seek to secure a proper reward and acknowledgment for its toil.

The rich man could fly from the contaminating association! The poor from necessity would be bound to the soil. Upon the rich would fall the present pecuniary sacrifice, but upon the poor would rest the perpetual record and presence of the wrong.

I have here assumed what I know to be an impossible contingency. An overwhelming military force may liberate the slaves—armed invaders from the North may destroy the value of the slave to his owner, and to mankind—John Browns may kindle the torch of servile insurrections; and the Southerner may live to see his dwelling in flames and his hearthstone made desolate; but all the power of their enemies cannot induce the freemen of the South, of any rank, condition, or occupation, to adopt the freed Africans as their fellow-citizens, or to tolerate any change in their relative conditions that would remove the barriers, social or political, which now separate the races.

But why should not good men consider the subject of slavery as it exists in the Southern States without allowing themselves to be influenced by unfounded prejudices, or sectional animosities, and look only to the results which it has achieved? Though they may be opposed to slavery in the abstract, is it more than just that the slave States should have the benefit of that inexorable necessity which, without any agency on their part, left them no alternative consistent with their safety but to adopt and perpetuate the institution of slavery? This conceded, examine and decide if the Southern States have not properly employed it in the interest of mankind, and with a due regard to the comfort and happiness of those who were thus placed under their charge and direction. If still there exist doubts, compare that system of labor with the systems of so called free labor, which civilized nations have adopted in order to achieve similar results. No friend of the slave States would fear the decision of any impartial, just, and intelligent tribunal.

LETTER IX.

Influence of Public Opinion—Origin of the Anti-Slavery Sentiment in England—Failure of schemes to destroy the value of Slave Labor in America—Revolting Inhumanity of the systems instituted to supersede Slave Labor—Comparison of the Slavery System with those proposed as Substitutes—Subjugation of India by England—A trial by the Moral Law.

THERE has been no period in the past when the policies of governments have been so much moulded by the general public sentiment of mankind as at the present epoch. Electricity and steam have brought countries once remote from each other into almost immediate contact; and the commerce which has been thus stimulated between the nations of the earth has brought about a mutual dependence which renders the productions of each important to the others. The facilities offered by rapid and constant communication are alike mediums for the transmission of truth and falsehood. Unfortunately, the latter travels with a celerity to which the former rarely attains. Upon the establishment of the Republic of America in the last century, with its boundless and inexhaustible resources, the adherents of the monarchical school, especially in England, imagined that they saw danger to all existing governments which were based on "the right divine," if the experiment should prove a success. How was this success to be averted? The great field for the production of the most important staples, with the labor which could alone develop them, was in possession of the Republic. How were these advantages to be rendered unavailable, and these sources of power to be destroyed? England did not require a Delilah to tell her in what consisted the strength of the young Samson. She set to work to shear the locks of the new Republic with an energy, and a zeal, and a disregard to cost, which no other nation than England knows how to put in practice.

Well does Britain deserve the title of Great! She is great in all things! Great in her virtues and in her vices; great in her physical strength; great in her prosperity, or in her adversity; great in the sacrifices she is ever ready to make to accomplish her policy; but greater still in the facility with which she can change her code of morals according to the exigencies of her pecuniary or political interests!

Slavery was abolished in all the provinces which remained to her after the American revolution, and the world from that day to this has resounded with her denunciations of the Republic for the toleration of that very slavery which she had established. Fortunately for the Republic and for mankind, the clamor against the slave States has been thus far unavailing. America has grown, as if by enchantment, from the lowest to the highest rank in the family of nations. The very existence of society, as at present organized, is dependent upon the products of that very labor which English pseudo-philanthropy has so vainly endeavored to destroy. In

vain, too, has she sought a substitute by which this dependence upon slave labor might be avoided. The world seemed ready to adopt any alternative however wicked, or inhuman, or cruel, *if it could only dispense with the form* of slavery existing in the American Republic. Failure has attended all these efforts, although some of them are still in existence. Let us briefly examine some of the more marked features of these substitutes for slave labor.

The British statesmen who instituted the moral war against slavery, hoped that in abolishing the institution, and leaving the slaves as freed men in the provinces in which they had been held in bondage, there would continue to result the same amount of production. This they expected to increase by the introduction of other Africans or Asiatics, who, instead of being slaves for life, should serve for only a limited period—say eight years, at a small stipulated rate of wages. The amount which should be paid to this class of laborers was of course fixed by the British employer—the savage, or semi-savage, as the case might be, being too ignorant to understand anything of the value of his labor. The system was supposed to possess a great advantage over that of slavery, as it did not involve the necessity of support to any who were too old or too young for active labor. Never perhaps did any nation have more at stake, in a pecuniary point of view, in the result of any one scheme, than did Great Britain in the issue of this experiment on a small scale, having for its object the substitution of a species of nominal free labor for that description of labor which existed in the southern States of America.

Upon the moment when the great English statesmen discovered that they could no longer compete successfully with the Republic in tropical productions, under the slave labor system, they resolved, if possible, to destroy that system, and to erect upon its ruins another, in which England would be without a rival, even though every christian power on earth were combined against her. If the substitute above referred to had been successful in achieving its purpose, slavery would have abolished itself, because of its unprofitableness. The new system would have destroyed the value of the slave, and the great struggle of the European nations having tropical possessions, would have been to develop, as rapidly as possible, a system of labor which, while being much cheaper, would at the same time have been put into operation without any violation of the public sentiment of the world. England, before the year 1860, could have thrown into her possessions, where slavery had been abolished, a number of laborers three times as great as all the slaves in America. These she could have taken forcibly or otherwise, as the exigencies might have demanded, from her vast and inexhaustible horde of subjugated Asiatics and Africans. There would still have been left for the cultivation of her immense Indian territory, the untold millions upon tens of millions of souls who inhabit that unhappy country, which has been reduced by a conquering and a superior race from civilization to barbarism; and whose liberties have been destroyed by the shedding of more human blood than flows in the veins of every enslaved African in America!

What magnificent visions of wealth and power and grandeur must have floated through the brains of the English statesmen, and the calculating christian philosophers, who conceived this scheme of aggrandizement! What were a few millions of pounds sterling in the beginning, to the results which they hoped to achieve! It was indeed worthy of an immense sacrifice, and great was the sacrifice they made to reach the promised, but ever receding goal! More money has, in one form or another, been expended by Great Britain, in this fruitless effort to discover a substitute for slave labor in tropical productions, than would have paid five times over for all the slaves she liberated.

This scheme offered to its originators a double advantage; for while it would have been, if successful, a source of unbounded wealth to European nations with foreign tropical possessions, its entire want of adaptation to the peculiar circumstances of the Republics of the new world, would have driven the United States of America from the field of competition for the great prize. I have already explained that it would be an act of political suicide, if nothing worse, for these States to introduce or to tolerate in their midst a barbarous, or a semi-savage population of a different race and complexion, who would occupy any other relation to the European masters than that of perpetual servitude. Nations having provincial tropical possessions, do not rest under any such restriction. The difference in this respect between the relative positions of Great Britain and the American planting States of the Confederacy, may be more readily conceived by supposing that the British Government were to introduce in the United Kingdom millions of Africans, who, after having served an apprenticeship of eight years, should be turned loose upon society as equal participants in the benefits and blessings of the English constitution. Although under such circumstances, even Mr. Bright might abate somewhat in his demand for universal suffrage, yet, though no other champions of the equality of races should spring up to claim for these the "rights of manhood," it will be readily admitted that the political, moral, and social evils which would result, would be a thousand-fold in excess of any benefits which might be expected from their presence. If Englishmen, who are sincerely desirous of witnessing the abolition of slavery in the American planting States, from pure and unselfish motives, will bring the matter home to themselves, they will readily admit that the total or even partial enfranchisement of four millions of black African slaves, amongst a population of eight millions of white Europeans, living under a Constitution which guarantees equality of right to its citizens, would be an act of madness!

But to return from this digression: While mankind should rejoice that this scheme which would have produced so much misery to the instruments whom it was intended to employ in its prosecution, has utterly failed in accomplishing the practical results hoped for, yet none can withhold from Great Britain the tribute of their admiration, for the boldness and grandeur of the conception, and the more than imperial profusion with which she has lavished of her immense resources the amount necessary to fairly test the feasibility of nurturing into life and giant manhood, this British offspring of the American revolution.

But all her sacrifices were unavailing. Too late it was discovered that the African would not work without a master! No stimulants of pride or ambition could move his soul to rise above the level which it would seem that the God of nature has assigned to him. While the productions of the slave States of America have increased in a ratio never before equalled in any country, the possessions of Great Britain, where this experiment was inaugurated, have been receding in the amount of their productions, until they now bear no comparison even to their former products. All, present to the eye of the observer a picture of unbounded desolation—a monument of the thwarted schemings of ambitious men, who hoped by this means to accomplish the double purpose of destroying the possessions of another, and of building for themselves a colossal power upon their ruins.

The failure of this scheme, which involved the impossible employment of nominally free African labor, led to the inauguration of another, far more revolting to every sentiment of humanity than the most cruel form of slavery, even in the days when Great Britain was the patron of, or participator in all slavery enterprises. This new scheme is known under the general designation of the "Cooly system," because the greater number of those who have been subjected to the horrors of this barbarism of the nineteenth century, have been Chinese. All the barbarous and semi-civilized nations of the world, however, have been subjected, in a greater or less degree, to the terrors of this revolting system. No other records of its enormities are necessary to convince the intelligent mind of its true character, than a simple detail of the plan and manner of its execution.

The Cooly broker, by means of his agents, seizes upon his unsuspecting victims wherever they can be found. These, when brought into the port for shipment, are confined in the most loathsome prisons, and are not allowed to hold any communication with their countrymen without. Upon the arrival of a purchaser, a paper writing is produced in the French, the English, or the Spanish language, as the case may be, by which these poor wretches are bound to work for their owner for the space of eight or ten years, at a promised rate of compensation varying from two to four dollars per month. The "free and unbiased assent" of the Cooly having been thus obtained, he is bound as a malefactor and conveyed aboard the ship which is to convey him to his destination. The ship obtains clearance, and sets sail with her living cargo of "free laborers," crowded to a degree of suffocation which, before the end of the voyage, reduces their number from deaths to about three-fourths of their original number. In many instances, this great mortality is frightfully increased. On board of one American ship which put into Manilla, in 1855, out of a cargo of four hundred and fifty souls, three hundred were smothered to death in one night from the closeness of the quarters in which they were confined! The end of their voyage at last arrives. Thrice happy those whose sufferings have already ended in death, and whose bodies have been cast into the sea. These "free laborers" are disposed of to the highest bidder, and are placed upon the plantations of the purchasers. The owner has only by contract an estate for eight years in the sinews of the freeman. His only interest, therefore, is to concentrate all the physical capacity of the man within that compass of time; and rarely indeed is it that there is any substance left in him at the expiration of his period of enslavement. If there is, What means has he to return to his native land? The miserable pittance allowed to him has in all probability been paid in such manner as to be exhausted before the period of his freedom commences, and he must sell himself for another term of eight years, for the doubtful prospect of again revisiting his far-off home. Mr Abbott, who has written a valuable work upon this subject, says in reference to the details of this inhuman system in Cuba:

> It seems to me, that human misery could sink to no lower depth. The doom of the Coolies is vastly worse than that of the slaves. Those wretched Chinese are lured to leave their homes upon the promise of being fed and clothed, and receive four dollars per month. Thus, at the end of eight years, they would possess $384. This seems like an immense sum to a poor Chinaman, to whom a cent a day is a very reasonable competence. *But none return!* They are sold upon their arrival for about $400. If their owner can wear them out in eight years, *so that they die, he of course has nothing to pay,* [for their wages, during their term of servitude.] If he cannot, he sends them to some distant plantation, or *sells them again for another eight years.*

This system has been attended with a partial success. So far as present gains are concerned, it has the great advantage over slavery of cheapness. It is impossible to obtain accurate statistics in regard to the numbers of human beings who have been thus sacrificed, to find a substitute for the slave system of America. It would probably be safe to say that the whole number, thus immolated during the last fifteen years, does not fall short of two millions of souls. With the stimulant of success, it cannot be long before the aggregate amount of those thus employed will exceed the entire number of slaves in the United States!

Where slumbers the philanthropy of the abolitionist of England, while this crime against humanity, more horrible far than the worst form which slavery has ever assumed, is thus lawfully prosecuted in the open face of day! Where sleeps the piety of Sharp's rifle clergymen of New England, while this enormous sin is robbing millions of semi-civilized human beings of liberty, of hope, of life! Alas, the fountains of their sympathies have been exhausted and absorbed by their devotion to the "little nigger baby robbed from his mother's arms," and, as taught by English abolitionism, so they believe that to hate anything but the slaveholder of America would be but an idle waste of the fire of their holy passions!

In instituting a comparison between these two rival systems, statistics are wholly unnecessary in arriving at just conclusions in regard to their respective merits. We may refer to practical effects to test the truth or soundness of our judgment upon doubtful points, but for arriving at just conclusions upon the question here at issue, nothing more is necessary than to examine the circumstances and terms under which they exist.

Under the slavery system in the United States, the slave is held as such from the cradle to the grave. At full maturity he is worth to the owner from ten to twelve hundred dollars. The latter has every stimulant of gain and self-interest to bring up the infant to manhood in the full possession of all his natural strength and health. He can only do this by sufficient food and clothing and rest from toil. When the slave has attained to man's estate the owner has an equal interest in preserving his health and physical strength to as late a period of his life as possible. This can be done by exacting only in a moderate degree the exercise of his physical strength. He must be sufficiently supplied with healthy nourishment—he must be warmly clad in winter; but above all, he must be made contented and happy in order to retain him at his full value. Any violation of these rules can only result in diminishing the value of the slave and the wealth of his owner. He may change masters, but always the same rules and regulations must be observed by the new proprietors; and this is the routine of slavery. If the slave is in full health and strength, he makes up twelve hundred dollars of the capital of his owner. If he is disabled by tyranny, or by improper or scanty nourishment, or by overwork, he is not only valueless, but an encumbrance and an expense; for the law compels the master to support his own slave under all circumstances, or in case of failure he is taken away and transferred to another. Does a man set fire to his own house for the purpose of looking upon the conflagration? Would he destroy the value of his property for the gratification of his spleen?

Such are the circumstances under which the slaves transmitted to the Southern States by Great Britain are now held. Englishmen should remember that there is as great a difference between the condition of the American slave of the present day and that of his ancestors when first kidnapped and sent a savage into their provinces, as between the mild government of their model Queen Victoria and that of the tyrant Henry the Eighth. Then he was a savage and a cannibal, while now he is civilized and a christian. I say nothing here of the actual condition of the slaves of the South, because I think the candid and unprejudiced mind can arrive at just conclusions without the aid of such testimony. Would that all the honest enemies of slavery could visit the slave States in person and see for themselves the workings of that system against which cupidity, malice, prejudice, and ignorance have erected such a mountain of calumny and hatred.

Let us consider further and compare the morals of the anti-slavery, or so called free labor system, which model Christian powers have inaugurated or tolerated as a substitute for slavery.

In the commencement, the horrors of the kidnapping and transfer of the Coolies or Africans, as the case may be, to the place of their destination, are the same in both; with this difference however, that comparatively few slaves are now introduced into America, and none into the Southern States of the Confederacy. However, I propose to consider that both are in active operation. Once arrived in the country where his services are to be rendered, the Cooly's condition and that of the captured African sent into slavery diverges. For eight years the Cooly is sold! for eight years he must, as a slave, obey the commands of a master! Suppose that the same master is the proprietor of a plantation worked by slaves in the planting States of the Union, and of another worked by the eight-year apprentices in Cuba. We have seen what would be his incentives to good and ill treatment in the former,—

how different would be his interests in regard to the latter! Eight years constitute a long period for ceaseless toil under a master who has no interest left in the victim after the expiration of that period. If he can only be worked to death there will be nothing to pay! Upon a reasonable calculation, how much of life and vitality would remain after this terrible drain of eight years, in a tropical climate, upon his powers of physical endurance? Could it be hoped that he would ever reach the end of a second term, though he had passed the first and lived?

Every truly philanthropic mind is forced to adopt the conclusion that this "substitute" is, upon the ground of humanity, not only more objectionable than the slave labor which it was intended to subvert, but that it is and, in its very nature, must forever be, under any and all circumstances, more cruel, more atrocious, more detestable, and more productive of human misery than the most revolting form in which slavery has ever been exhibited to mankind, even though we trace its history back to the period when English cupidity and Spanish cruelty first inaugurated the system.

If this species of traffic in human flesh is continued, as it has been prosecuted by the open sanction or secret connivance of the great powers, in less than half a century its victims will, in all probability, be greater in number than all the slaves in North America. Already they may be counted by millions, and yet no "tracts" nor "songs" have been sent over from England to America to be read and sung by the congregations, to stimulate fanaticism against the foul wrong. No pulpit, desecrated by political parsons, has rung with maledictions against the nations which permit the crime. No Sharp's rifles have been subscribed by New England clergymen, to assist with powder and ball in the extermination of the pirates who pursue this "nefarious traffic in blood and sinews." The skin of the Chinaman is not quite black enough to win their sympathies.

The anti-slavery party of England, however, has perceived that if the judgment of mankind is averse to the mild system of slavery which exists in the Southern States of America, it is scarcely to be hoped that, when the peculiar excitement of the day shall have passed away, the "Cooly system" will meet with even as much favor. It has, therefore, been unremitting in its efforts, to induce the nominal freemen in the despotic governments of Asia, to assist in supplying her looms with cotton. But the return of material has scarcely surpassed in amount the weight of the seed which she has distributed. They have penetrated every province and island embraced within the dominions of the Sultan of Turkey; but the Bedouin and the Druse, the Maronite, the Greek and the Armenian, the Christian and the Turk, alike refuse their tempting inducements.

The planting States of the South would cheerfully and gladly aid them in promoting the growth of cotton in other lands, because it would relieve them from their present isolation, and would build up a cotton interest, which would not be without its advantages to them, as well as to the consumers. No observant man can doubt, that the demand for cotton will keep pace with the supply, even although every field adapted to its cultivation, which is accessible to European markets, were called into successful requisition.

But, hitherto, all efforts to induce free labor voluntarily to engage in this branch of agriculture has failed, and for the British abolitionist, who is devoting himself to the work of emancipation in America, there is no resource left but INDIA. There lies that magnificent possession, which has been obtained at the expense of so much crime and injustice, and at a cost of human life, which years ago was estimated by millions. There are the untold, uncounted millions of a subjugated race, depressed by misfortune, exhausted in strength and physical courage, by their oft repeated, but fruitless efforts to shake off their unpitying oppressor; and powerless now for further resistance against the tyranny of an unrelenting master.

In estimating the sum of real philanthropy and regard for the rights of man, which may be accorded to British abolitionists for their efforts to eradicate the sin of African slavery from America, the unbiased mind naturally institutes a comparison between their practice in regard to India, and their precepts in regard to America. By what right does England hold India in subjection? By what law of morals can England lay claim to that extensive territory, on a far distant sea, and in another quarter of the globe? Has India ever menaced the integrity of the British Empire, or injured a hair of the head of any Englishman, who had not first entered its territory as a master and a conquerer? Did she make the conquest from any feeling of benevolence toward the human family? She found the inhabitants in the enjoyment of a great degree of civilization, and she has reduced them to barbarism; the African slave has been elevated from the most brutal barbarism to civilization. England found the inhabitants of ill-fated India rich and prosperous, and she has reduced them to beggary and want. All Britain has been enriched by the spoils which have been ruthlessly robbed from these helpless Asiatics. Their bodies have not been absolutely reduced to slavery, for that would have been not only impossible, but unprofitable. But she has taken away all of their substance, and, as admitted in Parliamentary Reports, she has, by tortures almost unheard of in the annals of civilized nations, compelled the miserable inhabitants to pay the assessments which were imposed upon them. What is this but the worst and most cruel form of servitude? for the master does not, in this case, leave even a crust of bread for his more than slave. If the enslavement of a comparative handful of Africans in America is a crime of such enormous magnitude, where can we find words to express the enormity of England's wrong to India?

But is England now to be excused by the moral law which is invoked against America, because it was the crime of her ancestors? No! for she does not surrender back to India her long lost liberties. She still clutches with a vulture's grasp, the dry bones of that carcass, from which she has torn the flesh; and shall not humanity hold her amenable to the same laws which she desires to impose upon the slaveholder in America?

What are the means which she has employed to maintain and to consolidate her power over India? The veins of every African, now a slave in the United States, do not contain as much human blood as has been shed for the accomplishment of this purpose. The English and American abolitionist is horrified that a Southern planter should "place an African in the cotton-field, whip in hand, to drive his fellow slave to his toilsome task." At this very moment of time, during a period of profound and unbroken peace, England has nearly three hundred thousand of the wretched inhabitants of India armed with sword and bayonet, and musket and cannon, paid out of the assessment upon the native races, who are employed to shed their brothers blood, if any resistance should be made, or murmur escape them, which might indicate a wish to shake off the chains in which they are bound. Is it for humanity's sake that Englishmen seek the emancipation of the slaves of America? The history of one day, according to the statements of the most reliable British authorities, would furnish a record of more misery, more destitution, more utter, hopeless, unpitied wretchedness, among the subjugated inhabitants of India, than would the history of *an entire generation of all the African slaves*, which their pseudo-philanthropy would set free. Here again the "tracts" and the "songs," sent over for "the American congregations" are silent. No moving story, or pitying verse, recounts the cruel fate of the poor Asiatic. No American pulpit resounds with eloquent denunciations of the damning crime and sin. No fierce and bloody-minded clergymen of New England, subscribed and forwarded the famous Sharp's rifle to the Indiamen, in their last great struggle against the wrongdoer. Alas! here again the unfortunate Indiaman's skin is not dark enough to entitle him to sympathy or assistance.

I do not wish to constitute myself an arbiter or judge between England and India. It is not my province even to decide whether more benefits than evils have resulted to mankind from the subjection of India by England. Whatever may be the abstract rights or wrongs involved in the issue, it is a practical fact, that to-day, as well as in all times past, powerful nations and superior races, subject and hold in dependence weaker nations and races; and it may be fairly assumed that such will be the case in all time to come. It is, and always will remain, an unsettled question, how far civilized na-

tions may go, in compelling indolent or wicked barbarians to change their brutal habits of life, and contribute their due proportion to the necessities or the luxuries of the civilized world. But British emancipationists may not justly complain if they are held amenable to the requirements of the MORAL LAW, by which they profess to be governed, and which they seek to enforce upon others. They may be justly brought to trial under the rules which they have instituted in their assaults upon the planting States of America; and by these they stand condemned, beyond the hope of a reversal, upon an appeal to any enlightened and unprejudiced tribunal.

However this may be, India is the field this class of British politicians hope will at the proper moment rise to increased importance, upon the ruins of the American plantations. Would it be too uncharitable in "a kinsman born," to intimate the existence of an impression upon his mind, that it is *chiefly* to this cause, that the African slave in America is indebted for their sympathies? May it not be that the eager interest with which they are now watching the progress of their battle in America, is stimulated primarily, or at least incidentally, by this hope of gain? Is it not possible, that behind the profuse protestations of a purely philanthropic interest, there may lurk a selfish purpose, which has had its influence upon the British emancipationists, who, according to a recent declaration of the LONDON TIMES, "have come up to the aid of abolitionism, in the present struggle between the North and the South?"

LETTER X.

Summary of the relative advantages of different systems of Labor—Results of the comparison—Characteristics of Great Britain—An Anti-Slavery Poem—Does not fairly illustrate John Bull—Reflections of a Philanthropist upon subjects suggested by the Poem—The institution of Slavery more Humane now than formerly.

I HAVE thus briefly glanced at all the various systems of labor which have been proposed as substitutes for the institution of African slavery in America. Each in its turn, has resulted in failure; or those which have been attended by a partial success, the judgment of all enlightened philantropists have pronounced to be, in every respect, more objectionable than the worst form of now-existing slavery. So far as practical results are concerned, we stand now precisely where we did when Wilberforce and his followers preached their first crusade against slavery. The confident predictions of that day, that free African labor and the cultivation of the rich soil of India by the subjugated natives would entirely supersede and render valueless the institution of slavery in America, have been proven to be idle dreams. American slavery has gone on increasing in value and importance until the present moment of time, when, if we could imagine such a calamity, its sudden suppression would produce more disasters and miseries to mankind than "war, pestilence, and famine." England, which is the great purchaser of cotton, admits that no other system can successfully compete in its production with slave labor. But many of her leading statesmen also insist that if the institution of slavery should disappear, the free labor of India, and of other tropical countries, would promptly engage in the cultivation of those articles which are now obtained almost exclusively from slave labor. They believe that the large number of laborers who would under such circumstances be added to the productive force, would be able to approximate to nearly the same results which are now achieved under the slavery system.

I can discover no reason for believing that these hopes would be realized. Still less can I see any interest which mankind has in making the experiment even with a certain prospect of success. I can perceive that such a consummation might possibly be serviceable in increasing the relative power and wealth of Great Britain, but I can also see that this increase could only result from a greater, or at least, a corresponding diminution in the sources of power and wealth now in the possession of the United States of America. I do not perceive that even by this exchange mankind would be the gainer in any way. But above all, I can discover no advantages in the proposed change which ought to induce America to strike so fatal a blow at her own power and influence; and unless our own folly or madness drives us to this act of self immolation, no earthly power, having the will, possesses the ability to deprive us of our control over that monarch of commerce which to-day exercises its peaceful dominion over the kingdoms of the earth.

In considering this subject, I have not only instituted a fair comparison in regard to the productiveness of "slave and free labor" in what are denominated tropical products—and, as my brief references have shown, to the advantage of the former, but, upon the question of *humanity*, we have tested American slavery by a comparison not only with those systems which have been employed to supersede it, but with the free labor system of England in the very heart of the empire, and under the shadow of the throne. I am well aware that the vast majority of those whose minds have been warped by long cultivated prejudices, will not see the advantages which have resulted to mankind through the instrumentality of the institution of slavery, nor the enormities of any other system which holds out the hope of gratifying their feelings of animosity. They will continue to shut their eyes to evils upon the one hand, and benefits upon the other, if these conflict with their theories; but the prejudices, the passions, the injustice of mankind, cannot make truth fiction, nor change right into wrong. Laudations of the system of free labor, as illustrated by its practical workings, not only in London, but throughout the greater part of the world, cannot put bread into the mouth of the starving, nor of itself bestow a real independence upon those who labor for their daily sustenance. On the other hand, the most moving picture of the horrors of slavery cannot destroy the existing fact that no other laborers in the same field have as many of the comforts of life, with as few of its troubles and trials, as have the slaves of the Southern States of the American Union. Neither can any amount of calumny which ignorance, or malevolence, or both combined, may heap upon the slaveholder deprive him of that inward consciousness that he has worthily employed the power which the Almighty has placed in his hands—that he has been instrumental in diffusing amongst the mass of mankind comforts and necessaries which have contributed in an eminent degree to their happiness, and that he has sent forth nothing which has ever added to the unhappiness, or increased the vices of his fellow men! With all this, he feels that in diffusing these blessings, and in adding to the wealth, influence, and importance of his native land, he has gone on improving the condition of those who have been his instruments for accomplishing so much good, until he can safely challenge a comparison in this respect with that of any similar number of laborers in the world!

In my comments upon the policy of the anti-slavery party of England, I have done nothing more than to test it by the rules which it has laid down as binding upon America. If these laws have condemned England, it is not my fault. There may be much that may be said in her favor, if it be admitted or claimed that the exigencies of her situation did not permit her to follow that straight line which the rigid rules of abstract right require; but many of her statesmen do not admit that the slave States of America shall be entitled to the benefit of such a plea, and impartial minds will decide that she has no right to an exemption which she is not willing to concede to others. The abolitionists of England have endeavored, by every means at their command, to stimulate the prejudices of the world against the planting States of America on account of negro slavery. If both were put upon their trial before a just and intelligent tribunal, which would be condemned as the criminal most deserving of punishment? which the most worthy of the approbation of mankind?

In my references to the English people and the English emancipationists, I have been necessarily obliged to regard them as a unit. I have been constrained to consider the acts of the Anglo-American abolitionists as expressive of the general sentiment of the nation; and who will say that I have even unwittingly been guilty of an injustice in the conclusions at which I have arrived? Suppose that an intelligent historian were called upon to describe the general characteristics of the British Government and people; he would say with truth, they stand preëminent for practical good sense, clear-sighted sagacity, self-will, self-confidence, obstinacy, contempt for the feelings, the opinions, and the interests of others, where they have an interest to subserve, selfishness, pride, a love of independence for themselves, with an overweening desire to destroy the independence of others, indomitable courage and boldness, and, above all, a readiness at all times to make any sacrifice for the indulgence of these propensities. But upon the other hand, who would not smile if the historian were to add, that they are characterized by the possession of qualities which come under the designation of tenderness, or sensibility, or sentiment, or an unselfish regard for the feelings or interests of others, or, in fine, that they are distinguished as a people for the display of what may be denominated the finer feelings of the human heart? It is fair to conclude that the smile even of an Englishman would degenerate into a more boisterous expression of merriment, if the said historian were to adduce testimony in support of their claim to the possession of these heart-sympathies, by quoting lines from the "tracts" or "pious songs" composed and sent from England into America, for the use of anti-slavery pastors, and their congregations; as for example:

> "I was a helpless negro boy,
> That wandered on the shore;
> Thieves stole me from my parents' arms:
> I never saw them more!"

I have said that the Englishman might laugh, but to the mind of the philanthropist, impressed by their pictures of the horrors of slavery, these touching lines might induce a train of reflections, which would awaken emotions far different from those which produce merriment. The thoughts might very naturally wander over the pages of English history which record the tears, and blood, and desolation of India. The ears might hear the cry of anguish which, in times past, has but feebly expressed the horrors which have attended the subjugation and progress of English dominion in other lands. The peculiar friend of *sombre colors* might behold, through the mists of the past, the embarkation of Africans doomed to hopeless and eternal servitude in Spanish mines, or upon the North American plantations of Great Britain. From the mast-head of the slave-ship floated the flag of that Britannia which "ruled the waves." Commingled with the wild shrieks of husband and wife, father and daughter, and of that "helpless negro boy, torn from its parents' arms," was heard alone the words of that tongue which have been immortalized by the writings of a Shakspeare and a Milton. Incredulous philanthropy might refuse to credit even the evidence of its senses, and exclaim, "It is a pirate ship and a pirate crew, who have stolen the livery of Heaven to serve the devil in!"

Show your authority, commander; leave not the incredulous to doubt about the lawfulness of your honorable calling. The Royal Charter is unfolded, which reads that after a long and bloody struggle among the Christian nations, Great Britain being of the victors, claimed and received as her portion of the spoils, the exclusive right to deal in slaves, and to transport the same from the coast of Africa.*

I have said that the institution of slavery, now in the United States of America, is so much more humane than that which existed under the rule of those who

---

* See the European treaties made during the wars of the Spanish succession.

Those are curious pages in history which record that the *madness* of the eighteenth century throughout the civilized world, embracing all the Christian powers of Europe without distinction, was the establishment upon the American Continent, by the most cruel and inhuman acts of barbarity of that same African slavery, which it has been the *mania* of the first half of the nineteenth century to eradicate, and that too, after the atrocious features of the slavery which they created had been supplanted by the mild and almost patriarchal system which now prevails, at least throughout the planting States of the Federal Union.

The solution of this apparent anomaly may be readily discovered in the great revolutions that occurred between the two epochs referred to, which robbed Europe of the greater portion of its North American possessions, and which promised, at no distant day, to free the entire continent of America from European domination. The slaves, with the territory they inhabited, thus changed masters; and the new possessors, from the condition of vassals, became the equals and the rivals of their former masters.

The enthusiasts who choose to imagine and to declare that this public sentiment of the nineteenth century in Europe, had its origin in a new revelation of the Divine will, or in some hitherto misunderstood or undiscovered law of Divine justice, and in a consequent loftier conception of public morality than was possessed by their ancestors, may gratify the vanity of the age by such a solution, but the intelligent reader of contemporaneous history will find no difficulty in arriving at the conclusion, that this revolution in public sentiment owed its origin and its development, not to *moral* but to *political* causes.

The Assiento was a contract or convention between the King of Spain and other powers for furnishing the Spanish dominions in America

first inaugurated the system, as scarcely to bear any resemblance thereto. In order not to tax the reader with the necessity of crediting the mere statement of a fact without proof, I beg to refer to some of the causes which have produced this change.

---

with negro slaves. The Spaniards having destroyed the native Indian races in their American Colonies, supplied the deficiency of laborers thus created by importing negroes from the coast of Africa. The Genoese first undertook to supply Spain with negroes at a stipulated price. They were succeeded by the Portuguese, and after them, the contract was transferred to France, and the trade yielded to that country enormous profits; insomuch that Great Britain coveted the contract. By the treaty of Utrecht, Philip V, being declared King of Spain, at the close of a bloody war in which all the great powers were engaged, and in which England and her allies were the victors, it was one of the articles of peace between France and England, that the contract referred to should be transferred from the former to the latter. Accordingly, a new instrument was signed in May, 1713, to last thirty years, and the furnishing of negroes to Spanish America was committed by England to the South Sea Company, an enterprise in which numbers of the royal family of England, the chief nobility, and many of the leading statesmen, as well as other citizens in every rank of life, were stockholders. In virtue of this treaty, England agreed to furnish Spain with one hundred and forty-four thousand African slaves, for which it was to receive pay at the same rate which had been paid the French. A condition was added, that during the first twenty-five years, only one half the duty should be paid for such as they should import beyond the stated number. By the treaty of Madrid, concluded on the 5th October, 1750, the right of England to this traffic for the four years not yet expired by former treaty, was re-transferred to Spain, and all claims against the Spanish Government growing out of the same were surrendered upon the payment by Spain to the British South Sea Company the sum of £1,000,000—about five millions of dollars. For a more detailed account of these transactions, the reader is referred to Anderson's Commerce, Robertson's History of America, and other contemporaneous historians.

Formerly the slaves were savages, and of course it was necessary to guard them with more vigilance. They did not speak the language of the countries to which they were transported, and they were for the most part, in fact altogether, distributed by the European powers throughout their colonies. The proprietors of the plantations often resided in the mother country, and governed their slaves by the employment of agents. Moreover, there was but a comparatively trifling value attached to slaves, and the loss of one or a dozen by bad treatment was of but small pecuniary importance.

Now, the slaves are civilized and speak the language of their masters. They may be left in the enjoyment of almost as much freedom of action, when unemployed, as they desire. They reside with their masters and form a part of the household, and their masters are themselves the political sovereigns of the country, in conjunction with their fellow citizens of the same race. Each slave has a large money value, so great indeed, that the interest upon the capital employed, with other incidental expenses, makes it the most expensive labor in the world. If free labor could be induced to cultivate the sugar and cotton fields, slavery might possibly abolish itself on account of its greater cost. The two races having existed together for so long a time, it is natural that both should now understand and adapt themselves to their respective positions. All these causes have produced such a modification in the practical effects of the system by the improvement of the condition of the slaves, as to divest it of almost all those features which at one time shocked the sensibilities of the world. It would readily be conjectured that such a result would attend the causes enumerated, without appealing to existing facts in corrroboration thereof.

In considering the probabilities, or rather the possibilities, of effecting the abolition of slavery in the planting States, and the substitution of another class of laborers, it is necessary to observe that there are difficulties in the way which have never attended any other scheme of emancipation in any other country. In the Northern States of the American Confederacy, when slavery became unprofitable, it was, in common parlance, abolished. This is not, however, literally true. As I have before said, no slave was necessarily made free by these acts. The dominant race rid themselves of a population which had ceased to be necessary or profitable, by selling them, before the day of emancipation had arrived, to the neighboring slave States. With England, so far as the great body of the nation was concerned, emancipation in her colonies was only a question of pounds sterling! The Africans had never been introduced into England itself, and by consequence thereof, the difficulty of greatest magnitude was not encountered—namely, the getting rid of the degraded population! Now, the slave States of the South cannot, as the Northern States did, make a profit out of emancipation, by removing them to a country where they would be more valuable; nor can they, as England did, get rid of the population by the mere sacrifice of their estimated money value. The slaves liberated in the South, in a body, must, of course, remain upon the soil. Supposing that, in a pecuniary point of view, the time should arrive when this course would be deemed most profitable, there arises the political difficulty that the institutions of the country are Republican in form, and all whom the laws recognize as citizens should have equal rights. This fact also precludes the Southern States from adopting the "Cooly system," or any other which involves the employment of Asiatics or Africans, to supply the place of slave labor.

Inasmuch, therefore, as the European races will not, to any considerable extent, labor in the production of cotton, rice, and sugar, it follows that with the abolition of slavery, the production of these articles in the United States would, to a great extent, cease. With the Governments of Europe the case would be different. They could transport any number of Asiatics or Africans to their colonies without any danger to their institutions, because the mother country would not be effected thereby. They could with impunity cover their islands and distant possessions with the most barbarous tribes, and protect their property against any threatened conversion to the use of these savages, by a few cannon. But to introduce such a population into the United States, in the midst of the families of the inhabitants, except under the system of absolute slavery, would be an act of suicide. It is not difficult to perceive that if the abolition of slavery in America can be accomplished, the United States, having no distant colonies, would cease from that moment to be formidable competitors in supplying the world with tropical productions.

My object in these letters, has been rather to state admitted facts than to make arguments in favor of, or against, any particular systems. That I have stated them frankly and without any coloring which could pervert their true meaning or significance, will not, I think, be questioned. Whether these facts will produce upon the minds of others the same convictions as upon mine, will of course be dependent upon circumstances. I am well aware that I have added no new light to the subjects about which I have written—the particular truths I have stated are known to all. My purpose, however, has been to present these isolated facts in a body, so that they could be considered together. In the investigation of a subject, in order to understand it, it is necessary to consider all the facts which bear upon it. Partisans often select a number of admitted facts, and by omitting another, establish a falsehood, without having stated an untruth. Oftener, still, they start out by the assertion of a proposition which none will deny, and leaping over a hundred truths, arrive at false conclusions.

Never has any subject been treated so unfairly as that of the institution of slavery in America. Its enemies start out with the declaration that one human being should not be held in slavery by another, and the abstract fact being generally conceded, they find no difficulty in concluding that the slaves should be set free and their masters consigned to eternal perdition! The slave States of the South have been required to submit the trial of their cause upon that single issue of abstract right. Every system of Government that has been invented by man, would be overthrown under the application of the same rule. Human institutions will not stand the test of a trial against abstract right! I have, therefore, chosen to examine the peculiar circumstances in which slavery had its origin—its progress, and its present condition. Admitting its imperfections, I have compared it with the good and evil of all other systems which have been devised to supersede it.

Great Britain, as represented by those who assume to speak for her, being the head of the anti-slavery party, as well as one of the most enlightened and powerful nations of the world, the enemies of the slave States of America could not object that, in trying slavery by the ordeal of a comparison with other systems of labor, I should have chosen those of one of the freest Governments of Europe. They charge the Southern States of the American Union with "the perpetuation of a crime against humanity," and by their grand moral influence, they have excited, in many parts of the world, a feeling of unkindness against the Southern people. They have stimulated the excitement of party struggles in America, and have materially contributed to enkindle a flame of sectional hatred, which threatens fatal consequences to the integrity and unity of the Republic.

I have therefore, in considering the defence of the South against these charges, continued the comparison which I had instituted in regard to the different systems of labor, and have made it embrace also the relative claims of the principal adversaries in the encounter to the respect of mankind, on the score of philanthropy and benevolence. I cannot hope that the enemies of the Southern States will reverse the decision which they have already made in favor of the powerful assailant, but I trust there will be individual instances of moral heroism in which truth will be allowed to triumph over prejudice, and justice be administered, despite the clamors of malevolence or ignorance.

It is to be regretted that the systematic and ceaseless assaults of the anti-slavery party of Great Britain upon the Southern States should render it necessary for them, in self-defence, to turn upon their powerful assailant and defend themselves by an enumeration of their own faults, vices, and crimes. It would be much more in accordance with the fraternal feelings which ought to animate the two great nations of Anglo-Saxon origin to institute comparisons in regard to the benefits rather than the evils which each have conferred or inflicted upon mankind. Nor do I doubt that there are very many Englishmen among all classes of society who deprecate these constant, and irritating, and unfriendly assaults upon a community of States which England has thus far known only by the benefits which she has derived from her intercourse with them. But however numerous this class may be, their power has never yet been sufficient to change or modify the policy or the preponderating influence of the nation as a whole.

Would that the great body of the English people could break the chains of prejudice in which they have been bound by designing leaders, and refuse to follow other counsels than the dictates of their own consciences and the promptings of their own interests! It is impossible that they can in their hearts cherish any feeling of animosity against those who have given such a direction to the legacy of slavery, which they inherited from British ancestors, as to offer employment and bread, and luxuries, which were previously attainable by the rich only, to millions of themselves and the poor of the world! Would that they could see in advance the evils which will inevitably fall with a heavy hand upon the toiling millions of their great country, should the mad designs of their ambitious leaders be crowned with success.

Leaving out of question that ridiculous affectation of sentimental philanthropy which is so peculiarly unbecoming and unsuited to the genius of the British character, there ought to be, and but for the influence of vain or wicked, or ambitious men, there would be a feeling of reciprocal sympathy between

Great Britain and the planting States of America. While neither is wholly dependent upon the other, each contributes materially to the other's prosperity. The planting States produce the raw material which England fashions into shape. The planter is after all but the overseer for Great Britain, while Great Britain is but the factor of the planter. Without considering the past, if there is any guilt in slavery it is shared alike by both, for in the products of slave labor they are joint partners. If there is moral turpitude in holding slaves, the guilt of those who knowingly participate in the profits accruing from the wrong, is the same as that of the active agents. By the moral law, as well as by the civil law, all who participate, either as principals or accessories, in any violation thereof are alike responsible and alike guilty.

Let the real philanthropists of Great Britain and her toiling millions call upon their anti-slavery propagandists to change for a season the field of their labors. Let them take up their abode within the benighted regions of Africa itself, and there devote their time and talents to the work of instilling into the minds and hearts of the natives the great and glorious principles of the British constitution. When they shall have succeeded in elevating four thousand—ay, four hundred of its sable inhabitants —its kings and nobles included—to the same rank and to the same condition of comfort and happiness which is now enjoyed by the humblest and most unfortunate of their four millions of fellow-countrymen in America, allow them to return and enjoy, in the plaudits of the really benevolent, the rewards to which they would then be so justly entitled. This field would be all the more inviting, because, even though they might fail in gathering and garnering the tempting fruits, it would not be necessary for them to pass through blood and strife, and over the desolated homes of their kinsmen, to reach the scene of their labors.

Although in the course of these letters I have taken advantage of such circumstances as might, even in the estimation of unprejudiced anti-slavery men, relieve the Southern States of all responsibility for the existence of slavery, yet I would be doing an injustice to the South and to my own convictions were I to rest her defence upon the plea of necessity. Neither will I claim that the shortcomings of those who are their assailants should shield the South from that just responsibility which she owes to God and man for the faithful performance of those duties which Providence has imposed upon her. Though I have commended to the lips of those who have instituted this moral war upon the slave States, the "ingredients of the poisoned chalice" which they had with so much skill prepared for others, it was not with the view to avert the judgment of that "evenhanded justice," which would hold the South to a rigid accountability for her own acts.

It may be a delusion—it may be as charged, that there is a fanaticism in the South as well as in the

North—it may be that the calumnies which malice and ignorance have heaped upon the citizens of the Southern States, and which have penetrated every civilized land, have blinded them to their real faults—yet the SOUTHERNER feels in his inmost heart the consciousness that whatever may be the judgment of to-day, history will record, and posterity will decide, that the slave States of the American Confederacy have been instrumental in diffusing among mankind as many blessings, with as little of evil or wrong, as any population of similar extent in this or in any other age.

LETTER XI.

Great Britain—Her interests in American Affairs—Public mind of Europe excited by misrepresentations against the South—The London Times on Sumner's last speech—"Republican" party of America—Its purposes hostile to the South.

In writing these letters from the old world, I have been led naturally to discuss the subject at issue between the North and the South in reference chiefly to the attitude occupied by Europe upon the same question. While disagreeing in opinion with those British statesmen who believe that British interests, or the interests of any other nation or people on earth, are injured by the institution of African slavery in America, I have not dared to suppose that they misrepresented the opinions of the British people. Although as a Southerner, I have much to regret and more to resent on account of the unjust strictures directed by them against the institutions and the people of my native country, I have no disposition to turn to account the feeling of irritation which this injustice has very naturally engendered amongst my fellow-countrymen. I have no desire whatever, even if I had the power, to disparage the claims of Great Britain to the respect of mankind. I admire the stern and obstinate zeal which she displays in maintaining her rank amongst the nations of the world. But above all, I admire that integrity of character in all the relations of private life which, to their honor be it said, is a distinguishing characteristic of Englishmen. Her history, upon the whole, is a record of great achievements of which the annals of no other nation furnish a parallel. Her governing classes of to-day are more distinguished for their intellectual attainments, and their natural and acquired capacities for discharging the functions of their high position, than any other aristocratic body that ever existed. Their Queen is not only a model sovereign, but more than this—a model woman. There are a thousand sympathies and interests which are common to the two great people of the Anglo-Saxon blood. But Americans should never forget that an apparently dominant party in England have announced that they have a deep interest which is in direct antagonism with the chief element of wealth and power in the American Confederacy. The question now at issue between Americans themselves is, shall this element of wealth and power be surrendered?

Although it is well known in America that the present contest between the North and the South is regarded by the British anti-slavery party with feelings of the deepest solicitude, yet there are perhaps few who are aware of the extent to which this feeling is entertained. The silliest calumnies which are set afloat by the abolition fanatics and presses of the United States are greedily read, republished, and with pictorial illustrations, circulated broadcast throughout Europe, and wherever else the English language is read or spoken. The false impressions thus created are instilled into the minds of the children in their very infancy—they are made to imbibe them with their mother's milk. They are taught that the most horrible atrocities are but matters of every day occurrence in the Southern States; that men and women, for pastime, scourge their African slaves to death, that the children of slaveholders are made to participate in these scenes of cruelty until they become as brutal as their parents. No calumnies are too gross for utterance, or too improbable to be believed. If their truth should be denied, the response is always ready—"We are bound to believe that which the Americans themselves tell us!"

The Southerner, knowing the falsehood and wickedness of these allegations, is almost tempted to doubt the evidences of his own senses. He knows that if there are faults in the treatment of slaves by their masters, they are, as a rule, the reverse of those which are charged by ignorant or malicious commentators. He knows that the feelings of kindness and affection between master and slave are cultivated to an extent utterly unknown to the intercourse of employer and servant or apprentice in his own or any other country. He believes that there are fewer instances of cruelty practiced by masters upon slaves in America than even by parents upon their own offspring in any civilized free State of the world; though he is also well aware that when such instances do occur, they are exceptional in both. The Southerner who reads or listens to the recital of these stories in a foreign land is silenced by the very magnitude and enormity of their falsehood! It is true that in England these atrocities are only charged upon the South, yet throughout Europe the geographical divisions are in a great degree lost sight of, and even those who originate them come in as "Americans" for a share of that obloquy which the malice and hatred of a senseless sectionalism seek to fasten upon a portion of those whom they call their fellow countrymen!

The political abolitionists of England, while earnest in their efforts to impose upon the ignorance and credulity of Europe by exaggerated and heart-rending descriptions of the horrors of slavery, are still more averse to the frenzied appeals of the abolitionists in the present contest in America between the North and the South. They believe that the abolition of slavery can only be accomplished by lulling the slave States into a fancied security—that violent denunciation reacts by placing conservative citizens upon their guard—that the true policy is, first to secure the power to control slavery, get possession of the government of the Federal Union and then they may, without hazard, strike down slavery and the slave power forever. In this view of the question, although the defeat of Mr. Seward before the Republican Convention was regretted because of his preeminent services in leading the Northern mind in the direction of abolitionism, yet the more sagacious anti-slavery politicians of England are satisfied that the nomination of a more obscure man will serve more effectually to blind the masses in regard to the ultimate designs of the Republican party. The late speech of Sumner, of Massachusetts, has therefore been regarded by them with manifest tokens of displeasure. They say that such ebullitions of malignity from those who have been elevated to the position of hero-martyrs are well calculated to arouse the conservative element of the Union to a sense of the real nature of the present conflict, which they insist should only be fully developed after they have succeeded in establishing themselves in power, and that Sumner's course is like that of an over-confident General of an army, who sends to his enemy on the eve of the battle a full and detailed plan of his intended operations. A brief extract from a leading English journal will better explain the more judicious, if less honest programme, which is furnished for the Republican leaders:

It is a part of the destiny of this country, that from its wide-spread dominions and universal interests, the concerns of no State are indifferent to it. *Perhaps the most important foreign question for England is, that of American Slavery.* Our relations with the United States, through trade and community of origin, are so close that it is impossible their moral condition should not affect our own. The rivalry which exists between the two countries makes it difficult to discuss any international subject without the chance of giving umbrage. . . . *We have the greatest interest in the decay* of this mighty evil. *The reputation of this country for wisdom* is at stake, for the negroes of the West India Colonies were emancipated *not only* on the ground of humanity, *but on the calculation* that *free labor was more productive* than that of slaves. These islands still lie at the threshold of the American Republic, and if the stars and stripes shall ever float over the walls of Mexico and Havana, the British Antilles will be exposed to all the influence of a pro-slavery propaganda. *How important then it is for us* that before these great territorial accessions, which seem inevitable, actually take place, *the system of slavery shall have been modified!* . . . John Brown himself has not done more harm to the cause of abolitionism in Virginia than a man like Mr. Sumner, when he drives the Southern Senators to fury by such a violent and uncalled for philippic as our American correspondent notices to-day. . . . *We must, in the name of English Abolitionism, protest against* these foolish and vindictive harangues. Scarcely has the frenzy caused by John Brown's outrage begun to die away, than out comes Mr. Sumner with a speech which will set the whole South in a flame. We can well believe *that the prospects of the Republican party* have been already damaged by it. Mr. Sumner is one of that class of politicians who should be muzzled by their friends. . . . We may predict that the man who first gains a victory for the cause of Abolition, will be of a very different temper to the Senator from Massachusetts.—*London Times, June* 18.

The influential journal from which I have made the foregoing extract is alike distinguished for its ability and its remarkable versatility. It does not represent the opinions of one man, nor of a political party, nor even of a class. Moreover, it never "makes war for an idea." Its chief ambition is, to present itself always to the world as a reflection—a daguerreotype, as it were, of the current public opinion of the day. If the picture taken does not seem accurate in its general outline or details, the indefatigable operator obliterates the impression and takes another, and if need be, another, until the likeness is thought to be without blemish or defect. Time, or altered circumstances, or both, may bring about a change, in which event, like a faithful photographist, the "Times" adapts itself to the times, tries it again, and again presents the lineaments of its subject to the world, in the garb, and with the lights and shadows, which will set it off to the best advantage. I will not quarrel with this most versatile operator, albeit the lineaments of the Southern features are painted now in sombre and gloomy and repulsive colors. I will bide our time, for I am sure the day will come when a brighter and a clearer light will shine around the sky-light window of the mammoth daguerrean; and I have an abiding faith that the Times will not then prove a laggard in presenting the picture to the world, in its new, and changed, and more flattering aspect.

But it is with the present, not the future, we have now to deal; and however much the true American may regret, that the public opinion of even a respectable body of Englishmen is reflected in the spirit of the foregoing paragraph from this leading and influential journal, the subject is one worthy of his serious consideration. We learn from this article that the crime of John Brown, and the blackguardism of Sumner, are only deserving of censure, by the moral code of British abolitionism, because, by exposing at too early a period the designs of the Republican party, the success of the abolition cause, in which England is said to have so deep an interest, will thereby be placed in jeopardy! It is not denied that John Brown and Sumner are both laboring earnestly in that cause which the anti-slavery party has so much at heart; but they are *indiscreet.* They are exposing the objects of the Republicans *before*, instead of *after*, the Presidential election; therefore such men should be muzzled! England has too deep an interest in the present struggle between the North and the South to sit by quietly, and give sanction by silence, to such an intemperate exposure of ultimate designs, as may arouse the country to a sense of the impending danger. England, says this journal, "has a right to protest in the name of English abolitionism," because not only are English interests deeply involved in the overthrow of American slavery, but *the reputation of England for wisdom is at stake*, because the emancipation of the negroes in the West India colonies, was not alone on the ground of humanity, but *on the calculation that free labor was more productive than that of slaves.*

There is a frank outspoken boldness in the manner in which the subject is treated for an English audience, very different from the policy enjoined upon the "Republican" leaders in the United States. Slavery, it is true, is treated as an enormous evil and a crime that should be abated, but it is frankly admitted that the crime and the evil does not consist in its "inhumanity" but in its declared antagonism to English interests and English dominion.

The John Browns and the Sumners are censured, not because they do not faithfully reflect the sentiments of the Republican leaders, but because such premature disclosures are calculated to weaken the Republican party, before its full strength has been consolidated preparatory to the final overthrow of the greatest of all the instruments which have contributed to the marvellous growth of the Republic, in all the elements of wealth, prosperity, and power.

This advice of the British abolitionists is certainly prudent, and exhibits much sagacity; but is it honest? If Sumner and Brown really reflect the spirit of the anti-slavery party, why should not the issue be fairly made up and presented to the people? If John Brown and Sumner have done no wrong, why should they be held up as objects of public censure, as men "who ought to be muzzled by their friends?" The Times says that British interests are too deeply involved in the issue of the present struggle, to allow that the success of the Republican party shall be placed in jeopardy by its indiscreet friends. But does this constitute any reason why American citizens, who have so much more at stake, shall not consider the question at issue in the true light in which it has been placed by John Brown and Sumner? Were the mere words of Sumner as soft and gentle as the music of the dying swan, would that change the purpose of his party? and though John Browns might cut the throats of their victims while praying for the repose of their souls, or while singing hymns of glory to the Most High, and uttering exhortations to the living to save themselves from a similar calamity, by conforming quietly to the requirements of abolitionism, would it change the true nature of the contest, or should it reconcile the Southern people to the chains which are being forged for them?

True Americans should bear in mind, that the interests represented by the anti-slavery party of England cannot be identical with theirs. If it be true, as they declare, that British power and wealth are to be increased by the success of the Republican party, American interests must suffer in a like ratio. If, as the Times says, "the most important foreign question for England is that of American slavery," it cannot be less important for America, because the hope of the party here represented, is to build up their own system of labor upon the ruins of the American plantations. In no other possible manner can English interests be promoted by the success of American abolitionism, and the consequent defeat of the party of free trade.

Is it true that England has the greatest interest in the decay of American slavery? If it be so, shall it be recorded in American history that the nation which failed to subdue three millions of our ancestors by the sword and the bayonet during a seven years war, conquered thirty millions of their descendants by sowing amongst them the seeds of discord without the loss of a single soldier? If it be so, and if British abolitionists succeed in piloting the "Republican" ship into the presidential harbor, well may they exclaim in the fulness of their triumph, "The defeat of our armies by a handful of rebellious subjects, was allowed by the providence of the Almighty, in order to prepare the way for the complete subjection to British interests, of ten times their number, at a later period in the world's history!"

In one thing, the London journal above quoted, has fallen into a grievous error. It urges prudence upon the part of the Republican leaders, for the sake of the great ultimate object which republicanism has in view. It censures Sumner and Brown for intemperance of acts and speech. The truth is, but for the Browns and the Sumners, there would be no Republican party. Blot out of existence the vindictive spirit of such men, and there is no appeal left to the madness of sectional fanaticism. If the leaders of the Northern mind were only to cultivate feelings of kindness and good-will towards the Southern people, there would exist no motive sufficiently strong to urge the Northern people to a crusade against the South. The abolition party would be reduced to a force so small, that no place-seeking politician would endeavor through such influences to attain to political honors.

I do not believe that all the Republican politicians, much less the Republican masses, desire to be considered as endorsing either Sumner or John Brown. Many, no doubt, hope at the proper moment to stay the tide of sectional hatred, and after having conquered the South by superior numbers, generously propose, upon the fulfilment of certain conditions, to leave them in possession of that which they already occupy. But these should remember that, *in the hour of victory, they must press forward, or be left behind* in a feeble minority, to be themselves taunted as they have taunted others, with the appellation of "dough-faces." If the Republicans are successful, *he amongst their leaders who falters in the work of destruction, will only work his own political downfall, without being able to arrest* his comrades and followers, maddened by the resistance which they have encountered, elated by success, and thirsting for revenge.

For the true American citizen, who would avert the threatened calamity, there is but one course left open which he can follow with any well grounded hope of success. All the parties which have nominated candidates for the Presidency, profess to find authority in the Constitution for all that they propose to do. Even Sumner says that the Constitution is upon his side, and that it does not confer any rights upon the slaveholding States in regard to slavery. But it is also a fact, that the hundreds of thousands of abolitionists who frankly admit, that in order to accomplish their purposes the *Constitution must be violated*, and its provisions set at naught—all the leading spirits who pronounce that sacred instrument to be "a league with death, and a covenant with hell"—all! all! all! are arrayed upon the Republican side, and are fighting their battle under the Republican banner, and have adopted as their candidates, the chosen standard-bearers of the "Republican party."

The conservative and patriotic friends of the Union which is but a creature of the Constitution, and which must perish with it, may well ask themselves if they can hope to preserve it in its purity, with such leaders and such associates.

Beautifully rounded periods in laudation of the Union will never save it from destruction, if that spirit in the Northern mind which menaces its destruction is not rebuked by both the North and the South. All the Constitutions which could be enacted, would be powerless to hold together a confederacy of sovereign States, where the animosities of the greater number are a constant menace against the tranquillity, the peace, and independence of the others. Parties may prove what they choose by written parchment articles of agreement, but all such compacts will be powerless to perpetuate a partnership that would be worth preserving, if the members thereof are repelled by a common sentiment of hatred. In this contest, it should be remembered that the North has no domestic interest at stake. It is not pretended that the South desires to interfere, in the smallest degree, in the affairs of the Northern States. No Southern man would accept of any privileges in the common territory, which were not enjoyed alike by every citizen of the Republic. The defeat of Republicanism would not deprive the North of a single right or privilege of sovereignty, while the success of abolitionism would place in jeopardy the liberty, the independence, the property, the very lives of the Southern people. While the triumph of the Republican party would seal the bond of hatred between the sections upon the very hearts of the people, too late, perhaps, its misguided followers would find that the fruits of their victory would be death.

LETTER XII.

Influence of Anti-Slavery Fanaticism upon Religion—Bible Authority on Slavery—Increase of Infidelity—Influence of the Clergy for Good and Evil.

In considering the evils which have resulted from the unceasing agitation of the anti-slavery question, its active influence in producing disbelief or skepticism, in regard to the truths of the religion revealed in the Holy Bible, cannot be overlooked, and should not be disregarded. The fanaticism of anti-slavery has been for many years past, of all other causes, the most fruitful source of infidelity, wherever its baneful influence has become a predominating passion. The philosophical mind may readily trace out the links of the chain which connect abolitionism with infidelity as cause and effect.

Slavery, as a political institution, or as a question involving certain political rights, has been a subject about which there has existed a variety of opinions. An investigation in regard to its influence for good or evil, leads us to consider the circumstances and causes which have produced such a relation between men. There are those, however, who condemn the continuance of such an institution without regard to the causes which brought it into existence, and without consideration of the results which may follow its abolition. Others excuse and tolerate it in consideration of various assigned causes; while others approve of it on account of its declared advantages, not only to those concerned, but to mankind at large. It may be discussed as any other subject would be, involving the rights of man, and incidentally the question in regard to its moral influence is considered.

The theoretical principle upon which a democracy is founded, is the absolute and unqualified political equality of its citizens. A limited monarchy invests a certain hereditary right in one or more persons to govern the subjects thereof under certain restrictions. An absolute monarchy invests one man with supreme and unquestioned power over the lives and property of his subjects. It does not follow that the monarch employs this power in perpetrating deeds of cruelty upon those over whom he is placed. Within these governments respectively, the inhabitants occupy various relations in regard to each other, which relations are established by the supreme authority of the State. From the earliest period of recorded history, to the present time, the relations have been those of proprietor and tenant, noble and vassal, lord and serf, master and slave. Men's minds, as I have said, differ in regard to the political advantages and disadvantages of the various relations thus established between man and man, as well as upon the moral influences of each. The great body of mankind live under the most absolute and despotic forms of government, the rulers of which, as before said, exercise unquestioned power over the lives, the personal liberty, and the property of the subjects. A smaller number are subject to governments in which the power of the monarch is more or less restricted, while fewer still are citizens of democratic governments. The absolute monarch exercises an authority over his subjects far greater than that which is held by a master over his slave; for in addition to the rights which are invested in a master, the sovereign may not only dispose of the life of his subject, but he may delegate his powers to another. The master holds his slave subject to the laws of the land, while the sovereign is himself the fountain of all power. Under very many governments in which the rights of the subject are protected by a constitution, the laws confer upon a creditor the right to dispose of the liberty of his debtor, and instances have occurred even in the history of our country, in which white citizens have been sold for a term of years to the highest bidder.

Mankind have discussed the relative merits of these various forms of government, from the beginning of time until the present moment, without having approached any nearer to a satisfactory solution than in the days when the chosen people of God by Divine command bought bondmen and bondmaids from the heathen round about, to inherit them as a possession for themselves and their posterity forever; or at that interesting epoch in the world's history, when after the terrible upheaving produced by the French Revolution had been calmed for a season upon the field of Waterloo, the victorious Monarchs under the inspiration of the mystic dreams of a courtesan, established that "holy alliance" which was to give peace and concord to all the nations of the earth forever.

The abolitionist of Massachusetts may believe with his whole heart that if the institution of African slavery be blotted out of existence, his native land will have touched the point of perfection in human government; while the extreme monarchists of the Old World may be as sincere in their conviction that the only existing human institution, more odious than that which is thus condemned by the Yankee leveller, is that very democracy upon which the American Government is founded. Yet who may say that the existence of any one of these different modes of government adopted by man is, *per se*, a sin against God? Has the Almighty ever made such a revelation to man? If so, when, where, and to whom, has the announcement been made? Where has the line of sin been drawn between an extreme democracy and an extreme despotism? If there is no record of any such announcement of the Divine judgment, how impious in man to say that he has penetrated the unfathomable designs of Omnipotence, and has discovered the line of demarcation? How is it that from the creation of the world to near the close of the eighteenth century of the Christian era, the now anathematized institution of slavery has existed, without any discovery having been made by mankind of its criminality or sinfulness in the sight of Heaven? During this period the Messiah himself has appeared upon the earth, and has left to us the record of his mission of mercy, in the sublime and heavenly precepts he has taught us; and yet, during eighteen hundred years, his disciples and followers never gleaned from his teachings a knowledge of the sinfulness of slavery!

Notwithstanding this, men have been found in this wicked age—aye! honored teachers of our holy religion, who have presumed to announce that the domestic institution of African slavery in America is, *per se*, a crime against the Almighty, and a sin which, without repentance, will consign the offender to everlasting punishment! Pulpits in England and in America have been employed to give effect to this impious doctrine. The deadly sins denounced in the Bible have, in effect, been held as the most trifling vices, compared to the great sin of the slaveholder. Churches have been set apart, not for denunciations of the sins which were practiced by their respective congregations, but of that which, if criminal at all in the sight of God, was the crime of another people! Clergymen have stimulated the passions and the fanaticism of their hearers, against the domestic institutions of a distant State, although it could not be pretended that the "crime and the sin" which elicited their eloquent and frenzied denunciations had ever been, or was likely ever to be, committed by a human being within the sound of their voices. As Peter the Hermit, in the days of the Crusades, preached to all Christendom that the crime of all crimes was to refuse to follow him to the Holy Land, to rescue the sepulchre of Christ from the hand of the Saracens, and that the virtue, the practice of which washed away all sins, was to follow him in his holy enterprise, so have the anti-slavery clergymen stimulated the fanaticism of their congregations against the declared offences of another people, to an extent which has, to say the least, blunted the perception of their own besetting vices and sins.

Whether or not the pulpits of the North have produced the prevailing excitement against the citizens of the Southern States, that it exists to a most fanatical degree, will not be denied. That it is the ruling and absorbing passion of multitudes of people, is fully established by the fact that the most sagacious, place-seeking politicians have severed their connection with old political parties, and are now sailing on the current of anti-slavery frenzy, as the surest and speediest way to political preferment.

The imagination of a well-meaning man being excited by false or exaggerated pictures of the horrors of slavery, and filled with the belief that the existence of such an institution is a crime and a sin against Heaven, very naturally seeks to find confirmation and authority for such belief in that great Book, which reveals the mysteries of the Christian's faith, and which he had been taught to believe was a sacred emanation from on high. He is startled first, by discovering that Abraham held as bond-servants, men and women, born in his house and *bought with his money!* He turns over the pages of the Holy Book, and he reads, (Leviticus xxv. 44—46:) "Both thy bondmen, and thy bondmaids, which thou shalt have, shall be of the heathen that are round about you; of them shall ye buy bondmen and bondmaids. Moreover, of the children of the strangers that do sojourn among you, of them shall ye buy, and of their families that are with you, which they begat in your land: and they shall be your possession. And ye shall take them as an inheritance for your children after you, to inherit them for a possession; they shall be your bondmen forever."

Finding nothing in the Old Testament to gratify the cravings of his morbid appetite, he hopes to find that which he seeks, in the teachings of our Savior and his apostles—he reads, (Ephesians vi. 5, 6:) "Servants, be obedient to them that are your masters according to the flesh, with fear and trembling, in singleness of your heart, as unto Christ; not with eyeservice, as menpleasers; but as the servants of Christ, doing the will of God from the heart."

He searches farther, and finds, (1 Timothy vi. 1:) "Let as many servants as are under the yoke count their own masters worthy of all honor, that the name of God and his doctrine be not blasphemed."

Again, he finds, (Titus ii. 9,10:) "Exhort servants to be obedient unto their own masters, and to please them well in all things; not answering again; not purloining, but showing all good fidelity; that they may adorn the doctrine of God our Saviour in all things."

In despair he continues his researches, in the desperate hope that perhaps there may still be some words of comfort in the little that remains for him to read. His eye is at length arrested by a passage, bearing an import, which startles his very soul. "Can it be I," he exclaims! He reads and re-reads, (2 Peter ii. 19:) "While they promise them liberty, they themselves are the servants of corruption: for of whom a man is overcome, of the same is he brought in bondage."

And when he discovers that Paul sends back Onesimus, the runaway slave, to his master, though with gentle words and a request, amounting almost to a command, that he be pardoned for having abandoned the service of his master, and thus fully recognizing the master's right, he is tempted to exclaim, in the bitterness of his disappointment, "the apostle of Christ a slave-catcher!"

While his researches inform him that, during the whole period of time of which the Bible furnishes a record, the institution of slavery existed; and that along with the evidences of its recognition by the holy teachers, whose writings adorn its pages, there is not a line or a syllable in which it is condemned, either by Christ or his apostles, the terrible doubt crosses his mind. There is a natural struggle between the passion that absorbs him and the religion which his mother taught him. He enters once more, and for the last time, the sanctuary where he had so often, in days past, listened to the words of love which fell from the preacher's lips, as he labored to impress upon his hearers the holy precepts of the meek and lowly Saviour. Alas! it is no gentle words of charity that fall upon his listening ear! Instead, thereof, again he hears the confirmation of his own belief: "Slavery is the sin against God and man, which calls aloud for the vengeance of the Almighty."

He reasons within himself: "Is not God perfection? Is he not allwise? If he had made a revelation to man, would it not have enumerated, clearly and distinctly, all the great sins which he condemned? If he had appeared upon earth, would he not, with his own lips, have pronounced a sentence of condemnation against the sin of sins which was practiced before his eyes?" Fanaticism triumphs! He throws down the Holy Book, exclaiming, "give me an anti-slavery Bible, and an anti-slavery God!" These are not my words, but words which have fallen from the lips of an excited abolition orator, and upon the ears of a gratified and approving audience of New Englanders.*

* "*We of the North want an anti-slavery Constitution, an anti-slavery Bible, and an anti-slavery God!!*" The author of this rather startling annunciation of Northern wants, has been rewarded, since the accession of the Republican party to power, by a first-class diplomatic mission abroad. The Government to which he was first accredited, very properly refused to receive him, but he was subsequently appointed to another, and he now holds the rank at a foreign court, of "Envoy Extraordinary and Minister Plenipotentiary of the United States of America."

But how could it be otherwise than thus? And who can tell how deeply this feeling of infidelity, or at least of skepticism, may have penetrated the hearts of those with whom anti-slavery fanaticism has become a controlling passion? If there are any who are ignorant of the extent to which this sentiment of unbelief is entertained, let him acquaint himself with the proceedings of anti-slavery anniversaries, and note the increasing numbers who openly avow their infidelity.

There is no human engine of good or evil so potent as the clergy—those who are acknowledged as the teachers of religion. In all ages of the world, this influence has been a controlling element among mankind. When it has been worthily directed towards cultivating the feelings of love, and of charity, and forgiveness among men, society has had reason to bless them as benefactors. But when, as has too often been the case, even in the history of our own religion, they have been instrumental in producing strife, and discord, and heartburnings, and misery, and bloodshed, society has had cause to regret that influence which their sacred calling secured for them.

It is not for me to judge of the motives of those who have contributed so powerfully towards building up that mountain of hatred, which may be said now to be common to a great number of the citizens of both sections of the American Union. Least of all, could I say that those motives have not had their origin in a benevolent purpose. The zeal to do good often degenerates into a fanaticism, which results in nothing but evil. Fanaticism begets a reverse fanaticism, and to the eye of the disinterested spectator, or to him who beholds from a distance, that which is transpiring, the acts of all appear as the acts of madmen.

We cannot but remember that the same sources of discord have existed since the foundation of the Union, and we should likewise bear in mind, that they will exist as long as the Confederation endures! We know that good-will did once prevail between the different members of the Confederacy, and why may it not exist again? If the clergymen of the entire North would resolve that, for twelve short months, they would preach nothing but Christ, and teach nothing but that which he taught: if they would, in good faith, call upon their congregations to exercise toward all mankind charity and love: if they would denounce, in the spirit of the apostles, the sins which they denounced, who can estimate the amount of good which that one year might bring forth? What a noble field is here presented in which to exercise the duties of a noble calling! How much of wretchedness, and misery, and wickedness, ay! perhaps of bitter strife and bloodshed, they might avert!

LETTER XIII.

Present attitude of Parties in the United States—Success of the Republican Party will accomplish Disunion—Its Measures examined, etc.

In the preceding letters I have endeavored to present a brief view of the origin, progress, and development of the institution of slavery in the Southern States of the American Confederacy. Although I may not hope that the facts I have stated will change the fixed opinions or convictions of any one, yet I trust they will not be altogether without influence in directing the attention of true Americans to the importance which attaches throughout the civilized world to the productions of slave labor, as elements in the wealth and power of nations. I am convinced that such an investigation will lead the dispassionate observer to the conclusion that, if the Southern States "are blinded by their passions to the evils of slavery," the anti-slavery party of Great Britain is not blind to the disastrous effects which its destruction would entail upon the material prosperity of America. That there should be a party in the United States, formidable as to numbers and respectability, co-operating with these in the accomplishment of such a result, either by the force of circumstances or a common sentiment, is well calculated to excite the wonder of mankind. If it be true that this British party represent, as they say they do, the feelings and opinions of the English people, then are the "Republicans" fighting the battle of England far more effectively than did the British soldiers and Hessian mercenaries who contended in arms against our ancestors in the days of the revolution. That this party should be sufficiently formidable to present a candidate for the presidency, with a strong probability of success founded upon the common action of all the free States of the Confederacy, and that such should be the issue, and the only issue pending in such a contest, is a startling fact, the importance of which cannot be over-estimated, because it strikes at the very foundation of the compact upon which the Confederacy has been erected.

The subject of slavery, as a question of morals, or political economy, or expediency, or abstract right and wrong, is one which like all others that affect the interests or passions of man, may be a subject of legitimate discussion; about which mankind may differ, as upon other questions in which the interests of the human family may be involved. The Southern States may naturally seek to remove the prejudices against them, which artful enemies have succeeded in exciting. They may be willing to present their cause at the bar of an enlightened public opinion, as an individual may seek to remove unfounded imputations against his honor or integrity. But the South does not mean thereby to admit that the other States of the Confederacy *have any right to vote away* the political privileges which they claim to have inherited from the founders of the Government, and over which they retained entire sovereignty when delegating certain powers to the General Government.

Great Britain may defend her various systems of free labor, and endeavor to prove that, upon the whole, they are respectively liable to fewer objections than any others which she could substitute; but though she might fail in leading mankind to her conclusions, she does not mean to intimate that, if mankind differ from her in opinion, they have therefore a right to change or in any manner to modify her domestic policy. America has just the same right, if she possessed the power, to subvert the internal laws and customs of England, as the Northern States have to modify, or alter, or in any manner to interfere with the domestic institutions of the slave States. All the citizens of the Republic beyond the limits of the slave States, may believe that slavery is a wrong and a sin in the sight of God and man. They may believe that it was a virtue in Europe to establish an institution which it is a crime in the Southern States any longer to tolerate; yet whatever may be their opinions upon the abstract merits of the controversy, or upon the morality or expediency of slave labor, there exists no other external authority than that of violence for any interference with the domestic institutions of the Southern States. This can only be accomplished by illegal means, and would be an act of revolution, which would release the South from the compact of Union.

Do a majority of the citizens of the free States desire to dissolve the political bonds which unite the Confederacy, or to re-organize the Union upon a different basis from that established by its founders, in order that they may contrôl the domestic institutions of the Southern States? and do they wish by these peaceful means to declare or to accomplish their purpose? The interrogatory seems to assume the possible existence of a public sentiment which at this distance seems almost beyond belief; and yet the dispassionate mind cannot reject the conclusion, that such a feeling or wish lies at the foundation of that party which has entered into the contest for the presidency under the title of Republican.

What are the facts which present themselves to our view in investigating the causes of the present deplorable state of feeling among the citizens of the United States? Upon what special issues does the Republican organization ask for the support of the Northern States? for it does not expect or desire a single electoral vote in the slave States. The only issue they present—the only support they ask—the only idea they illustrate is anti-slavery, pure and simple! designedly and sedulously disembarrassed of all or any side issues. They expect no aid from any except anti-slavery men, and they appeal to no passion, but that of hatred for the slaveholder! In justice to that party, it must be supposed that they have a purpose to accomplish, and that such purpose must be inimical to the slave States. It cannot be that the leaders would stimulate such a torrent of vindictive passions between the sections of a Confederacy, which in their hearts they cherish, for the mere purpose of obtaining power and place. I give them credit for other motives.

But suppose this to be the true and only object of the politicians, and that these appeals are successful in accomplishing their designs. What would it signify? Could it be interpreted to mean anything but the expression of an abstract wish on the part of the majority of the Confederacy to dissolve the Union, or to reconstruct it upon another basis, which would leave with them the Constitutional control of the question of slavery in the Southern States?

Upon the hypothesis that the Republican party has no political purpose to subserve in opposition to the rights of the Southern States, by such an expression of anti-slavery feeling, the force of its significance, as a demonstration of sentiments averse to the longer continuance of the Union, is doubly enhanced. Truthfully interpreted, according to the rules of common reason, such an expression of antipathy to the Southern States or their institutions, conveying no intimation of a design to give a practical effect to their victory by any act inimical to slavery, would mean, that they had ceased to regard the Union as worth maintaining. After the expression of such a deliberate sentiment of repugnance to the fifteen Southern States or their domestic institutions, would they not be driven by the force of public opinion without, as well as by their own feelings, to repudiate a longer political association with those whom they had thus formally insulted and pronounced unworthy of respect; or to attempt their subjugation and, if successful, hold them as vassals? Would it not be, in effect, a virtual dissolution of the Confederacy upon the terms previously existing? The unbiased mind can arrive at no other conclusion, than that such a result would of itself, and in itself, dissolve the union between the two great geographical sections. The chain of the Confederacy would be broken! The fragments might, for temporary purposes, be re-united by a flaxen thread, but its power of cohesion would be gone forever.

Conservative citizens of the Northern States should not delude themselves into the belief, that this is the mere expression of an idle threat on the part of the South; for the result would be accomplished against the wishes and in opposition to the united protest of the Southern States!

But upon the more plausible supposition, that the Republican party has a political purpose in thus consolidating into one mass the anti-slavery sentiment of the North, without any admixture of other ingredients, it becomes important to discover what that purpose is. Is it that this anti-slavery party desires to secure the reins of the General Government in their own hands, in order that they may control the institution of slavery within the States? This would involve a palpable violation of the Constitution, and could only be accomplished by violence.

The announcement of such a purpose, is of itself an overt act of hostility to the Union, which would be utterly inconsistent with an intention to maintain the existing Confederation. The act of consummation would be revolution. Although this is the avowed object of the extreme abolitionists, and is doubtless the purpose of many who do not give public utterance to their designs, yet it is fair to presume, that those of the Republican party who still cling to the Union and the Constitution as the anchor of safety, have in view the accomplishment of their anti-slavery purposes by other methods. We read in all the Republican journals of the more moderate and conservative school, the declaration of a design to prohibit the farther extension of slavery, by excluding it from the territories. I presume that I shall not be charged with representing the anti-slavery party unfairly, when I assume this to be the ground on which every member thereof, embracing every shade of opinion, is willing to stand.

If a proper degree of fraternal feeling existed on the part of the Republican party towards the Southern States, it might be urged, even if such a prohibition could be legally accomplished, that it would be unkind to the white race, and cruel to the African, to insist upon its enforcement—ungenerous to the citizens of the South, because it would debar the Southern States bordering upon the Free States, from abolishing slavery for all time to come. The Northern States were not only permitted to rid themselves of slavery without cost, but also of the slaves, by transferring them to the adjoining slave States. Here they were purchased by the Southern planters, and by this simple process, these objects were accomplished without involving the loss of a single dollar. The North having thus disposed of its slaves, would it be equitable to deny to the border slave States a similar privilege? Does there not rest upon the North a moral obligation to leave open this one avenue to the consummation of the same results, should the institution of slavery cease to be profitable, or be rendered from any other cause undesirable? But suppose the number of Africans go on increasing in the same ratio as they have done since the foundation of the Republic; within the lapse of a comparatively brief period, the African population would be equal to the present population of the entire Union. When we add to this the natural increase of the white race, it is easy to perceive that no greater curse could be inflicted upon the posterity of the Southern States, than thus to confine the Africans for ever within their present limits. It is appalling to contemplate the tyranny which, for the protection of the white race, it would be necessary to exercise over such a multitude of African slaves, confined within such narrow limits; unless indeed, the ever menacing danger of insurrection should drive the great body of European races to seek a more secure asylum, and thus leave the country in the possession of the Africans. I know there are those who would say that this is the consummation they desire, but these are madmen with whom it were folly to reason. Let sane men, however, who do not act upon a principle of revenge, or blind hatred, make for themselves an estimate founded upon data already furnished by our history, of the probable extent of the population of the Southern States within a given period, under such a prohibition of emigration. They will find that like all the radical short-cut roads of abolition philanthropy, it leads not only to evil for the master, but is also cruel and unjust to the slave. The smaller the number of slaves among any given population of the dominant race, the better is their condition, and the more abundant their comforts; while every increase, either in reference to territory or population, draws more closely around them the restraints imposed by their condition of servitude. Intelligent practical anti-slavery philanthropy, would seek to increase the area of slavery, when it could be accomplished without increasing the number of slaves, rather than by circumscribing increase its hardships.

Thus is it ever with the schemes for the amelioration of the condition of the slave, which have their origin in free States. They are dictated, primarily, by a feeling of animosity to the master, and all end in disaster to the slave, for whom there is such a noisy demonstration of sympathy.

But as I intimated in the outset, the feeling of unkindness or hatred for the South, forms too important and essential an ingredient in the composition of the Republican party to justify any appeal to their magnanimity, or to any sympathies they might be supposed to entertain for the African. The only present defence of the South, therefore, against such an aggression upon her equal rights, rests in the Constitution. So long as the Union is maintained, that is the final arbiter of all disputes. I know that the provisions of that instrument may be violated—I am well aware that by a wide latitude of construction, a false meaning may be attached to certain phrases, yet the undeniable principle which lies at its very foundation, is the equality of the States, and their absolute sovereignty over their domestic affairs.

If these reserved rights were respected in good faith by all the citizens of the Republic, ages and ages might pass away without the occurrence of a single act which could destroy the harmony and the unity of the Confederation. What a magnificent prospect and reward is thus held out to the true patriot, to restrain within the boundaries of the Constitution, his generous efforts to improve the condition, or reform the vices of his neighbors! Alas! there are those who will not brook any restraint which interposes an obstacle to the gratification of their passions or their personal ambition.

If under the Constitution, a dominant section may appropriate for themselves all the property in lands, belonging to the General Government, they may certainly make the same disposition of every other species of property. Upon the same principle they may accumulate a surplus of money in the Treasury, and divide it among the States of the same dominant section. If the government of the United States may, under the provisions, and according to the true intent of the Constitution, exclude from the territories any one article which is recognized as property by any one State, then it may prohibit the introduction of any species of property whatever. Even if there were not a slave State, no statesman in the formation of a charter of Confederation between independent States, however homogeneous might be their internal regulations, would confer upon Congress the power of excluding from the common territories, any property recognized as such by any one of the States. If it would be absurd to suppose the existence of any such power in a Confederation of States, having similar local Constitutions, how can it be inferred that either the slave or free States which formed the Constitution of the United States would have authorized the exercise of such power by Congress?

To declare that the citizens of one State shall not enter upon the territory of the General Government with their property, and that the citizens of another State may, strikes down the very cornerstone of the Constitution. It would be a violation of every principle of common justice. For if these territories are common property—that is if they have been bought by the common purse, or the common valor of the Confederacy—then there exists no power, except by the exercise of brute force, to exclude any one State from an equal participation therein.

If this exclusion cannot lawfully be made by the Congress of the United States, which might be supposed, at least, to represent the will not only of a majority of the States, but of the people, much less can any inferior power accomplish the same end. For to suppose that a superior can delegate greater power to a subordinate than he possesses himself, is absurd, and not to be believed.

Neither if such unlawful power is attempted to be exercised on the part of such inferior, can the general Government close its eyes and refuse to see or to redress the wrong. The supreme power is bound to prevent a wrong if within the compass of its means; or failing in this, it must redress the wrong; otherwise it is not sovereign.

I am aware, that here is the great stumbling-block for many honest citizens who, from conscientious motives, from education, or from prejudices, do not desire to legislate in favor of slavery; or in the language of the Republican politicians, they are opposed to the establishment by Congress "of a slave code for the territories."

Neither does the South ask for the establishment of a slave code, in the sense in which it is here meant. But the Constitution confers upon them and their property the same rights as are conferred upon the free States and their property. The citizen cannot protect himself, because he has transferred that right to the Government which, having assumed it, is bound to perform that duty; otherwise such citizen is an outlaw.

Government is the natural protector of all its citizens. It is bound alike to each. This is the foundation upon which all its powers rest. The government which from inability fails in the performance of this duty, is no longer entitled to the allegiance of the citizen, unless there is a reasonable effort made to redress the wrong. But where the Government refuses to perform this duty, it abdicates, and is no longer the Government.

It follows, therefore, that when the Government of the United States refuses or fails to protect the South in its equal rights, it abdicates its authority; and, ceasing to be the Government of the slave States, cannot rightfully claim their allegiance. By such an act, it becomes only the Government of the States which it protects.

Even though the North might gain a temporary triumph by the abrogation of the equal rights of the South, yet one day or other it would be made to recoil upon herself. However that may be, no other construction can fairly be placed upon the Constitution; and however objectionable may be its provisions, it is the duty of good citizens to conform to them, in letter and in spirit. When they seek to violate or fraudulently to evade its requirements, it is an act of revolution. It is disunion

LETTER XIV.

A Confederacy could never be established which did not recognize the equality of the States—Position of Parties illustrated—Aggressions of the South and North considered.

WITHIN the Republican or anti-slavery party, there are many who are willing to admit the importance of the Confederacy to the general safety of the whole, but who detest the Constitution which recognizes the institution of slavery, and thereby imposes upon the Government the necessity of giving the same protection to the slaveholder and his property as to the Massachusetts manufacturer and his looms. I have already referred to the absurdity of assuming the existence of a government which would not give full and ample protection to all its citizens. I have said—and it will scarcely be called in question—that when a government refuses to protect all its citizens in their constitutional rights it virtually abdicates, and is no longer entitled to the allegiance of its citizens; and in a confederacy like that of the United States, it is, in effect, a dissolution of the Union.

But let it be supposed that, by common consent, and without any popular excitement or unkind feeling between the citizens of the several States, the Union were dissolved into its original elements. The first impulse of many who are now, perhaps, unwittingly engaged in the work of destruction, would be to re-establish some sort of union as a protection against foreign aggression. Let it be supposed that, in accordance with this sentiment, a convention should be called to settle the terms on which the new union should be established. It assembles: every State is represented; the organization is completed, and the President announces that all is ready to proceed to the dispatch of the business which called them together. Fifteen slave States and eighteen free States are represented.

A grave member from Massachusetts rises and says:—"Mr. President: Before proceeding to arrange the details of the terms upon which these thirty-three independent states may form a union, for purposes of common defence and other great objects of interest to each, it is necessary to declare the terms upon which new States, formed out of the common territory of this confederacy, may be admitted as integral parts of the proposed Union. As I do not desire to awaken any angry or even unkind feelings by making any special reference to certain crimes and sins of enormous magnitude, which are tolerated and legalized by fifteen of the States here assembled, I propose to accomplish my purpose in another way. The Constitution of my native State is perfect in all its parts. It is the result of the matured wisdom of the greatest statesmen of this or any other age. Does any member of this Convention find in that charter of our liberties any single provision to which a rational objection ean be made?" After a pause, during which there is a profound silence, the gentleman from Massachusetts continues: "I do not desire, Mr. President, to force this Constitution upon any of the States here represented; and it would be alike a departure from the great principle of liberty to insist, absolutely, upon the adoption of this Constitution by a new State before being admitted as a member of our Confederacy. I therefore propose to adopt the following article defining the terms upon which new States may be admitted, to-wit:—

"ARTICLE I. Any territory of the United States, having the requisite population, and complying in other respects with the provisions of this Constitution, may be admitted into the Union as an equal member thereof, *Provided* the said territory has adopted for its government the Constitution of the State of Massachusetts. But if said territory asks for admission under a Constitution with provisions similar to the provisions of the Constitution of North Carolina, it shall not be lawful for such territory to become a State of the Confederacy."

After the member from Massachusetts has taken his seat, a Republican from New York rises and says:—"Mr. President: Though there is an entire coincidence and agreement between the distinguished gentleman who has just addressed the Convention and myself, in regard to that sin against God and man which is tolerated, and encouraged, and made lawful, by fifteen States here represented, yet, I cannot admit that the Constitution of Massachusetts is the only one which establishes and confirms the sublime principles of equality and fraternity which are set at naught by the fifteen States before referred to. The proposition of the gentleman ignores the existence of a North! Like most of his countrymen, (I say it with all proper respect, and without designing that the remark shall be interpreted in an offensive sense,) the member from Massachusetts can see nothing which is worthy of admiration beyond the limits of his own State. It is notorious that the visions of Massachusetts statesmen are bounded by the view from the summit of Bunker Hill. Let me tell that gentleman that there is a North! a glorious North, proud of her achievements in the past, and ready now to make any sacrifice in defence of her honor and her equal rights. Allow me, furthermore, to declare in direct terms, and in the outset of our proceedings, that the Northern States will submit to no invidious distinctions! They will enter this Union as equals, or not at all! It is well for the gentleman to be promptly undeceived. Massachusetts is not the North, nor is the North Massachusetts. She forms but a small integral part, and to that extent she may ask consideration; but when she demands that hers shall be the model Constitution of all new States, she insults that great North whose very existence she ignores. This self-exaltation may be appropriate enough on Boston Common or in Fanueil Hall, but it is a species of sectional arrogance which is altogether misplaced in the halls of a Convention, assembled to form a union between independent States. I therefore propose a substitute for the proposition before the Convention, and ask for its adoption. It is as follows:

"Any territory of the United States with the requisite population, etc., etc., may be admitted as a State into the Union, *provided* the said territory has adopted for its government, a Constitution similar in its provisions to the Constitution of any one or all of the eighteen Northern States here represented. But if said territory asks for admission under a Constitution with provisions similar to the provisions of any one of the fifteen Southern States, it shall not be lawful for such territory to become a State of the Confederacy."

A member from Vermont rises to address the Convention, and says: "Mr. President, I am a plain, straightforward, out-and-out Abolitionist. I can discover no good likely to result from mincing this question. I have not had the opportunity in my native mountains to acquire the art of expressing my thoughts without calling things by their right names. The two gentlemen who have preceded me, deal their blows against vice and crime, without daring to name them, for fear of giving offense. Now, Mr. President, I am not afraid to speak my sentiments boldly and above board! The crime of all crimes, the sin of all sins, the enormity above all enormities, the existing libel upon humanity, which is alike offensive to Vermont and to the Almighty Ruler of all things is, the crime, the sin, the enormity of slavery, as legalized by the fifteen Southern States here represented! Our most eminent divines have already made known that before the tribunal of Heaven there will be no mercy for the slaveholder. The Churches of the North have announced for him a similar fate; then why should we make Heaven angry, by putting on our kid gloves when we handle the monster? I have therefore to propose in lieu of the two propositions now before the Convention, the following:

"The territories of the Union, being the common property of all the States, may be lawfully occupied by all the citizens of the free States with their property of whatever kind. But it shall not be lawful for citizens of the slave States to reside with their property upon any of the lands which are now, or which may hereafter come into the possession of the Government. No State shall ever hereafter be admitted into the Union whose Constitution tolerates the existence of slavery."

It is unnecessary to follow up this assumed discussion, or to enumerate the arguments by which the movers and opponents of these respective propositions would defend their proposed measures. But we may fairly conclude that the representatives of the slave States would propose, in lieu of the propositions referred to, something like the following:

The States forming the Confederacy are in all respects equal. The sovereignty surrendered by each to the General Government is the same; and in all other respects the sovereignty of each State within its own limits is supreme.

All territories, lands, or other property which may come into the possession of the General Government, being alike the property of all the States, must be held as such. Whenever a territory shall be opened for settlement, it shall be alike free to all the citizens of all the States. Immigrants from any State of the Confederacy may lawfully take with them any property recognized as such by the laws of their own States. The duty of protecting its citizens being an essential condition of sovereignty, the citizens of the respective States shall be fully protected by the Government of the Confederacy, in all their rights in the territories, against all aggressions whatsoever.

Whenever a territory having sufficient population, etc., etc., makes its application for admission as a State in the Union, it may be admitted as an equal member of the Confederacy with whatever Constitution the citizens thereof may adopt, provided it be republican in form. The said Constitution may contain any one or all of the provisions of the Constitution of any one of the original States composing the Confederacy.

It will not be denied that the first three propositions above considered, represent fairly the views and opinions of the more moderate and conservative portion of the Republican party, while the latter embraces every claim or demand that any portion of the Southern States have ever made in regard to this subject. The South desires nothing more than the recognition of its equal rights, and it will be recreant to honor and liberty if it ever submits to accept of anything less.

It is scarcely necessary to discuss the probabilities of the formation of a new Confederacy upon any terms which would accord with the principles of the Republican party. Such a consummation would be simply impossible. The Constitution under which we have hitherto lived, undoubtedly confers upon the Southern States the equal rights which they would demand under any other which might be proposed. It therefore follows that the Republican party is not only founded upon the principle of opposition to the present Union, but to any other Confederacy which it would be possible to erect upon the ruins of that one which they now in effect seek to overthrow.

Am I mistaken in my opinions in regard to the intentions of the Republican party? Are there any portion of citizens who give it their support, who desire to maintain the present Union, upon the terms demanded by the Constitution? In short, do they mean nothing in derogation of the rights of the South, by uniting in the establishment of a great sectional organization founded upon the single idea of opposition to the domestic institutions of the South? If they propose no measure hostile to the slave States, why do they give their countenance to the establishment of a great political anti-slavery party? Is there any proposition from any quarter to reëstablish slavery in the free States? Has the South ever sought either directly or indirectly, or does she now seek, to exercise any control over, or in any manner to interfere with, the domestic institutions or governments of the free States? Does the South deny the North any right which the Constitution accords? Or does she ask for herself any thing more than the recognition of her equality under the great charter of confederation? If to these interrogations there can be none other than a negative response, I repeat, why should there exist in the United States a political anti-slavery party, if it does not propose some change or modification of the existing institution of slavery, or involve some denial of the rights of the slave States? Republican partisan leaders would answer, that their organization was established to resist "the aggressions of slavery." I must confess that I find it impossible to conceive what particular acts are here referred to, for, of all the institutions which exist, that of slavery is the least aggressive. When, however, the heated partisan is obliged to furnish an illustration of the nature of these aggressions, he refers usually to the unfortunate collision in the Senate chamber between a Southern Representative and a Northern Senator. This Senator was attacked and beaten by a Southerner. It is not necessary to discuss the merits of that affair. The act was that of one man; but if the deed was as atrocious as it has been represented, by what harsh epithet may we denounce the crime of John Brown? What is there about Sumner that should excite to a greater degree our feelings of pity or compassion, than the helpless victims of John Brown's brutal propensities for murder! Sumner still lives to utter calumnies which ought to be sufficient to gratify the most morbid appetites of his followers. The victims of John Brown and his confederates are in their graves. Yet, strange and startling truth, the very men and women, who, if their power of performance had been in accordance with the force of their will would have immolated the whole South, to have avenged the "crime" against Sumner, find but little to condemn in the conduct of that monster murderer, Brown, except *his indiscretion!* His "zeal," they say, "was without *prudence*, but his *motives* were *pure* and *honest!*"

Nothing has occurred within a quarter of a century more significant of the unhappy state of feelings existing in the Northern States against the South, than the effects which the two events referred to have produced in the public mind. And I may add that it furnishes a fair index to the influences which abolition propagandism has produced upon the morals of its adherents.

I have only referred to this subject to show that the chief aggressions complained of by the abolitionists, even admitting the propriety of classing the cases referred to in that category, have been exceeded a thousand fold in enormity by aggressions upon the South. At most, they are not of sufficient magnitude to authorize or justify conservative men, in giving their support and influence to a party, which can only accomplish its openly avowed designs, by a palpable repudiation of the Constitution by which the Union is maintained, and which can only accomplish its measures by the sword. If there are citizens who are in favor of preserving the present Union, but still propose to give their support to the Republican candidates, may I ask them how they can reconcile the two? They cannot accomplish the political object they may propose under the present constitution, then why should they give expression and form to such abstract desire? Is it to gratify or to give expression to a feeling of hatred against slavery? Let them not delude themselves. Men do not hate vice, but the vicious. They do not hate murder, but the murderer. Neither do men hate slavery, but the slave-holder. Vice, murder, slavery, are mere words which convey to the mind the idea of certain acts, which acts must be performed or brought about by intelligent human beings, otherwise no passion of hatred could be excited. Now let me ask the sincere friend of the Union, how he supposes the Union can be maintained, or how he can think that the Union ought to be maintained, when he and others constituting a majority of all the States of one section, being a majority of the citizens of the Confederacy, declare thus solemnly and formally that they have given their support to the candidate of their choice, with the sole object of giving expression to their feelings of hatred against the citizens of fifteen States of the Confederacy. Can a love of the Union as it now exists, animate those who cultivate and give expression to such feelings in regard to one entire section of the Confederacy? Or can they expect to excite a feeling of love for any Union whatever, in the breasts of those against whom such an irritating warfare is kept up, on account of the existence of a domestic institution, for the creation of which they are not responsible, the continuation of which has become an inexorable necessity, and the management of which is, and of right ought to be, under their exclusive control?

LETTER XV.

Duty of Citizens—Republican Measures are the results of unfriendly feeling; not the cause—Spirit of the Republican Party inconsistent with a desire to maintain the Union in its integrity.

MAN cannot engage in any work which yields a greater revenue of good than in softening the asperities of his fellow-men against each other. In the present contest in the United States, is it the duty of every good citizen to pause and look steadily and calmly into the probable future of such a struggle. Let him not deceive himself by delusive hopes, but watch the current of passing events, and see with his own eyes in what direction we are tending. Let him pause and listen to the roar of that cataract whose ominous mutterings can now be distinctly heard, even upon the far-away shores of the Bosphorus, from whence I ventnre to send forth upon their uncertain errand these words of admonition.

It should be borne in mind that there is a feature peculiar to the present attitude of parties in the United States which distinguishes it from all others that have hitherto existed. In the past, parties have been organized in support of and in opposition to certain measures of State policy, which were sustained or opposed without any direct reference to geographical lines. The people naturally arrived at different conclusions in regard to the merits of these measures, and as their judgments or their interests dictated, they have arrayed themselves on the one side or the other. The discussions growing out of these differences of opinion have at times produced more or less of bitterness, and personal as well as sectional unkindness. But it will be noted that these antagonisms originated in the previously existing differences of opinion in regard to questions of public policy. Now, this state of facts is totally reversed. The measures advocated have grown out of a previously existing feeling of animosity, and have no other foundation upon which they rest for support. The proof of the truth of this proposition exists in every man's mind who will consider of this one fact, namely: if every trace of bad feeling, or hatred, or sectional animosity were removed from the breasts of the people, the questions which are now discussed and fiercely sustained upon the one side, and opposed upon the other, would instantly and of themselves disappear.

Without considering the abstract merits of the measures proposed by the anti-slavery or Republican party, if a contingency could arrive which would remove from the minds of its adherents and supporters, all purely personal ill will or exasperated feeling against the Southern people, its presidential candidate could not upon the present issues obtain the electoral votes of three States of the Confederacy. It is impossible that a party in the United States sufficiently formidable to carry a half dozen

States, or even one State, could be formed out of citizens who desire to maintain the Union, the inevitable effect of whose measures would be, to take away from the Southern States their equal rights, to render their domestic peace insecure, and to aid the anti-slavery party of Great Britain in their effort to bring the Republic into disrepute, unless they were sustained by the passions and prejudices of the electors. The friends of the Union in this contest should act upon this existing fact, that the angry passions which the Republican leaders may make available to their success are not founded upon the measures they propose, but the measures owe their existence to the angry passions. To address these by controverting the policy, the propriety, or the justice of their measures, would be fruitless, so long as the feeling referred to exists in their breasts. To eradicate a disease, the physician must go to the root of a malady. Those who would labor effectually for the defeat of Republicanism should direct their efforts to remove the unfounded feeling of animosity which has been implanted in the hearts of its supporters. The war of the Allies against Russia brought their armies to Sevastopol. During the pendency of the struggle, the besiegers and the besieged erected their fortifications and defences, and planted their batteries, to meet the exigencies which the varying events of the siege brought forth. Peace was finally made, and the works of the defenders as well as of the assailants, are now neglected and in ruins. Just as war measures are resorted to by nations, when an angry state of feeling exists between them which forebodes hostilities, so stand the parties to the present contest in the United States. The bitterness of feeling which prevails against the South, and the fortifications which are being erected from whence to assail the slave States, have produced counter defences. Remove the feeling which produced them, and the fortifications and the defences will alike tumble into ruins. Eradicate this sentiment of animosity from the Northern mind which, while exasperating the South, yields no advantage to the North, and it would be worth more than all the slave codes which the South could ask or a united Congress grant. If the feeling is too deeply rooted to be obliterated, the most stringent laws which could be enacted would be powerless to protect the rights of the Southern States. Let then the friends of the Union and the adversaries of political sectionalism deal their blows at the foundation upon which the superstructure of the anti-slavery Republican party has been erected. Strike down the corner-stone of the edifice, and the walls and domes and towers will fall into a mass of indistinguishable ruin. This duty, this glorious privilege, I might say, falls upon the true men of the North. Hundreds of thousands have, up to this hour, withstood all the appliances of proffered rewards upon the one hand, and the certainty of political death upon the other. If they should succeed in arresting the calamity which now threatens the Confederacy, a grateful posterity will unite them in their hearts with the fathers of the Republic. If they fail, the consciousness of having discharged their duty will be a reward of far more value than any which would follow their defection from the cause of their country.

Those who would labor with a reasonable hope of success in the great contest which must now soon be decided, should remember that the specific measures proposed by the Republican party are mere outposts or decoys sent forward to draw off the attention of their adversaries from the true point to be assailed. These may be readily overthrown by an appeal to the Constitution, and an exposition of the true principles of equality, which are the foundation upon which the superstructure of the Confederacy has been erected. But of what avail would be this? Others would be proposed; more skirmishing parties would be sent out, which, though driven in, would leave the main body intact, and as strong as at the beginning. Thus would the strength of the national party be frittered away in fruitless contests, with insignificant bodies of the enemy, and upon the very ground which that enemy selects.

The only hope of success for the national party which holds out the prospect of a victory that will be enduring in its results, consists in their ability to eradicate, or, at least, to soften the spirit of animosity towards the Southern States, upon which the Republican party alone relies for success. The proposal to exclude the citizens of slave States from the territories—John Brown insurrections and murders—incendiary publications and incendiary emissaries distributed among the slaves, and the counter propositions of those who are assailed, are all effects, not causes. Remove the causes and the effects disappear. Let, then, the main attack be directed against the spirit which dictates a wish to inaugurate unfriendly legislation against the South.

A citizen of the North may be conscientiously opposed to the institution of slavery. Be it so! If there should be a proposition to introduce slavery into his State, let him oppose it. But he has no right to assail a neighboring sovereignty for differing with him in opinion, in regard to the management of their domestic affairs. I know it is contended that in a free country a man has a right to say what he pleases; but the fact is, that in a free country, of all others, there is a moral responsibility resting upon each citizen not to exercise that power indiscreetly. A man has the power, and he may also have the legal right, to say and to do many things which are very wrong; but if more evil than good results from what he says and does, he has no moral right to do the wrong! There may be a dozen partners in trade, who have engaged each to contribute to the joint stock an equal amount, and to share equally in the profits. Seven of the twelve may assail the private characters of the five, and that of their families. They may insist that for fear of spreading the infection of their sins by their example, the women and children shall not be permitted to leave their houses. In furtherance of this good work they may go farther, and say that the children of the five shall not be permitted to occupy or enjoy the use of any of the estates or farms, which have been purchased out of the joint profits of the partnership. The power to make such a proposition cannot be questioned. The legal right to ask that such a disposition be made, may be also conceded. But would not such a suggestion be equivalent to a demand that *the partnership be dissolved?* Can it be supposed that the five would consent to continue the "union" upon such terms, in the face of an agreement that they should be equal partners? Or would a longer continuance of the association be either desirable or proper, after such declarations had been formally embodied and presented, as the only terms upon which the majority would thereafter consent that the business should be conducted?

Whether the causes which should produce this state of feeling be regarded as real or imaginary, would it not be the duty of the seven, in lieu of demanding a proportion of the common estate for their own use, to which they could not justly lay claim, to say frankly, "We do not like you personally; we object to the manner in which you are raising up your families; we are shocked by the conduct of your wives and daughters; therefore we propose that the partnership be dissolved, and the estate be equitably divided, according to the letter and spirit of the terms on which it was created?"

So may it be said to the supporters of the Republican party: Your unfriendly and constant assaults upon the Southern States, their institutions, and their people, are utterly inconsistent with the position you occupy to each other as partners and associates. The language of your ceaseless tirades against slavery and the slave States, are carefully collected by the enemies of the Republic in Great Britain, and disseminated in every land where the English language is read or spoken. These are translated into every tongue, and the world exclaims: "What horrible monsters those Republicans must be, when, according to their own statements, they tolerate a political union with the incarnate fiends who perpetrate such enormities against their fellow-creatures!" If, therefore, nothing can eradicate or soften these feelings, they should act like men who really feel strong moral convictions, and frankly repudiate the political bonds which unite them to so much sin. If they do not urge this as a sequence, how can they expect to secure the respect of mankind by continuing, for mere gain, that confederation which they believe to be a "covenant with hell?" Let every man, then, bring home to himself the true question. The spirit which animates the Republican party, and the feeling of animosity, which is its prime element of strength, is utterly inconsistent with a desire to maintain the present Confederacy, except from the most sordid considerations. Let this issue be fairly and honestly presented; and why should we doubt that tens of thousands, who have drifted into this great gulf of sectionalism, will once more turn their faces towards the shore, and swell the ranks of that civic army which is now engaged in, perhaps, its last struggle for the Union in its entirety, by the preservation of its integrity. Remember that now is the time for action! This occasion lost, and in all human probability all will be lost! Sectionalism once triumphant, no human power can restrain the onward march of the victors towards that goal to which their hopes have been directed. The war of subjugation against the South once inaugurated, who can estimate the terrible consequences of the conflagration which will be enkindled? Let those in the North who believe that, from their superior numbers, there would be an easy victory, and a prompt surrender, remember that the South will enter upon the struggle with the conviction, that while defeat *may be annihilation*, submission *would be death!*

LETTER XVI.

The madness of the hour—In Europe the Dissolution of the Union is expected—A few words to Northern Enemies of the South—Conclusion.

AMID the din of arms, and the roar of artillery, and the smoke of battle, and the mad fury of men excited by the contest and eager for blood, there is small hope that the voice of one man calling upon the combatants to lay down their arms, would be either heard or heeded. Neither can I hope that the words of one, whose only claim to be heard is, that he is a fellow countryman, though for a time resident in a distant country, will be listened to by the excited parties to the great, perhaps the final struggle *at the ballot-box*, for the union, the liberty, and the equality of the States, which now moves the heart of the great Republic! It may be that even before we are called upon again to celebrate the anniversary birth-day of the Father of his Country—the immortal first President of the Confederacy—opposing armies of his fellow-countrymen may be struggling in deadly strife upon the soil of that Virginia which gave him birth, within sight of the now quiet capital on the banks of the Potomac, which bears his name, and upon the very grave where he lies buried! In view of the impending storm, the spectacle now exhibited in the United States is indeed a sad one.

The history of the past teaches us that at times, nations are seized with a madness which it were even a worse madness to attempt to combat by an appeal to reason. This insanity, if I may so denominate it, though it may have its beginning originally in a sentiment of philanthropy, or even love, terminates by merging every other feeling into the single passion of hatred! It is vain to attempt to deny the startling truth—such is the present aspect of that madness which seems to pervade the people of America! If ever in the inception or progress of this contest, one single element of love or consideration for the slave entered into the thoughts or hearts of the principal assailants in this sectional struggle, it has been supplanted, buried beneath the passion of hatred, which that contest has engendered! We who are removed far from the scene of this struggle—far from a knowledge of the under-currents, and personal jealousies of the mere political contest for place and power—see and know full well, that it is not *love*, but *hatred* on which the sectional politician relies for success; and it is that feeling or passion, which gives to the present unfortunate contest its vitality. There is no practical issue but that of *hatred.* The success or defeat of aspirants for office depend altogether upon the degree of hatred which their appeals may produce in the popular mind! There is no single element of success, and no appeal which can secure success for the Republican party but that of *hatred!* Americans should not for a moment disguise this fact.

There has been a time in the brief history of the great Republic, when the adherents of despotism in the old world, regarded with distrust and dread, and the lovers of freedom, with hope and satisfaction and pride, the progress of the great experiment in democratic government. Now how changed! Both look forward with a confidence, inspired by hope upon the one hand, and by despair upon the other, to a speedy disruption of the Confederacy—civil war—exhaustion—anarchy—and then the repose of despotism.

For myself, while I, as an American citizen, will never admit to be true, the declaration of even moderate monarchists of the old world, that a government founded upon democratic principles, bears within itself the germ of its own dissolution—that the turbulance of universal freedom, and the tyranny of mere numbers, or dominant geographical sections, must end sooner or later in the destruction of the liberties of the minority, to be followed by the despotic rule of a single tyrant—yet I confess that the events of the last few years, and the unnatural struggle which they have engendered, involving in its progress no practical issue of good to either, except that of mere sectional domination, and in the future nothing but disaster to both, has made me at least less hopeful of the result.

Never before in the history of any other nation, have we evidence of so rapid a march from the weakness of infancy to the full development of a hardy manhood, as has been illustrated by the brief career of the American Confederacy. It is the pride of Americans, at home and abroad, to direct special attention to this undeniable truth. Whether that growth in greatness is to be checked, destroyed, or continued, is certainly to a considerable extent involved in the final result of the present controversy. It may or may not be, that the present struggle between men for political power, will terminate the contest for sectional supremacy. But whenever it is decided that a *geographical division of the Republic*, owing its cohesion *to sectional animosity* only, and its success to *mere numbers*, shall triumph over its numerically weaker but combined confederates and equals, it were worse than madness, it were idiotcy to suppose, that with unfettered limbs, and the liberty of free action on the part of the oppressed, they would not sever the political bonds which united them to their oppressors.

It is quite true that the mere peaceful dissolution of these constitutional bonds of union, and the establishment of smaller and more homogeneous nations, would not of itself abrogate the principle of liberty upon which our free institutions are founded. But such a separation, accomplished under auspices which would leave so much mutual bitterness in the hearts of the people, which by destroying our unity, would leave us comparatively defenceless as against foreign aggressions, all involving the necessity of large standing armies, make the probability strong that our present form of freedom could not long survive.

How can these calamities be avoided? Madmen may answer, "By crushing our enemies beneath our heels!" But it is to be hoped, that a majority of the citizens of the Republic are not thus held in bondage by their angry passions, and that the voice of reason may yet penetrate the minds of numbers sufficiently formidable to arrest the onward march to such a catastrophe. Let us not surrender until to hope would be madness!

If the will exists, the means are at command to avert such a calamity, without any surrender of political rights, and without any abandonment of matured convictions in regard to politics, morals, or religion. The citizens of the dominant section are called upon simply to deal fairly and justly with their fellow-citizens of the South. They have but to do unto others as they would that others under the circumstances should do unto them. Let patriots make no effort to disguise from themselves or others, the true and only questions involved, but in a frank and manly spirit, such as would become the monarchs of a great nation, seek only an equitable solution. The *nature*, the *origin*, and the *objects* of the present struggle, we have already considered. We have seen what interests are involved, and *who*, if any, will be the beneficiaries upon a division of the spoils among the victors.

It will be readily conceded, that in a struggle of parties for political supremacy in a confederacy of

States, the result of which should be brought about by a combination of certain States, composing a section distinguished by geographical lines, and presenting but one single issue, and that issue being an expression of hostility to the domestic institutions of the weaker by the stronger section, and depending for success upon the ability of the latter to create a feeling of hatred for the citizens of the former, could not be regarded otherwise than a menace against the independence and the equality of the States thus assailed. Success under such circumstances, would of itself amount to a declaration on the part of the majority, of the dissolution of the Confederacy upon the terms previously existing. That which would follow would be nothing more than to arrange the details of separation or reconstruction.

When I say that there is no practical issue involved, except the expression of an abstract feeling, or sentiment, or passion, I of course refer only to that portion of the Republican party, who profess that it is not their intention or desire to curtail the equal rights of the Southern States, nor to destroy or attempt to modify the institution of slavery within their respective limits. If this be true, then between them and the South there cannot be an issue, for the most extreme Southerner neither asks nor desires any thing more than this. For people of the North who really entertain these sentiments, intentions, or opinions, to unite themselves to the Republican party, could not have any other significance than simply to announce an irreconcilable feeling of animosity against the Southern States. Upon any other hypothesis, why should they combine with those whose avowed or apparent purpose is to destroy the institution of slavery? It must be remembered that this party is founded, by the avowal of its leaders, upon the sole question of slavery. They must have some object, some purpose to accomplish; and we are bound to conclude that this purpose or object, being supported only by men of anti-slavery opinions, must have some practical anti-slavery design, and that design must have reference to the slave States of the American Union, and must contemplate some change, or modification, or the destruction of that institution. Otherwise the existence of such a party would be impossible; for it is absurd to suppose that a party can exist without a purpose, at least upon the part of its founders and leaders.

It follows, then, that if the Republican party embraces sane men amongst its leaders, it must have a purpose. Being founded solely upon the single sentiment of anti-slavery, its purpose must be *inimical to the slave States.* Now, why should those who have no wish to interfere with the institution of slavery where it exists, and who do not desire to curtail or to destroy the equal rights of the South, give their support to the Republican party, with which they differ, and thus withhold their support from the opposing party between whom and themselves, on the only practical issue, there is an entire agreement?

Whatever may be the individual exceptions, it

must be presumed that those who give their support to the Republican party in the present struggle, do so for the purpose of interfering with the rights of the slave-holding States, or with a view to give expression to a feeling of antipathy or hatred for the people of those States. That such should be the only issues in a great national election for the choice of a President, should of itself awaken the earnest attention of every citizen, who in his heart desires the perpetuation of a Union which has been attended with so many blessings. Let no Northern man deceive himself in regard to the results of a victory thus obtained. If he be a high-minded, honorable man, and will for the moment imagine himself to be a citizen of a Southern State, he would require no other index to the consequences that would ensue, than the promptings of his own heart. No threat, no declaration, no warning voice from the South, could add to the firmness of his convictions, in regard to the feeling with which such a sentence of condemnation would be received by those against whom it would be directed, or the consequence which would surely follow.

To the individual exceptions above referred to, or rather to the large class of citizens of the North from whence these exceptions come, the hopeful American can only look for the means of safety from the storm which now threatens to engulf the Republic. So far as regards mere numerical strength, the North is unquestionably the strongest; and if the artful appeals of the anti-slavery party, and of other enemies of the South, can accomplish a Union of the entire North, so far as mere voting is concerned, slavery may be considered as already abolished, and the slave States prostrate before their more powerful adversaries.

To you, citizens of the North, who have gained much, both in honors and in wealth, from your intercourse with the South, and who are now found in the ranks of her enemies, let me address a few words at parting: You have been made rich by the spoils you have derived from your improvident and free-hearted neighbor. I cannot believe that you are yourselves so mad, as with your own hands, to destroy the goose which supplies you, day by day and year by year, with its golden eggs; but you are exposing it to dangers which, in a few short months, you may be powerless to avert. The South pours annually into your lap the tribute of its almost boundless resources, for which you pay nothing in return, but hard words. You confide too much in the forbearance and long-suffering of your benefactors. The South has proven to you that she is willing to be fleeced—that she is willing the proceeds of her labors shall build up your palaces, and yield you the means necessary to support them. Be content, and do not, in uncalculating wantonness, place the last feather upon the back of the patient camel.

The South would lavish freely of her wealth and the blood of her citizens to maintain and uphold the dignity and honor of the Union, and she would glory in its perpetuation to the latest posterity, if it might be preserved upon the same principles on which it was established. But if you force upon her the alternative of surrendering her rights, or of withdrawing herself from the Union, be assured that her free citizens will, with one voice, accept the latter, and start forward with hopeful hearts in the new career which will open up before them. You ought to be convinced that the South can do without you, and that her boundless sources of wealth would be augmented, instead of being diminished, by the separation. It is not by any means sure that such a result would follow in that North which, strange to say, seems to have nothing so much at heart as to render a longer union impossible!

You insultingly proclaim to the world that "the South is a burthen" to you, and that "she herself is so fully satisfied of her dependent condition that she could not be kicked out of the Union"—otherwise you would be gratified if she would take the determination to retire and leave you alone, the glorious champions of liberty, unstained by unhallowed associations. These are harsh words; and it is not surprising that the hot blood of the Southerner should mount with a redder glow to his cheek as he listens to them, and ponders to discover their significance. But may not the words you now so scornfully utter be but the words of the vain boaster? When the hour of consummation would arrive, can you not imagine that some of the golden visions of future prosperity and wealth, which have made tranquil the moments of your repose from the cares of life, would melt away forever in the presence of the stern reality before you?

Be assured in time that, if you force upon the South the issue, she can and will pursue her separate career, in whatever direction and with whatever success may be decreed by Providence; and if you will let her go in peace, she will thank you, and will wish you God-speed, while bidding you a reluctant though an eternal farewell. If, however, your passions, or your pride, or too tardy a consideration of your temporal interests, should make you seek her overthrow, though your number be greater, millions of freemen, with strong arms and chivalrous hearts, will meet you with a bloody welcome when you cross the border. Should the first encounter result in the triumph of the invader, they will, with one voice, pray the God of battles *to prosper the right*, and they will defend their homes and their firesides in every city, on every mountain, and on every plain, from the Potomac to the Rio Grande, and the shores of the Gulf of Mexico; and you will never accomplish your purpose, whether it be to emancipate the slaves or to enslave the freemen of the South, until their last dollar shall have been expended and their last soldier shall have fallen before your victorious legions.

If, however, you still believe that soft words, spoken hereafter, when the crisis comes, will induce the South to forget the past, and shut her eyes to the hard fate which is being prepared for her, do not, let me conjure you, over-estimate your influence in the hour of victory, over the excited politicians, and the maddened, deceived masses, who are respectively your leaders, and instruments. Be warned by the fate of others, who, in times past, have fruitlessly essayed to stay the tide of popular passions, which they themselves had artfully put in motion. The reflection that, in losing all yourself, you compass the destruction of your enemy, will not, in the hour of your affliction, be held to be a sufficient compensation for your own downfall.

Before you drive the South away forever, remember, that although you are of the same race and lineage, and your governments are founded upon the same general principles, the slave States have retained an element of conservatism in their domestic institutions, which, however repugnant to your prejudices may be its features, has hitherto reacted upon the entire Confederacy, and has had a powerful influence in preserving the whole from the dominion of that radicalism and license which murders liberty while professing to fight under its banners. Remember, that however happy may be the people who live under the protecting flag of a free government, there lurks in the very heart of every purely democratic republic an element which may be developed in the form of the most hideous despotism. When passion, instead of reason, sits enthroned in its councils, and in the hearts of its citizens, that latent element of tyranny may be developed into acts of more unpitying atrocity than any single despot whose foot has ever pressed upon the necks of slavish subjects, would dare to perpetrate. That element once aroused to action, farewell to all your hopes of future greatness. You may, in terror or in anger, direct its fury, for a season, against a common foe; you may make desolate their hearthstones, and leave their dwellings in ashes, but as sure as Heaven's laws are always executed, *it will return to fasten its deadly fangs into your own vitals!*

In concluding these desultory letters on the issue involved in the pending contest for the presidency, I may be pardoned for saying, that no mere party feeling—no wish to promote the success of this or that individual aspirant for the presidency, on account of any personal predilections for the one, or any unkind feelings for the other, has had the slightest influence in deciding me to write them. Separated by oceans, and continents, and seas, from my native land—standing, as it were, upon the outermost verge of the civilization of the Old World, beyond which all is darkness—in the midst of decaying empires, whose history, for many centuries, is crowded with the records of dazzling achievements—surrounded on every hand by the melancholy memorials of once powerful kingdoms and republics, whose greatness and whose dominion, annihilated by the sectional dissensions of their own citizens, have passed away forever; the splendor of whose glorious deeds, in the day of their pride, has only been exceeded by the magnitude of their ignoble fall; whose descendants have for ages lived, and groaned, and died, the despised and slavish subjects of a foreign master; I have asked myself, if the unhappy fate of subjugated and degraded Greece, is but a prototype of that which is in store for the great Confederacy of the New World!*

So far as the solution of this question depends upon the preservation of the federal Union, I admit that I am less hopeful than at any previous period of my life. I see the indications of an unswerving purpose, on the part of the North, to obtain a triumph over the South, by means of its numerical preponderance; and well I know the spirit with which the South will meet the issue thus presented.

---

* Only eight months after the above letter was dispatched to the United States, the writer received a letter from a most intelligent and accomplished Greek lady, who has devoted her life to the task of raising up her fellow-countrymen from the degraded position they now occupy, containing the following reference to American affairs:

"I learn that the excitement against African slavery in your country has culminated in the choice of an anti-slavery President, and I perceive that the result has given great joy to your adversaries in Europe. I likewise discover, through the same source, that the South will resist, and that a great war between the opposing sections will, in all probability, ensue. I tremble when I think of such a catastrophe! I cannot but remember that, during the entire period of the greatness of my native Greece, slavery existed in a form certainly much more to be deprecated than the African slavery of your country. When Greece tumbled headlong from the pinnacle of power to which she had ascended, it was not from without that the terrible blow was dealt, but from the sectional dissensions and wars between her own children, which ended by plunging them all into irretrievable ruin."

In view of the impending calamity of a conflict, whose beginning seems almost at hand, but whose end is shrouded in impenetrable gloom; with a vivid appreciation of the disasters which may soon involve us in a common danger, if not a common ruin; in the character of an humble citizen, whose passions have been calmed by the startling proximity of the menacing danger, I have addressed these words, and now send them forth to my fellow-countrymen. That I am a Southerner, by birth, by education, and in all my hopes for the future, I am free to declare; but I am also an American, protected in a foreign land by the flag of the Union, and every day I live I appreciate more highly the value of the great Confederacy which that star-gemmed banner symbolizes. Priceles, indeed, compared to the pecuniary sacrifices necessary to maintain it in its integrity; priceless, even compared with the blood which might be shed in defending it against a foreign foe; *but detestable as a tyrant, and valueless to freemen, when it can only be upheld by a sacrifice of the honor and the independence of its members.*

LETTER

TO THE

RIGHT HON. HENRY LORD BROUGHAM.

CONSTANTINOPLE, Feb., 1861.

MY LORD: Two events of recent occurrence—trifling in themselves, except when regarded in connection with the peculiar circumstances of the times in which they occurred—have contributed more towards the identification of your lordship's name with the political convulsion which the year of our Lord one thousand eight hundred and sixty-one is now witnessing in America, and with the anti-slavery movement, in which it has had its origin, than all which you have hitherto accomplished, during your long and brilliant career as an English statesman.

With a zeal which has known no flagging—with a resolution which was appalled by no probable or possible consequences—with an ability which is fully accorded by your adversaries—and with an earnestness which would seem to preclude any doubt of your sincerity, you have labored for the overthrow of that institution of African slavery in America, which has existed from a period long anterior to the incorporation of the Republic in the family of nations.

In this lifetime labor, however, you have been identified with others of your compatriots, who have exhibited the same pertinacity of purpose, and who have probably acquired a reputation almost equal to your own as the great exponents of English sentiment and English policy.

It has been the fortune of your lordship through the instrumentality of the two events referred to, to inscribe your name far above those of your fellow-laborers, in the roll of the recognized exemplars of British sentiment and British policy.

The first of these occasions offered to your lordship the opportunity, in an assembly of distinguished dignitaries from almost every nation of the civilized world, of proclaiming, in effect, your belief in the equality of the races of man, and the special claim of an African then present to be regarded as a worthy and fit associate for the noble Peers of England.

If your lordship had been contented with the utterance of this simple expression of opinion, it would probably have been forgotten by those who were your auditors, almost as soon as uttered. If, by any accident, a representative man of the millions of Anglo-Saxon blood and Anglo-Saxon color, who have sighed in vain to attain to that social rank and station which you so readily accorded in that august assemblage of princes, and nobles, and statesmen, to this sooty African, had bestowed a passing notice upon this paragraph in your lordship's speech, the subject would doubtless have been dismissed after a brief commentary, with the very natural and charitable observation, that a Peer of England had an undoubted right to choose his own associates, and might be expected to comprehend better than another the qualifications and characteristics of those who should be regarded as worthy of such association.

But your lordship entertained a deeper purpose. You desired to hold up to obloquy a great nation on the opposite side of the Atlantic; and, in order to startle your audience by the magnitude and the enormity of its crimes, you proclaimed the presence of the diplomatic representative of that nation which held in the bonds of slavery millions of a race of people, of which you then and there presented a faithful type, and to whom you assigned an equality of social rank with the noble order of which your lordship, in the estimation of your fellow-countrymen, is a faithful representative.

Your lordship's design was skilfully, and artistically, and dramatically executed. To be received and acknowledged as a peer, in such an assembly, was certainly, in your lordship's estimation, to be placed upon a pinnacle of social and moral elevation which few could hope to reach; while the doom of the slaves upon the plantations of America was a degradation beyond which there was no lower depth. The worthy representative of the oppressed, and the official representative of the hated oppressor, were both present before you. Both were in a foreign land, and both were strangers, and your guests. Disregarding these pressing claims upon your forebearance—acting, it may be, upon the conviction that the claims of God and humanity were more than paramount to all other considerations, you held them up, as it were, to the gaze of your audience as representatives of the victim and of the enslaver—of virtue and of vice—of freedom and of despotism—of all that was worthy to be loved, and of all that should be hated.

The occasion was one which precluded reply or explanation. The generous, the refined, the intellectual, the noble representative of a despised and down-trodden race, stood revealed before your sympathizing audience, in all the majesty of injured innocence; while there, too, stood the spoiler—the embodiment of the stupendous crime of his country.

It would probably be presumptuous in me to question the good taste displayed by your lordship, either in your choice of the occasion, or in your manner of treating one of these stranger guests. I am willing to concede that your lordship should know better than I the rules of politeness and good breeding proper to be observed in an assemblage of nobles and high dignitaries, gathered together in the great capital of the civilized world, and presided over by the Prince Consort of England's noblest Queen. Upon this collateral point, I would not dare to make up an issue with your lordship, the more especially as your audience, by the applause with which it greeted your remarks, has already recorded its verdict in your favor.

The main purpose of your lordship was achieved —the contrast you suggested startled the world by its magnitude. The irrelevancy of the subject to that which your auditors had assembled to consider, gave to the incident a notoriety which was magnified by its very isolation; while the event has been perpetuated in the memory of the multitude by the princely character of the audience before whom the scene was so dramatically enacted. From that moment, America has recognized in the questionable gallantry of your achievement, the qualities which have made you the great champion of British abolitionism.

I will now pass to the second event, which has served, in a still greater degree, by expanding the field of your operation, to strengthen and to confirm you in the position which, by common consent, had been previously assigned to you. But, before entering directly upon the subject, allow me to refer to an incident which occurred, not a great while ago, at a spot more than three thousand miles distant from that great centre of civilization in which your lordship moves.

A *murderer* in another continent closed a long career of crime under the gallows! There was nothing peculiar in this fact, for such has been often the fate of murderers in England, in America, and elsewhere. But this was a villain of no ordinary stamp. His victims were not stalwart men alone, but defenceless women and little children. He did not slay in the glare of the noonday sun, as a common robber at the head of his band of retainers, but he killed in the quiet hours of the night, and the slumbers of innocence were startled by the death-shrieks of his unsuspecting victims. But his crimes had not their beginning in those for which he suffered an ignominious death. They extended over a series of years; and the last, for which with his life he paid the forfeit, was by no means the worst. I myself have seen and known the unhappy victims of his earlier crimes. I have seen and known the happy wife and mother—happy in the innocence and purity of her life, though humble in her station—and I have seen her again in all the desolation of a childless widowhood. Dreadful, indeed, were the scenes through which that poor woman passed during the brief space of one short night. She was sleeping in fancied security when the spoilers came to her humble log cabin, and passed through the unbarred door to the bedsides of her sleeping husband and children. Your lordship knows the rest, and I will be brief. They were four when they lay down to rest, that dreadful night. The morning dawned upon the living woman, surrounded by the lifeless and mutilated bodies of her husband and children.

The chief criminal in this drama of blood, emboldened by immunity, changed the scene and enlarged the field of his operations. At Harper's Ferry, he again unsheathed his bloody dagger, and again was the hour of midnight made terrible by the death-struggles of his unwatching victims. Am I not right, then, in saying that John Brown was a villain of no ordinary stamp? *Sane* men, in a contemplation of the magnitude of his crimes, have said that he was *mad*, while *madmen* have exalted the *demon* into a *saint*, and mourn for him as a martyr in a holy cause!

It was upon the 3rd day of December, 1860, that his friends and partisans assembled in the city of Boston, to celebrate the first anniversary of his martyrdom.

Previous to that time, a letter had been addressed to your lordship by the "Committee of Managers," inviting you to be present upon that occasion, and to join in that celebration.

Those who knew the fact that such an invitation had been addressed to your lordship, were eager to learn in what manner you would respond. The first impression would naturally be, that your lordship would treat the missive with the dignified silence and disdain with which a nobleman of your lordship's exalted standing might be expected to meet a gross and studied insult; or, that your indignation, obtaining the mastery of your better judgment, might induce you, in that burning eloquence of words, which your lordship can so readily command, to hurl back the insult in the faces of your traducers; or, milder and more humane than either, and, perhaps, more in consonance with the gentle manners which might be expected to distinguish those through whose veins flows gentle blood, you would have responded, "It is not *my sins* but *your insanity*, which has led you to believe that I could hold fellowship with the partisans and admirers of an assassin. Go! you are madmen, and I forgive you."

These thoughts, I confess, were my thoughts, and that I give them voice here will show to your lordship that I did not rank you amongst the vicious and blood-thirsty fanatics with whom a common sentiment, upon a single point, had served in some measure to identify you. Besides, I will add, that my high respect for the exalted order to which you belong, as well as the position in which you stand towards the occupant of a throne, induced in my mind the belief that you would, in some manner, exhibit your horror of the crime of assassination, and with such an emphasis that even madmen might never again give expression to the thought that an English nobleman could have any sympathies in common with either assassins or their partisans.

Pardon me, my lord, if I, in unconscious ignorance, did not estimate, at their proper value, the refined principles of that "higher law" which have been incorporated among the doctrines of that so-called great humanitarian anti-slavery party, of which you are so distinguished a chief.

At first view it might occasion surprise that the "philanthropists" of Great Britain should seem to shut their eyes to the spectacle, and their ears to the wail of woe which rises up around them from the millions of the unhappy, the destitute, and depressed, of their own race and kin, who live through life a lingering death, while they have only eyes to see, and ears to hear, and tears to shed over the reputed wrongs of a handful of Africans upon the far-off shores of a continent beyond the Atlantic. But it is necessary in charity to remember that the degradation and wrongs of the one are familiar to them from youth to old age. It is an oft-told tale, to which they have become accustomed, familiar, and perhaps indifferent from its constant repetition. They are probably appalled by the magnitute of the evil, and ask to forget its existence and their obligations by the exhibition of redoubled zeal in the cause of those whom their imaginations, excited by heart-rending romances, picture as the victims of sorrow and oppression in a far distant land.

From this brief but not unnatural digression, I will return to the subject of the invitation which was given to you to participate in the celebration in memory of John Brown, the great American murderer. Permit me to refresh your memory with the first lines of your response to the committee in your own language:

"SIR: I feel honored by the invitation to attend the Boston Convention."

Upon reading these few emphatic words, I paused and re-read the letter of invitation which had been addressed to you, to discover if I had not, in my hasty perusal thereof, misunderstood its import and object. I beg to quote its words:

"*My Lord:* A number of young men, earnestly desirous of devoting themselves to the work of eradicating slavery in the United States, respectfully invite you to meet them in a public convention, to be held in this city on Monday, the 3d day of December. * * * * * It seems to them that the anniversary of the death of John Brown, who was killed for attempting to decide this problem in the mode that he believed to be the most efficient, is an occasion peculiarly appropriate for the discussion of our duty to the race for whom he suffered. * * * * * It would be a work of supererogation now to defend John Brown, and a useless waste of time to eulogize him. Leaving both these duties to the coming ages, *let us seek to continue his life by striving to accomplish what he left us to finish.*"

It is true ,my lord, that you modified somewhat the only legitimate interpretation of your first emphatic endorsement. True, as "the representative of the anti-slavery party in England," you avowed a wide difference of opinion between those you represented and the promoters of the Harper's Ferry expedition. True, you denied that John Brown was a real martyr. True, you declared your opposition to the encouragement of negro insurrections, because "*they might prove less hurtful to the master than the slave.*" True, you intimated that the surest means of accomplishing your cherished schemes of American negro emancipation was under the form of law, through the instrumentality of a recent political change in the Government of the Republic! But preëminent above all other considerations which are suggested by a perusal of your letter, stands forth the declaration that you "*feel honored* by the invitation to attend the Boston Convention!"

What a spectacle is here presented, and how fruitful a theme for reflection! An English nobleman shaking hands across the ocean and transmitting pleasant messages to *such* an assemblage, convened for *such a purpose!*

It is, perhaps, not unworthy of a passing thought, that while some of your admirers have hailed your letter as furnishing evidence of the conservatism and moderation of British abolitionism, many have regarded your slight deviation from the bloody path of an extreme fanaticism as too great a concession to the dictates of an uncalculating and weakly-relenting humanity.

I confess that upon this subject there is a chasm between us, so broad and so deep, that I have not the hardihood to attempt to fill it up. I cannot hope even that anything will ever occur to reduce the breadth of this impassable gulf to smaller dimensions.

But pardon me, my lord, if I suggest the possibility that you may not have fully appreciated the deep significance of the first sentence of your memorable letter. Did you reflect upon the powerful influence which your slightest word of encouragement might exercise upon the furious madmen whom you addressed? Do you believe they will fail to infer that while you disclaim sympathy with John Brown's plans of emancipation "because they are less likely to result in injury to the master than the slave," you will, nevertheless, regard it as an honor to be invited to attend the celebrations consequent upon the death of other martyrs in the same cause? Do you excuse yourself, my lord, with the thought that it is only the assassins of slave-holders in America who are worthy to be treated with so much kindness, respect, and forbearance? Have you forgotten from whom, and under whose auspices, American slaves were acquired as chattels? May I be pardoned for saying that in the family of the writer there is a slave, bought and paid for by my ancestor from a British subject in a British province, under the solemn sanction and approval of British laws, and who is now held as a slave under the guarantee of a British title deed? Should another John Brown, under the pretext of giving freedom to this slave, slay the owner thereof, and for his crime suffer a felon's death, would your lordship feel honored by an invitation to attend the anniversary celebration of his "martyrdom?" Your lordship has already answered the interrogatory in the affirmative.

The day may come, my lord, when "even-handed justice will commend the ingredients of the poisoned chalice to your own lips." There are more shining marks for the assassin's dagger than the slave-owners of America! Millions of lives stand between the honored felon and the accomplishment of his bloody work of philanthropy; a thousand times your lordship might have the privilege of acknowledging "the honor" of invitations to attend and participate in the celebration of events similar to those which were enacted at Harper's Ferry, and as often might "English philanthropy" palliate or excuse the crimes in which they had their origin, and still there would be a sea of living blood coursing through the veins of slaveholders! There are millions of the human race who, bound in the chains of political servitude, are ready to believe that they behold but one living man standing between themselves and the liberty to which they aspire! that one life less, and the fetters would fall from their liberated limbs! You may truly believe, my lord, that no such danger may threaten England's Sovereign. Even madmen would not strike at one whose noble virtues have added a brighter gem to the British Crown than was ever placed there by the valor of British arms. But England's best and noblest Queen must die, and be succeeded by sovereigns who may not imitate her virtues. If a British nobleman, of such world-wide reputation for statesmanship and philanthropy as your lordship, endeavors to instil into the public mind the belief that it is a *real honor* for an honorable man to be invited to join in rendering homage to the virtues, the moral worth, and the philanthropic services of an *admitted midnight assassin*, whose only *virtue*, or *worth*, or *service* in the cause of humanity, whose only claim to distinction above other cut-throats, beyond that notoriety which always attaches to the most revolting murderers, consists in the fact that he killed ostensibly in the cause of the so-called great humanitarian anti-slavery movement of the age; you need not be surprised, if others, who have real or imaginary wrongs to redress, may, while rejecting your peculiar idiosyncrasy, accept this as a means of redress. There are those who from the depths of their bleeding hearts, and for the redress of grievous wrongs which they themselves have suffered at the hands of their own race, would feel and say "If this be a real honor, which a British nobleman may covet, how much more honorable to be invited to participate in saturnalia of nobler blood!" May Heaven grant that neither your lordship nor any other may ever again be called upon to acknowledge the honor of an invitation to join in the celebration of such a feast!

But your lordship's response has satisfied me that though you may be a *fanatic*, you are not a *madman*. Though you may move fearlessly upon the brink of the precipice, you will not plunge bodily into the abyss into which you invite others to descend. You will not place in jeopardy that which you conceive to be the policy of England, by permitting it to be fully identified with the crime of assassination—the more especially as you imagine that you perceive in recent political events a more effectual means of accomplishing your ends, with less probability of injury to the slave than the master.

I come now, my lord, to consider a paragraph in your letter, which, containing, as it does, a grave personal charge *against myself*, constitutes within itself my claim and my apology for addressing you. Your lordship may mentally respond to this announcement, that not the most insignificant thing alive was farther from your thoughts than the unknown writer who now demands and *exercises* the privilege of repelling your unjust imputations, that *he* has never once "passed between the wind and your nobility," and that you have, therefore, never given to him a cause of offence.

In order to refresh your lordship's memory, I beg to refer you to the closing sentences of your response to the Boston committee. The following is your language:

> In the elevation of your new President, *all friends of America, of its continued Union*, of the final extinction of slavery, by peaceful means, *all friends of the human race must heartily rejoice!* They will, let us hope, find in him a powerfully ally, as his country may expect to find an able, *a consistent*, and an honest ruler. I have the honor to be, your faithful servant, BROUGHAM.

I have italicized that portion of the above paragraph to which I claim the right of response. While I will not pause to consider the phenomenon which is exhibited in your expressions of friendly regard and sympathy for, and confidence in, an American President; yet, I beg to say, that it at least furnishes evidence of a wonderful change in the sentiments of British politicians in regard to the chiefs of the Republic. At the end of a long night of horrors and misrule, your lordship sees bursting over the horizon the bright and glorious sunshine, which is hereafter to illumine the career of the Republic. By the early light of this dawning luminary you imagine that you behold in the not distant future, the end of that terrible conflict between brothers and fellow-countrymen, which you hope will in its results be less hurtful to the slave than his master. You, perhaps, imagine that in a very brief period the nation which Great Britain failed to conquer with her mighty sword, even in the dawn of its infant existence, will have fallen an easy victim to that subtle policy, by which you and your co-laborers have endeavored to arm its citizens in a fratricidal war. If the merit of a deed may be measured by its success, I grant that your lordship, as the representative of British policy, may boast that you are upon the point of achieving a greater triumph by the subtle arts of diplomacy, than has ever been won by British arms, during a long and brilliant and bloody career.

In contemplating the possibility of such a catastrophe, one is tempted to exclaim, Was ever nation before so wooed, so won! Your own King Richard had less cause to hope for success, when he sought to win the widow of the murdered Edward. And in surveying the victory you have achieved, you may well recall the words in which he vaunted his victory over the weak Lady Anne, and, with a slight change of phraseology, apply them to your own triumph:

> I'll have her, but I will not keep her long:
> What! I, that killed her husband, and his father!
> The bleeding witness of her hatred by,

> With God, her conscience, and these bars against me,
> And I, no friend to back my suit withal,
> But the plain devil, and dissembling looks—
> And yet to win her! all the world to nothing!

Were this communication addressed to my fellow-countrymen, instead of to your lordship, I might beg them to remember this farewell injunction of the Father of his Country—the immortal Washington:

> Against the insidious wiles of foreign influence, I conjure you to believe me, fellow-citizens, the jealousy of a free people ought to be constantly awake; since history and experience prove that foreign influence is one of the most baneful foes of Republican Government.

I might pray them to consider that foreign nations rarely, if ever, mingle in the internal conflicts of a rival power, for any other than selfish purposes. I might point to the long and brilliant career of your own great country, and demand in vain to be informed of a solitary instance in which the foot-steps of Great Britain might be traced upon the soil of a foreign land, except in the accomplishment of her own agrandizement. I might say to them, and I might prove that British anti-slavery fanaticism is but the creature and the servant of British policy, owing its origin and its development to what was supposed to be a political necessity, and that though your lordship might *write* as a fanatic, you have never failed to remember *that you are also a British politician!* Yes, my lord, if I thought that my voice would be listened to in the madness of the hour, I would appeal to my countrymen, with the earnestness of conviction, to resist with all the energy of a determined will, and to repel as an insult not to be forgiven, every effort of the foreigner to embroil them in fratricidal conflicts, even though attempted under the garb of philanthropy. I would say to them, that however gratifying it might be to have the sympathies, and to win the smiles of the great of other lands, the hopes which may be built thereon will prove delusive; the promises of succor will, in the day of adversity, be forgotten, and all the bright anticipations which may have their origin in such an association, will, like the apples of Sodom which tempt the eye of the traveller upon the shores of the Dead Sea, turn to ashes on the lips!

Perhaps, though, your lordship's visions of the future of the Republic may prove delusive. Perhaps your own unguarded words, written in the first flush of an anticipated but not yet fully accomplished victory, may of themselves induce a momentary pause in the mad career which you and your associates have inaugurated. Perhaps, when they read your lordship's letter, a *burning thought* of days long past, when, as a band of brothers, their fathers, by their bloody valor, conquered liberty from their hostile invaders, may penetrate their hearts. Perhaps the retrospect may reinaugurate once more that feeling of fraternity which animated their ancestors "in the days that tried men's souls." Or, if they cannot agree to live together as brothers in one family, that they will, in memory of a glorious past, with all its heart-thrilling associations, in memory of the blood of their sires, mingled together upon many a hard-fought battle-field, consent at least to part as friends. The end may not be yet, my lord. Out of the *clouds* may emerge a *sun*, more resplendent than even that which seems to you now to be setting in a starless night.

But your lordship, plunging into the arena of party politics in America, hails the recent defeat of that political organization, which has ruled and guided the destinies of the Republic from the first moment of its existence to the present day, as an event in which "*all friends of America—all friends of the human race must heartily rejoice.*" If your lordship should happen to remember that, during brief intervals in the history of the Republic, parties known by other names have obtained a temporary ascendency, I need scarcely remind you that these were but branches of that great organization which has just been defeated, divided as it was into three parties, each claiming that it adhered most closely to the distinctive principles of the old Democratic party. All of these, therefore, go to swell the ranks of those whom your lordship declares, *in effect*, to be *the enemies of America and of the human race.*

This is a most harsh judgment, most harshly enunciated—to say nothing of its implied condemnation of the statesmen and citizens who have passed away, and whom we, their sons by blood and inheritance, have been taught to regard as "true friends of America." It is certainly, when considered in reference to the source from whence it emanates, a most overwhelming condemnation of the millions of American citizens who struggled to avert its downfall, and who still cling to its fallen fortunes, and to its great distinctive principles, as the sheet-anchor of the hopes of the Republic. The charge is as sweeping as it is harsh. You will not grant that ONE "friend of America, or of the human race," can feel any regret at the occurrence of the event you commemorate.

The Heaven-doomed city of olden time, even after its destruction had been ordained by the fiat of Omnipotence, was allowed a respite from its terrible fate, in answer to the prayer of one *real* friend of humanity, who said: "Behold, now, I have taken upon me to speak unto the Lord, which am but dust and ashes—peradventure ten righteous men shall be found there;" and the Lord, admitting the doubt, and ever tempering justice with mercy, delayed the execution of his judgment with a promise that if ten righteous men could be found in Sodom, the city should be spared for their sake.

More inexorable in your judgment, though but a man; under the influence of your own antipathies, and upon the testimony of their enemies alone, you condemn unheard millions of your fellow-men, and deny that, amongst them all, there lives one friend of his country or of the human race, whose righteousness might plead in behalf of his fellow-countrymen to save them from the doom of Sodom.

While the world may give your lordship credit for a more profound knowledge of those subjects which concern the general good of the human race, than the unknown writer who now addresses you, I cannot doubt that an impartial public would decide that an American citizen, whose destiny has been cast within the limits of the Republic, ought to understand as thoroughly, and to appreciate as fully, the qualities which distinguish a "true friend of America," as any British nobleman, however high his rank, or however exalted his endowments as a British statesman.

This consideration emboldens me to declare, in my right as an American-born citizen, and as the representative of a sentiment held in common by millions of my fellow-countrymen, that it is not *I*, nor *they*, who are the enemies of America. If it must be that one or the other of us, my lord, is an enemy of the Republic, it is *you*, who, from your high and noble rank, disdain not to stoop to a fellowship with the openly-avowed friends and followers of assassins! It is you, who, by acknowledging yourself to be honored by an invitation to participate in demonstrations of respect for one of the foulest murderers whose deeds have found a place in the records of crime, place the lighted torch and the dagger in the hands of the incendiary! It is you, who, from your safe retreat, may laugh to scorn the horrors of such a contest, thus enkindle the flames of a fratricidal war in a distant land, and all *in the prostituted name of humanity.*

There are many who do not rejoice over the event which has filled your lordship with so much satisfaction. These mourn over a result which places in imminent peril one of the noblest—pardon me if, with the old pride of an American, I say, *the* noblest fabric of a government that has ever been constructed by human intelligence.

You delude yourself, my lord, if you believe that all "friends of America" and of the "human race" share your sentiments of joy upon the occasion you celebrate. Millions of the downtrodden and the oppressed of other climes now mourn over the peril which menaces the overthrow of "the great Republic," without knowing, or caring to comprehend, the domestic questions which have produced the danger. During eighty-five years, it has been a beacon of hope to the weary and heavy laden, and should its brightness be quenched by that dark and clouded night, upon whose gloomy and fitful shadows we may even, at this moment, be gazing, believe not, my lord, that the announcement of the catastrophe will be a message of joy to the hearts of "all the friends of the human race!" No, my lord: you may or may not represent the sentiments of the high and noble order to which you belong—I would fain hope that you do not—but you do not express the sentiments of the million!

If your lordship really believes that "all friends of the human race" are rejoiced at the overthrow of that political organization which, commencing with Washington, has been perpetuated in power to the present day, descend a little, I pray you, from your elevated position in the social scale, and seek enlightenment from those whom you may encounter. Ask of the wandering exile from his native land, who, for the crime of seeking freedom from the thraldom of despotism, has been doomed to revisit the home of his childhood no more for ever, if *he* rejoices at an event which threatens to extinguish the brightness of that light, the contemplation of which has been to him, and to his fellow-sufferers, a thing of joy, of life, and hope, in the gloomiest moments of his despondency!

I would ask no nobler epitaph upon the tomb of that party, whose defeat your lordship commemorates as an event which should be hailed with joy by every "friend of the human race," than to record in simple and brief words, this fragment of its history:

"The political organization which inaugurated the revolt of the Thirteen American Colonies of Great Britain; which conducted the war of the Revolution to a successful close; under whose auspices the Confederation of free States was established; and which ruled and guided the destinies of the Republic during the firrst eighty-five years of its existence, perished in the year of the Christian era one thousand eight hundred and sixty-one."

Whether its fall was a consequence of its crimes, its virtues, or its misfortunes, let posterity determine.

And may I be pardoned, if, in casting a glance into the unrevealed future, I venture the prediction, that even though the Republic itself should perish to-day, the incidents of its brief, but brilliant career will be remembered, and the grandeur and sublimity of the great principles upon which it was constructed will be appreciated, and the memory of its founders and of their successors, who ruled it, will be honored, when London, with its Kings, and its Nobles, and its Commons, will have been, like Egypt's ancient capital, with its monuments and its inhabitants, mingled together in undistinguishable ashes?

It would be profitless for me to indulge at greater length in the reflections to which the two events I have referred to, and your lordship's connection therewith, have given birth. I am unwilling to offer to you, my lord, any defence for the local policy of the political party in America to which I belong. Nor, on the other hand, will I make any attack upon that in whose success your lordship seems to feel so deep an interest, and whose cause you commend with so much zeal. I do not recognize in Englishmen, or any other foreigners, the right to interfere in those domestic questions which concern Americans alone, and which they should be left free to settle among themselves. I cannot admit a foreign tribunal to judge between us, any more than I would claim for America the right of interference, under similar circumstances, in the internal affairs of England. But, my lord, you have invited a comparison by which I am willing that my country shall be tested. You have, by the energy of your assaults upon the institution of

African slavery in America, indirectly challenged an examination into the manner in which subjugated races have been ruled by your own country, and you seem to invite scrutiny into your own connection, as a nation, with the institution of African slavery in the past, as well as in the present era.

I, in turn, challenge an investigation and a comparison, and I am willing to accept "all friends of the human race" as our umpires. I am willing that both shall be tried "by the laws of God and humanity," and that the inquiry shall have for its object the determination of the question: Which has so governed as to achieve the greatest good, with the least evil, to those over whom Providence or cupidity has called them, respectively, to bear sway? Every friend of the Southern States of America is willing to stand or fall upon the result of such an investigation and comparison.

I have a high respect, my lord, for the great nation in which you hold so distinguished a rank. I am satisfied that many, very many, of its noblest citizens of all classes deprecate the officious interference of British politicians in the contests of political parties in America. But my friendly regard for individual citizens of your country does not blind me to the fact that English influence has been a principal element in the sectional troubles which now distract my country. Chief among the leading journals of England is one which, by the common consent of all Europe, is the great exponent of English sentiments and English ideas. In

America, it is equally recognized as the unrivalled European defamer of the Southern States and their inhabitants. While you, my lord, in conjunction with your associates of the same school, stand at the head of the pseudo-religious section of the political anti-American-slavery movement of England, the *Times* leads that other branch of this formidable politico-religious organization, whose moral principle can only be effectually aroused to a healthy action by means of a thorough perception of certain concomitant temporal advantages.

To show to you, my lord, that I do not over-estimate the influence which, directly and indirectly, you have exercised in producing the present political troubles in America, and that I have not misconceived the nature and motive of your action in regard thereto, I beg to submit to you the following brief but *pointed* extract of a leading editorial article from the London *Times:*

Will any one, however, say that it is *not mainly* to the *ceaseless exertions*, to the philanthropic energy, to the entreaties, to the persuasion of this country, *that the anti-slavery party in the States owes its strength?* *Blot out England, and English sympathies, and English power* from the map of the world, and *the battle betweem the North and the South* would be fought on the other side of the Atlantic on very different terms. So far, then, as this, Englishmen are as one with each other on this question. Slavery shall not be in our own dominions—could we have gone one step farther and annihilated the peculiar institution, in all other countries as well as in our own, the problem would, in the main, have speedily received a satisfactory solution, This, however, was beyond our power, and consequently *we find* ourselves in this anomaly, *that we, without a slave popula-*

tion, must compete in the markets of the world with other countries which have slave populations, and that with respect to tropical productions.

To these few bluff words, the purport of the last four lines of which is a key to Anglo-American, anti-slavery philanthropy, I may add that the persistent misrepresentations against the Southern American States, which have emanated from this British party, have excited unjust and wholly unfounded prejudices against my countrymen throughout Europe. I cannot hope that in a day, or a year, these prejudices can be removed by any exposure of that narrow and thoroughly selfish policy which, decked in the garb of humanity, has given tone to the sentiments of Europe upon American affairs. But in the confidence that a returning sense of justice will induce your lordship to listen to the defence made by one whom you have accused as an enemy to his country and to the human race, I propose, after the lapse of a few weeks, which will be necessarily occupied by other engagements, to do myself the honor of again addressing you.*

I may not hope that the judge who has already pronounced against me, in terms so emphatic, will be induced to reverse his pre-determined judgment;

---

*The publication of the letters here referred to, is now superseded by those which fill the greater part of this volume. Although they were written antecedently to my announcement to his lordship, yet, as they cover the points at issue, I submit this volume to "the true friends of America," as well as to "all friends of the human race," as a redemption of my pledge.

but I will not despair of obtaining a reversal of your sentence before a tribunal composed of the "friends of the human race," until longer to hope would be fanaticism.

The small grain of mustard seed, which I throw upon the ground, may be choked by the foul weeds amongst which it is cast, and never see the sun; but it may be that from this little seed may grow and "wax a great tree," and that the "fowls of the air may lodge in the branches of it," and that beneath its shade a few, at least, of the noxious plants, from the midst of which it grew, may wither and perish!

I have the honor to be, most respectfully,

Your Lordship's obedient servant,

JAMES WILLIAMS.

THE RESULT AND ITS CONSEQUENCES.

Interest excited abroad by the last canvass for the Presidency, and its results—Amazement at the consequences—The South tranquilly living under the same laws as before, while the North is in a state of Revolution—Atrocities of the invaders—Fremont's Proclamation—Spectacle presented to mankind—Nature of the late compact of Union—Reserved rights of the States—While the Monarchies of Europe are upholding, the Lincoln Government is denying the rights of the people to self-government—The Union of South and North is opposed to the freedom of the former, and the happiness of the latter, and can never be restored—Characteristic differences between them—"Puritans," "Cavaliers"—The South will stand higher in the estimation of the civilized world after separation—The only issue is subjection or independence—Providence smiles upon the Southern people—Through the murky clouds the sunlight is already visible—President Lincoln's declaration that the States derived their powers from the General Government disproved, Note to page 288—The nature and terms of the compact of union between the States considered, Note to page 293.

At the time when the series of letters which occupy the larger portion of this volume, were written, the South was making its last appeal to the North for justice, and was engaged in its last great struggle at the ballot-box, against its unrelenting adversary. When the letter to the distinguished British statesman, which succeeds the series referred to, was addressed to that gentleman, the result of the election had been already announced, and the States which had composed the Union were trembling in the balance, between the alternatives of a peaceful separation and a war of subjugation against the seceding States. It would seem to be proper, in order to complete the connection between the cause, the effect, and the results, that something should be added upon the subjects indicated at the head of this chapter, as a sequel to that which goes before.

The result of the election for the Presidency of the United States in 1860—during the pendency of which the preceding series of letters were written in the Old World, and forwarded to America for publication—together with the immediate consequences flowing therefrom, are now events accomplished and ready for the pen of the historian. Never before has any political contest in the New World created so deep an interest throughout Europe, as that which terminated in the installation of one section of the Union, embracing eighteen States, into all the powers of the General Government, and the consequent practical exclusion of the other section, embracing fifteen States, from all participation in the management and control of a Confederacy of which they formed so important a part.

The interest excited by that struggle, in view of the internal changes which it was thought would be likely to follow, have been intensified and deepened into an absorbing passion, in presence of the actual consequences which have succeeded swiftly upon the heels of the Northern victory at the ballot-box.

All Christendom stands amazed—electrified, as it were—in presence of the stupendous spectacle which is this day presented to mankind in that country, which, a few short months ago, was properly regarded as the living embodiment of the principles of freedom.

Eleven of those States have withdrawn from the old Union—have resumed their sovereign powers—and in the exercise of their inalienable rights, have formed a separate Union, under the style of the "Confederate States of America." The four remaining slave States are ready and eager to unite themselves with their brethren in the Confederate States, whenever they can throw off the chains and shackles with which they have been fettered by the Government of the United States in the exercise of a despotism more ruthless, cruel, and vindictive than any which has marked the career of any civilized conquerors of modern times.

The present attitude of the respective Governments, which are now contending in arms for political dominion over the soil of the South, presents to the philosophical and inquiring mind some curious phenomena. That portion of the late United States, which is spoken of, by superficial observers of passing events, as being "in a state of revolution," seceded from the late Union, and formed another, without any change whatever in the internal organization of the States composing it, and without suspending, for a single instant, the operation of the laws by which the citizens of each had been governed. The acts accomplishing secession and creating a new Confederacy, had no more influence upon the *status* of the citizens, than the withdrawal of France and Sardinia from a European alliance, and the formation of a separate compact, would produce upon their subjects. In both instances, the acts referred to might be accomplished without any knowledge on the part of the inhabitants, so far as it would effect their relations to their respective Governments.

The Confederacy thus established assumed upon the instant of its creation the powers which were confided to it by the States composing it, and is now firmly established, not only in the regular exercise of its legitimate functions but in the hearts of the people.

Under the benign administration of this government, the rights of its citizens have been everywhere respected, and the laws have been faithfully executed. The liberty of the press has been maintained inviolate. No citizen held in prison for a political offence has been deprived of his right to a trial before the civil tribunals; and so far from arresting non-combatant subjects of the United States who might be within the limits of the Confederacy, a law has been enacted by the Congress at Richmond, giving to alien enemies forty days in which to make their preparations for departure, and offering them free egress from the jurisdiction of the Confederate States. These are the circumstances and condition of that country which, in common parlance throughout Europe as well as the United States, is said to be "in a state of revolution."

On the other hand, the Government of the United States, which is said to be engaged with all its power in putting down the attempted revolution in the States of the South, and in suppressing "the great rebellion," is itself in the throes of a terrible revolution. The stupendous encroachments upon the constitutional rights of its citizens which have marked the administration of the Government since the inauguration of the present President are without a parallel in the history of any other nation. The liberty of the press has been abrogated and many journals, both secular and religious, which have expressed a doubt in regard to the policy of continuing the war of subjugation against the South, have been either suppressed by the direct orders of the Government or destroyed by mob violence.

An inconsiderate word, uttered in the confidence of private friendship, is employed as a pretext for consigning the offender to a prison. Men are arrested while engaged unsuspectingly in their private avocations—transported to distant fortresses beyond the limits of the State in which they reside—incarcerated in dungeons—deprived of all means of communicating with their friends—and from first to last are kept in utter ignorance of the cause of their arrest and detention; and as if to complete the parallel between the tyranny inaugurated by Lincoln and that which marked the career of Robespierre and Danton, even women and young girls are arrested and incarcerated, by a simple order from a commanding officer, and without even the forms of law, upon suspicion of disloyalty to the government of Washington. The right of the citizen to petition Congress has been refused, and the petitioners in New York arrested. The writ of *habeas corpus* has been suspended, or rather abrogated, by the sole authority and at the discretion of the President, as to time and place. He has also delegated this usurped authority to his military commanders. All these acts, unheard of in the previous history of the country, and unparalleled in enormity by those of any other government of the present age, are perpetrated, not against those who are said to be "in rebellion," but against the citizens, and within the legal jurisdiction of "loyal States" who profess to be as earnestly desirous of upholding the government properly administered, and of re-uniting its dissevered elements, as the President himself or his advisers.*

*The only justification which is attempted for these various outrages, is the plea of necessity. This might avail them with mankind if they were defending themselves against invasion, but they are themselves the invaders against an unoffending people, for the avowed purposes of subjugation and virtual robbery. To declare the mere expression of an opinion adverse to the prosecution of such a war to be "treason," is against the practice of all civilized nations, and cannot be commended by any friend of liberty.

Such having been the conduct of the United States Government when dealing with the "loyal States," the

---

The following are among the leading newspapers, the circulation of which have been suppressed by order of the government: In New York City, the Journal of Commerce, News, Day-Book, and Freeman's Journal; in Pennsylvania, the Christian Observer; in Missouri, the Journal, Missourian, and Herald. Those suppressed by the mob are the Standard, (Concord, N. H.), Democrat, (Bangor, Maine,) Farmer, (Bridgeport, Connecticut,) Sentinel, (Easton, Pa.), and the Republican, (Westchester, Pa.) The New York Herald was assailed by the mob, but was spared on becoming a government paper.

Nothing can more clearly illustrate the utter subjection of the people of the North themselves to the despotism which in a few short months has robbed them of every vestige of their former liberty, than the following extract from the card of the editor, M. E. Masseras, of the "Courier des Etats Unis," a French paper published in New York, on retiring by order of the Government from the editorship of that paper. He says that in future the paper will confine itself simply to the news of the day, as that is all which is permitted, and that he himself will retire until the time arrives when he will be permitted to speak his sentiments. He concludes as follows:

"To-day as in April—still more than then—I am convinced that war will not save the Union, and, that, on the other hand, it will destroy the Republic. I am satisfied that the majority of the nation submits to a war which it does not approve, without believing in the happy termination about which it seeks to delude the people. I am satisfied that the war is the work of a party, who will push it to the last extremity, without hesitating at any means to maintain its supremacy. In all this I see nothing but oppression, ruin, then as a last consolation, inevitable revolution. And as the situation in which the press is placed only leaves me the choice between blandly praising everything or holding my tongue, I decide upon silence."

The belief on the part of the Washington government that such extreme measures are necessary, proves conclusively that there must be a strong feeling of disapprobation on the part of the people against the war.

treatment administered to those which are said to be in "a state of rebellion," or to have sympathies in common with the Confederate States, wherever they have been in whole or in part placed in a state of subjection, may possibly be imagined. The occupation of that portion of the border of Virginia which has fallen under the ruthless dominion of the invaders, has been marked by deeds of the most wanton cruelty, rapine, and violence. Every blade of grass has been destroyed, whole villages and towns have been burned to the ground, and their inhabitants driven forth without pity. Every foot of territory over which their armies have trodden, presents a picture of utter desolation. Throughout another entire State, the writ of *habeas corpus* has been suspended, and the civil authorities have been entirely superseded by military rule. The commander of this military division—a vain despot, who seems only ambitious of acquiring a wider notoriety of infamy, than any other person engaged in the same occupation—has issued a proclamation, declaring as forfeited, not only the property, but the lives of all persons who may be found in arms against the Government which he represents. *

---

* EXTRACT FROM FREMONT'S PROCLAMATION.—"In order, therefore, to suppress disorders, to maintain as far as practicable, the public peace, and to give security and protection to the persons and property of loyal citizens, I do hereby extend and declare established martial law throughout the entire State of Missouri. . . . All persons who shall be taken with arms in their hands within these lines shall be tried by court-martial, and if found guilty shall be shot.

"The property real and personal, of all persons in the State of

These acts are done within the limits of a State, four-fifths of which would hail the advent of a Nero as a deliverance from the despotism of that "paternal" Government, which has, by its ruthless deeds, banished every vestige of liberty from all territory over which it exercises dominion!

These are not the exaggerated statements of an excited adversary, but facts of public notoriety, every one of which has been derived from official

---

Missouri, who shall take up arms against the United States, or who shall be directly proven to have taken active part with their enemies in the field, is declared confiscated to public use, and slaves, if any they have, are hereby declared freemen.

"All persons who have been led away from their allegiance are required to return forthwith to their homes. Any such absent without sufficient cause will be held to be presumptive evidence against them: the object of this declaration is to place in the hands of the military authorities the power to give effect to existing laws and to supply such deficiencies as the conditions of war demand."

The proclamation from which the above paragraphs are extracted, appears to be an exact copy in substance of the proclamation of John, Earl of Dunmore, the last British Governor of Virginia. This State paper, so celebrated in Virgina annals, must have been the immediate source of Fremont's inspirations. It is to be regretted that the lesson then taught to tyrants, that vindictive and ferocious deeds, in the conduct of a war, defeat the very objects which they were intended to accomplish, seems to have been lost upon the chief of the present United States Government, as well as upon the tools who are willing to be his instruments in perpetrating the barbarities of a common vengeance. The United States Government may murder its prisoners, and rob them of their property, as both President Lincoln and his military commanders have officially declared they would do; *but mankind would accuse the Confederate States Government of criminal weakness, if it failed to follow the consummation of these threats, by a terrible retribution!*

The proclamation of Lord Dunmore, bearing date 17th November,

documents which have been authoritatively published in the columns of leading Journals in the interest of the Government of the United States.

Nay more, as if the ruler of this once free people were resolved while destroying the liberties of his subjects, to eradicate every impediment to the exercise of his usurped authority, and to annihilate the last and only remaining bulwark of the people

---

1775, by a mere change of names and dates, would be the proclamation of the Republican General, with only a trifling difference in the mere words. Lord Dunmore says:

"To defeat such treasonable purposes, that all such traitors and their abettors may be brought to justice, and that the peace and good order of this colony may again be restored, which the ordinary course of the civil law is unable to effect—I have thought fit to issue this, my proclamation, hereby declaring, that until the aforesaid good purposes can be obtained, I do, in virtue of the power and authority to me given by his majesty, determine to execute martial law, and cause the same to be executed throughout this colony; and to the end that peace and good order may the sooner be restored, I do require every person capable of bearing arms to resort to his majesty's standard, or be looked upon as a traitor to his crown and government, and thereby become liable to the penalty the law inflicts upon such offences, such as forfeiture of life, confiscation of lands, etc., etc. And I do hereby further declare all indentured servants, negroes, or others appertaining to rebels, free that are willing and able to bear arms; they joining his majesty's troops as soon as may be, for the purpose of reducing this colony to a proper sense of their duty to his majesty's crown and dignity."

The proclamation of the commanding general of the United States in Missouri—the spirit and objects of which, have been sanctioned by the President and his Cabinet, and applauded by the people of the North—ought to satisfy the last lingering doubt upon the minds of all, that the intention of the North in the formation of the Republican party was to obtain and to exercise control over the domestic institutions of the Southern States. That it was the original design of this

against the encroachments of a central despotism, he has in effect abrogated the sovereign rights of the States—reduced them to the condition of mere counties or townships—and as if to add insult to injury, he proclaims officially that the States of the Confederacy never had an independent existence, and that they derive all their powers from that

party to carry out their pledges to foreign abolitionists, cannot for a moment be questioned. If a commanding general has a right to give freedom to the slaves, surely the right of Congress to do so cannot be questioned. The resistance of the South has only hastened the denounment of a foregone conclusion. The only difference between the position which the South would have occupied if she had remained a passive witness of her own enslavement, and her present attitude consists in this, that in the first instance she would have been degraded by an unresisting subjugation by the North, while now, if she perishes, it is while nobly fighting for all that is dear to freemen; and if she triumphs, all the proclamations of the petty despots who have sprung up like mushrooms under the reign of terror which has been inaugurated by Lincoln, will remain null and of no effect, except as a record of perpetual infamy, against those who have employed the authority confided to them, in attempting to crush out the last vestige of constitutional liberty.

It were worse than folly for any one having a personal interest at stake, to doubt any longer in regard to the past or present intentions of the North. If there should be any citizens in the border States who hope to retain their property by submission or subserviency to the North, let them also bear in mind, that they will only retain possession thereof at the pleasure of the North. If the Government possesses the right to manumit slaves for one offence against the Government, they can do the same thing as a punishment for another. In short the assumption and practical exercise of such an authority under any circumstances, is equivalent to an entire subjection of all Southern States which submit to the authority of the Government of the United States—which is now nothing more than the government of the North.

General Government of which he is the chief ruler. *

Strange spectacle of mad ambition! The head of a once free, powerful, and respected nation murdering not only the substance, but the very forms of liberty among his own subjects, that he may employ them the more readily in destroying the liberties of others!

Strange spectacle of wickedness! The President of a once mighty Republic, deriving its powers from the consent of the governed, hurling his armies of mer-

* EXTRACT FROM PRESIDENT LINCOLN'S WAR MESSAGE TO CONGRESS, JULY, 1861.—The States have their status in the Union, and they have no other legal status if they break from this. They can only do so against law by revolution. The Union, and not themselves separately, procured their independence and their liberty by conquest or purchase. The Union gave each of them whatever independence and liberty it had. The Union is older than any of the States, and in fact it created them as States. Originally, some dependent colonies made the Union, and in turn the Union threw of their old dependence for them and made them States. Such as they are, not one of them ever had a State Constitution independent of the Union."

President Lincoln may be an excellent rail-splitter, but it is clear that he is not an expert at hair-splitting. He tears up sovereignties by the roots, and casts them at his feet without deigning to show to his faithful subjects how he had reached conclusions so adverse to the doctrines universally acknowledged previous to his advent to power. To say nothing of the belief entertained by the States themselves, that they were once sovereign, and that they only transferred a very limited portion of that sovereignty to the General Government, over which, in an evil day for his country, he was called to preside as the chief ruler, mankind will be curious to understand, what disposition he means to make of the following brief extract from a document which gave to the United States, or rather the States united, their first fully recognized legal claim to independence and sovereignty:

cenary soldiers against eight millions of freemen, living in contented happiness under a government of their own choice, for the purpose of coercing them by fire and sword, to become his dutiful subjects!

Strange spectacle of weakness! The very people who should defend with their life's blood the rights which are thus set at naught, and who are at once his victims and instruments, rattle the chains which despotism has placed upon their once free limbs, and shout for the war of subjugation against the freemen of the South! They raise their manacled hands

---

Extract from "Provisional Articles signed at Paris, November 30, 1782, *by the Commissioners of his Britannic Majesty, and the Commissioners of the United States of America."*

"ARTICLE I. His Britannic Majesty acknowledges the said United States, viz: New Hampshire, Massachusetts Bay, Rhode Island and Providence Plantations, Connecticut, New York, New Jersey, Pennsylvania, Delaware, Maryland, Virginia, North Carolina, South Carolina, and Georgia, to be free, sovereign, and independent States, and that he treats with them as such; and for himself, his heirs, and successors, relinquishes all claim to the government, propriety, and territorial rights of the same and every part thereof."

After President Lincoln shall have satisfactorily explained that this recognition did not mean what it declares, the world has a right to ask him how he reconciles the act of war which he has instituted, and is prosecuting with so much ferocity, with the positions assumed in his speech delivered in the Congress of the United States, January 12th, 1848, from which the following words are extracted, viz:

"Any people whatever, being inclined and having the power, have the right to rise up and shake off the existing government, and form a new one that suits them better. This is a most valuable, a most sacred right. Nor is the right confined to cases where the whole of an existing government may chose to exercise it. Any portion of such people that can, may revolutionize and make their own, of so much territory as they inhabit."

towards heaven, and pray that God may prosper their enslaver!

Strange spectacle of madness and folly! Nineteen States of a Union once embracing thirty-four members, without the pretence of a wrong to redress, or an insult to avenge, invade with a great army, the territory of their former confederates, murdering their citizens, plundering them of their property, burning their dwellings, committing atrocious violence upon their wives and daughters, and leaving upon the track of their sacrilegious hosts, nothing but ruin, and desolation, and woe amongst the inhabitants, and "all to win back the alienated affections" of those whom they call their brothers!

Of a truth may it be repeated, that while the "rebellious States" have passed without a revolution or an internal commotion, the period of transition into the new Confederacy, the "loyal States" which still adhere to the old federal Union, are themselves in the agonies of a revolution involving changes in the organic principles upon which the Government had been previously administered, scarcely less startling in its magnitude than that which was inaugurated by the eloquence of a Mirabeau, in the days of Louis XVI., which terminated by driving the Bourbon from the throne of France forever.

So far as it may affect the result of the war in which the two countries are now engaged, a decision confirming the right of the Southern States to withdraw from the late Union would be unavailing. Whether the acts of the now Confederate States be regarded as secession by right of sovereignty, or rebellion by authority of the people, they will maintain their independence by the sword, which they will never return to its scabbard, until the last hostile invader shall have been driven from their borders!

Nevertheless, a due respect for the opinions of our fellow-men, and a natural desire to justify our acts and to secure for ourselves the respect, if not the sympathies, of the civilized world, make it a duty incumbent upon the citizens of the South to show clearly the causes which impelled them, in defence of all that they held dear, to sever the political bonds which united them with the States of the North. These causes have already been fully stated, and the opinions of disinterested men every where have undergone a revolution, which promises, in due time, to correct the erroneous views which were at first entertained. The impartial historian will declare that the circumstances under which the Southern States resumed their independence, and declared their determination to defend and maintain it, by an appeal, if necessary, to the arbitrament of arms, would have justified the adoption of that measure, even though they had previously formed but an integral part of a consolidated sovereignty. But they were not thus bound to their late associates. They joined them in a compact, but they never surrendered to them their sovereignty. They formed with them a Union for certain specified purposes, and delegated certain clearly defined powers, but by express stipulation in the articles of agreement which were concluded between them, all the powers not specifically conferred upon the federal Government, were reserved to the States. There was no arbiter appointed to decide in case of a disagreement, so that the right to determine the sufficiency of the causes which impelled them to a separation, was and remained with them, and them alone. The Government of the United States might, or might not, have been stronger and more durable if the States had transferred to it all of their sovereignty; but we are considering what was, and not what might have been. The very name by which the Government was known indicated unmistakably that it was not consolidated into a single State, but was the admitted representative of several sovereignties. The causes which induced the original States of the Union to guard with so much care their State sovereignty, can be readily discovered by considering the peculiar circumstances in which they were placed. The territory embraced an extent of country large enough for a dozen empires, each one of which would have rivaled the greatest Powers of Europe. There already existed an antagonism between the Northern and the Southern States, and their domestic institutions were still more widely at variance. If these Governments had been consolidated into one, slavery might have been abolished, or made universal, throughout the whole. The States therefore retained their sovereignty, for the reason amongst others, that they desired to avoid giving any pretext to the General Government for attempting to control their internal affairs.*

*One is almost tempted to smile at the flippant insolence with which the Northern people charge the Southerners with being in a state of rebellion against them! In America, they call it "the rebellion of the Southern States," but in Europe, they speak of it as "the rebellion of the Southern provinces." There is no doubt that the North is laboring to accomplish this end, but as it has never yet had a beginning, the South can scarcely be said to be in rebellion against anything, except *the intentions* of the North to enslave her. There are those, however, who speak of the rebellion of the Southern States against the Government of the United States, without considering that such a thing, under existing circumstances, is absurd and impossible. If there were a Monarch upon the throne, there might be a rebellion among his subjects, but the people were the sovereigns of the late United States, and to say that the people of the South are in rebellion, is to say that the sovereign has rebelled against himself, which is absurd. Moreover, suppose that the North is right in declaring that the Government of the United States was the representative of a single sovereignty, namely, the people of all the States. The people of the Southern States have refused to constitute any longer a portion of the sovereignty of the whole, and having separated themselves from all political association with the North, it follows that the Government of the United States is the agent of the Northern people alone; and, as the Southern people cannot be in rebellion against themselves, if it may be said that they are in rebellion against the Government of the United States, and the people are the sovereign, it follows that the South must be regarded as in rebellion against the North. This would assume that the Southern people were never sovereign, but that they were subject to and owed allegiance to the North. We do not find this in the bond.

During the war between the Thirteen Colonies and Great Britain, Articles of Confederation were adopted by the Colonies, by which it was provided that "the Union shall be perpetual." Notwithstanding this, another convention subsequently assembled, which adopted the present Constitution of the United States. Article VII. provided that "the ratifications of nine States shall be sufficient for the es-

The only pretext upon which the Northern United States may justify the unprovoked war which they

---

tablishment of this Constitution, between the States ratifying the same." In effect, this Constitution was ratified at first by only a portion of the States composing the previous Union, (each at different dates and in its sovereign capacity as a State.) So that the right of secession is fully admitted, by the fact that the late Union was created by States which "seceded" from the previous Union, three of which, in their acts of ratification expressly reserved the right to secede again. Virginia, in giving her assent to the Constitution, said:

"We, the delegates of the people of Virginia, duly elected, etc., etc., do, in the name and in behalf of the people of Virginia, declare and make known that the powers granted under the Constitution, being derived from the people of the United States, may be resumed by them whenever the same shall be perverted to their injury or oppression."

The State of New York said that "the powers of Government may be re-assumed by the people whenever it shall become necessary to their happiness." And the State of Rhode Island adopted the same language. It is clear that when these States speak of the people of the United States, meaning the States united, they spoke authoritatively for the people of their own States respectively; for when they speak of the re-assumption of power by the people, it is manifest that they refer to the people who previously held it. Now, what people held this power originally? It was the people of the States respectively whose independence had been recognized separately, and by name, by George III., and not the whole people of all the States as a unit.

Furthermore, in order that no inference might ever be drawn prejudicial to the rights of the States, the Constitution was amended after its ratification in such manner as to state that "the powers not delegated to the United States, nor prohibited by it to the States, are reserved to the States respectively, or to the people."

The right of secession has been distinctly affirmed and admitted by almost every President, and in turn by almost every State of the Union, since the celebrated Resolutions of Virginia and of Kentucky

are now waging against the Southern Confederacy, might, with equal propriety, be employed by Eng-

---

in 1798. The former were drawn up by Mr. Madison, and the latter by Mr. Jefferson. The first Kentucky resolution was as follows:

"1st *Resolved*, That the several States comprising the United States of America, are not united on the principle of unlimited submission to their general government, but that by compact under the style and title of a Constitution for the United States, and of amendments thereto, they constituted a general government, for special purposes, delegated to that government certain definite powers, reserving each State to itself, the residuary mass of right to their own self-government; and that whensoever the general government assumes undelegated powers, its acts are unauthoritative, void, and of no force; that to this compact each State acceded, as a State, and is an integral party; that this government created by this compact, was not made the exclusive or final judge of the extent of the powers delegated to itself; since that would have made its discretion and not the Constitution the measure of its powers, but that as in all other cases of compact among parties having no common judge, each party has an equal right to judge for itself, as well of infractions as of the mode and measure of redress."

This was the interpretation given to the compact of the Union by Jefferson and Madison, and the fathers of the Union. To come down to the interpretation of more modern times, it may be stated that Van Buren, Polk, Pierce, Buchanan, and perhaps others, were elected respectively to the office of President upon platforms embracing *specifically* the above recited resolution. It will be remembered that upon this declaration of principles, Mr. Pierce received the votes of every State in the Union except three, and one of those has time and again given her adhesion to the same principle.

To show how this subject and the subject of coercion was regarded by the framers of the very Constitution under consideration, I close with the following extracts from the debates in the federal convention for forming a Constitution, 1787:

"Mr. Edmund Randolph, of Virginia, presented a series of resolutions as a basis of a form of government. The sixth resolution suggested, amongst other matters, that the National Legislature

land, or France, or Russia, if either of these powerful nations should attempt the subjugation of all Europe, upon the ground that the existence of

---

ought to be empowered to 'call forth the force of the Union against any member of the Union failing to fulfil its duties under the articles thereof.' See Madison Papers, Vol. 2d, page 732.

"Mr. Madison observed, that the more he reflected on the use of force, the more he doubted the *practicability*, the *justice*, and the efficacy of it, when applied to people collectively, and not individually. An Union of the States containing such an ingredient, seemed to provide for its own *destruction*. The use of force against a State would look more like a declaration of war than an infliction of punishment; and would probably be considered by the party attacked as a dissolution of all previous compacts by which it might be bound. He hoped that such a system would be framed as might render this resource unnecessary, and moved that the clause be postponed. This motion was agreed to unanimously. See Madison Papers, Vol. 2d, page 761.

"Mr. Patterson, of New Jersey, moved a series of resolutions, as a basis of a plan of Government. Ib., Vol. 2d, page 863 to 867.

"His sixth resolution suggested, 'That if any State, or any body of men in any State, shall oppose or prevent the carrying into execution such acts or treaties, the Federal Executive shall be authorized to call forth the power of the Confederated States, or so much thereof as may be necessary, to enforce and compel an obedience to such acts, or an observance of such treaties.' Mr. Patterson's whole plan, including the sixth resolution, was voted down.

"Col. Alexander Hamilton said, 'The great and essential principles necessary for the support of government, are' five in number, which were respectively enumerated and commented on by him. The fourth was '*Force*, by which,' he said 'may be understood a *coercion of laws, or coercion of arms*.' After commenting on a coercion of laws, he continued, 'A certain portion of military force is absolutely necessary in large communities. Massachusetts is now feeling this necessity, and making provision for it. But how can this force be exerted on the States collectively? *It is impossible. It amounts to a war between the parties.*' Ib., Vol. 2nd, page 881.

other nations upon its borders was a constant menace against the integrity of its own dominions.

The moral spectacle which is exhibited to the

"Col. George Mason said, 'He took this occasion to repeat that, notwithstanding his solicitude to establish a national government, he never would agree to abolish the State governments, or render them absolutely insignificant. They were as necessary as the general government, and he would be equally careful to preserve them.' Ib., Vol. 2nd, page 914.

"Mr. Luther Martin agreed with Col. Mason as to the importance of State governments: he would support them at the expense of the general government, which was instituted for the purpose of that support. . . . At the separation from the British Empire, the people of America preferred the establishment of themselves into thirteen separate sovereignties, instead of incorporating themselves into one. To these they look up for the security of their lives, liberties, and properties; to these they must look up. The Federal government they formed to defend the whole against foreign nations in time of war, and to defend the lesser States against the ambition of the larger. They are afraid of granting power unnecessarily, lest they should defeat the original end of the Union; lest the powers shonld prove dangerous to the sovereignties of the particular States which the Union was meant to support, and expose the lesser to being swallowed up by the larger. Ib., Vol. 2nd, page 915.

"Mr. Madison said, 'It had been alleged (by Mr. Patterson) that the confederation, having been formed by unanimous consent, could be dissolved by unanimous consent only. Does this doctrine result from the nature of compacts? Does it arise from any particular stipulation in the Articles of Confederation? If we consider the Federal Union as analogous to the fundamental compact by which individuals compose one society, and which must, in its theoretic origin, at least, have been the unanimous act of the component members, it cannot be said that no dissolution of the compact can be effected without unanimous consent. A breach of the fundamental principles of the compact by a part of the society would certainly absolve the other part from their obligations to it. If the breach of *any article by any of the parties*, does not set the others at liberty, it is

civilized world by the United States Government, even apart from the bloody horrors of the desolating war which it is now waging, is enough to arouse in the bosom of every true lover of liberty an agony of grief and shame. Through seven long and dreary years, the immortal founders of that government continued in arms against a mighty foe, in defence of the great principle that the people had a right to determine the character of the government under which they lived. They won the victory after a long and doubtful struggle, and forthwith proceeded to establish their own political institutions, upon the great principle which they had proclaimed during the progress of their struggle.

Let us for a moment glance at the political condition of the nations of the earth at that turning point in the world's history. It was scarcely more than three quarters of a century ago, and many who were living then are living still. Of all the nations of the

---

because the contrary is *implied* in the compact itself, and particularly by that law of it which gives an indefinite authority to the majority to bind the whole in all cases. This latter circumstance shows that we are not to consider the Federal Union as analogous to the social compact of individuals: for if it were so, a majority would have a right to bind the rest, and even to form a constitution for the whole; which the gentleman from New Jersey would be among the last to admit. If we consider the Federal Union as analogous, not to the social compacts among individual men, but to the conventions among individual States, what is the doctrine resulting from these conventions? Clearly, according to the *expositors of the law of nations*, that a breach of *any one article by any one party, leaves all the other parties at liberty to consider the whole convention as dissolved.*"

globe, there was not one holding a high rank, which recognized the right which was thus proclaimed by a handful of Americans, as inalienable to the people. All Europe held that the source of all legitimate earthly power was the monarch, and that the monarch derived his authority from the Almighty. If the people came into the possession of any rights, they were indebted therefore to the gracions sovereign who conferred them. Now, how changed! England, which was the adversary of America in that contest, big with great results, proclaims to-day from the Throne, from the Parliament, and from the people, its adhesion to that great principle. France —that mighty France, which proclaims to the world that she will go to war for an idea, or fight for an abstract principle of right or justice, is ruled over by the third and greatest Napoleon, in conformity with the will of the people, deliberately proclaimed at the ballot-box. Victor Emanuel is the elected King of Italy, recognized as such by some of the great powers of Europe, upon the specified grounds that he was the chosen of the people. The King of Sardinia ceded to the Emperor of the French, his right to the sovereignty of Savoy and Nice. These little principalities, hid away amid the rugged and barren slopes of the Alps, were only incorporated into the empire of France after the question of transfer had been submitted to the people to be effected by the change, and ratified by their votes. And even the Sultan of Turkey, in obedience to the demand of the great powers of Europe, headed by the autocrat of Russia and the Emperor of Austria, has conceded to the people of Moldavia and Wallachia, and other Christian principalities within his dominions, the right to elect the prince who may rule over them.

The people upon the various occasions referred to, may or may not have exercised wisely or even independently the privilege which was conceded to them, but the principle and the right is granted and acknowledged by the very fact of claiming to exercise authority by virtue of the sanction thus accorded. The governments of Europe do not submit the election of their rulers to the people at stated periods, but the great point has been gained, that the people have an inherent right to be regarded as the original fountain of power. The consequence is that almost all the governments of Europe profess to exercise dominion in the interests of their subjects, and with their approbation.

At the very moment when the enlightened public sentiment of mankind has recognized the validity and binding force of the sacred principle for which the fathers of the American Republic contended single-handed, only eighty-five years ago, against the opinions and practice of the whole world, their degenerate descendants are waging an exterminating war against eight millions of freemen, in order to compel them at the cannon's mouth to surrender the government of their free choice, and come under the dominion of a power which in the depths of their hearts they abhor. The vain pretext that the armies of the Union are hurled upon the South in order to relieve the majority of its people from the tyranny of a minority which holds them in subjection, will no longer avail them, since the terrible routs of Manassas Plains, and Bethel, and Oak Hills. The world will say with truth, whatever way its sympathies may run in the contest, that there can exist *but one impulse, and one heart,* amongst a nation of eight millions of people, whose armies can successfully meet and vanquish in battle the hosts which eighteen millions of their own race, acting under the impulse of an undivided purpose, can direct against them.

Whatever may be the fluctuating fortunes of war, every intelligent observer, who will calmly survey the attitude of the two parties in the struggle, must see that it can only terminate in the establishment of the independence of the South. The North declares in the face of the world that it is fighting for the restoration of the old Union, a result which, in the very nature of things, is not only improbable, but impracticable. Even though their victorious armies should desolate every district, and destroy every village and every city within the limits of the Confederates States, and carry mourning into every dwelling, the consummation of such a purpose would be still farther removed beyond the verge of probability. Every vestige of a Union sentiment, upon the part of the people of the South, has been already burned out of their hearts, and seared over as with a red hot iron, by the vindictive deeds and no less atrocious designs of their former confederates. It could never have entered into the thoughts of those who inaugurated this war of subjugation, that the South would ever again receive, as brothers, the ruthless foe, whose hands were dripping with the blood of her murdered children.

It is absurd to attempt, by force, to compel a people to enter or return to a political union, whose existence can only begin, or be perpetuated, by consent. It is scarcely to be credited that any portion of the Northern people can now look to any other end to the present conflict, than the complete independence, or the utter enslavement and subjugation, of the South to a military rule.*

---

* However it may detract from their claim to a reputation for candor, it is due to the leading spirits of the war party in the North to say, that, in Europe, they do not pretend amongst their friends that they have any hope, or even wish, to restore the old Union. The writer did not leave Europe until after the war had already commenced, and having been several years resident in that country, he had opportunities of becoming acquainted with the real plans of the anti-slavery party in America, because there, they threw off the disguise, which it was still necessary to wear in America. When "the war for the restoration of the Union" was proclaimed in America, the world said, in the words of Douglas, "war is eternal separation." The representatives of the war party in Europe said "No! it is death to the former Union of free and equal States, but war will acquire the South for the North, and she will hold it under military rule by right of conquest." They spoke, unreservedly, of breaking up the old Constitution, and establishing a consolidated government of the States of the North, and then, after the conquest of the South, they would divide it into military districts, and hold them as provinces. They referred, with great self-complacency, to historical

When such is the issue, and the only issue presented, the South knows well that, whether the war endures for one year, or five years, or a generation, she must fight on until her victorious legions establish her independence.

Any why should such a result be deplored by any friend of liberty? The old federal Union had played its part upon the political stage—it had answered the purpose of its creation, by sustaining the power of the infant Government until the Republics which formed it had attained to manhood. The great continent of North America was never designed, by the wisdom of Omnipotence, to form but a single, undivided, and indivisible Power. The State of Texas, alone, embraces territory suffi-

parallels, which they said established that, by a law of nature, Southern people were always subjected, sooner or later, by Northern invaders. It is certain that at least one of the proselytes to this opinion was recalled from Europe, and is now holding one of the highest positions as a military commander in the "Union" army. His conduct, since he assumed command, proves conclusively that his feelings and opinions upon this point have not undorgone a change.

In this connection it may not be out of place to state a fact which may not be generally known, namely, that the first great impulse given to the inauguration of this war, came from certain parties in Europe, whose anti-slavery sympathies had led them to form an intimate alliance with many of the Republican leaders in America. When the information crossed the Atlantic that there was a small probability of a compromise, by which the integrity of the South would be guaranteed, and that Mr. Seward, and other prominent Republican politicians were trembling in the balance, the frantic violence of some of their European allies was almost equal to that of the Northerners on the occasion of the fall of Sumter. They taunted their American friends with the charge of timidity and incient for a vast empire. The old Union has had its day, and it has passed away forever. No human agency can restore it to life. It has perished by the fiat of Omnipotence, and by the unchangeable will of the people of the South.

The North and the South are of the same race,

---

sincerity, and told them that if their own previous statements were to be relied upon, the South had been so completely enervated by slavery that their subjugation could be accomplished almost without an effort, and with but little bloodshed. They further insisted, that whether the South was permitted to secede, or to remain in the Union upon a new compromise, it would result in an indefinite perpetuation of slavery; whereas, after many sacrifices and disappointments, the North had at last made itself master of the position, and that it would seem to be an act of folly and imbecility to lose the present golden opportunity. So that at the very moment when the Americans were dreaming of peace, Southerners who were in Europe did not doubt that there would be a bloody war, for we knew a fact of which Europeans seemed strangely ignorant, namely, that the South had the will and the military force to offer a successful resistance.

In corroboration of the fact that the foreign impulse referred to, had a powerful influence in inducing a change of policy in the United States, the reader has but to refer to the speeches and writings of the recognized leaders of that party about the time referred to. In order not to encumber this note with an unnecessary number of proofs upon this point, I will extract some brief paragraphs from a journal which has always been recognized as the leading anti-Southern paper in the United States.

From the New York Tribune of Nov. 26, and Dec. 17, 1860.

We hold with Jefferson to the inalienable right of communities to alter or abolish forms of government that have become oppressive or injurious, and if the cotton States shall become satisfied that they can do better out of the Union than in it, we insist on letting them go in peace. The right to secede may be a revolutionary one, but it exists nevertheless, and we do not see how one party can have a right to do, what another party has a right to prevent. Whenever a con-

speaking the same language, but they are, and always have been, from the beginning, two peoples. Circumstances, coupled with a once existing political necessity, for a time united them, but they never mingled. They were as oil and water preserved for a season in the same bottle. Confined upon every

---

siderable section of our Union shall deliberately resolve to go out, we shall resist all coercive measures designed to keep it in. We hope never to live in a Republic, whereof one section is pinned to the residue by bayonets. . . . . If ever seven or eight States send agents to Washington to say "we want to get out of the Union," we shall feel constrained by our devotion to human liberty, to say "let them go!" And we do not see how we could take the other side, without coming in direct conflict with those rights of man which we hold paramount to all political arrangements, however convenient and advantageous.

From the same, of May 1, 1861.

But, nevertheless, we mean to *conquer* them—[the Confederate States] not merely to *defeat*, but to CONQUER, to *subjugate them.* But when the rebellious traitors are overwhelmed in the field, and scattered like leaves before an angry wind, *it must not be to return to peaceful and contented homes!* They must find POVERTY at their firesides, *and see* PRIVATION *in the anxious eyes of mothers, and the* RAGS *of children.* The whole coast of the South, from the Delaware to the Rio Grande, *must be a* SOLITUDE, save from the presence of a blockading squadron, so that no relief shall come in to the beleaguered people from the sea. It is in the power of the West literally to *starve her into submission.*

I select from another leading organ of the party in power at Washington, the following brief extract, which is only important as exhibiting the model after which the war, or rather the massacre, against the South is to be conducted.

From the New York Times, May 1, 1861.

How shall the United States government wage the war? Whoever has to die, it is better to die *by the guillotine,* than by a cancer. Then up with the axe, and down with the head, and let the slide fall.

side, and shaken up with a sufficient degree of violence, they pass through and through each other, creating an ugly, excited compound, covered with froth and filled with bubbles. But remove the external force, give both an equal chance and a moment's quiet, and they separate upon the instant, under the influence of a mutually irresistible repulsion.

"Puritanism"—a word of terrible significance, both in English and in Anglo-American history—is not developed into fanaticism by a long process of incubation. It is born fanaticism, fully matured in all its hideous proportions, at the very instant of its conception. It has shown itself capable of great achievments both for good and evil; but even in its blandishments it strikes terror into the hearts of those on whom it fondles. It appeared first in England, in the form of a great pestilence of living men, professing to be heaven-descended. They went forth to battle with shaved heads, but strong arms, and unconquerable hearts, and they varied the monotony of killing their fellow-men, by singing psalms over their victims. The wickedness of England may have induced the All-wise Ruler of the Universe, to visit it with this pestilence, and the result may have been a purification, but the medicine was not the less nauseating to the patient. It performed its work there, and partially disappeared; although leaving seed which took root and which has not even yet been eradicated. In the meantime, a sufficient number for a colony tooktheirflight to the bleak and barren coasts of New England, where it still rules and reigns without a rival. Leave it alone to operate upon itself, and it develops great achievements; but whenever it is brought into contact with others, it exhibits the same spirit which, under the direction of Cromwell, shivered the power of his royal rival for regal honors. It is a pestilence which was doubtless sent upon the earth for a wise purpose, but a merciful Providence surely never designed that its power should be perpetual in any one country. Eternal punishments are only inflicted by our benevolent Father in heaven, in the eternal world.

The "Puritan" exiles, who established themselves upon the cold, and rugged, and cheerless soil of New England, and the "cavaliers," who fixed their destinies in the ever-blooming, smiling, sunny South, did not bear with them from the mother country to the shores of the New World any greater degree of congeniality than existed amongst them at home, previous to the commencement of their perpetual exile; and there has been but little perceptible change in their relations since. It does not matter which was or is the better, or which the worse. Others may settle those points according to their tastes, their judgments, or their prejudices, *but they are different*—always have been, and always will be.

The one drowned or burned women, according to the tastes or humors of their judges, on satisfactory proof that they were witches, holding nightly communications with the evil one; the other would have been charmed to make the acquaintance of these curiously gifted ladies, and would have bestowed upon them more than a due share of their proverbial hospitality. The one will employ force, if necessary, to convince an adversary of his error; the other cares but little whether his fellow-men believe as he does, if he is permitted the full and free enjoyment of his own opinions. The one wishes to compel every man to enter the gates of heaven by the road which he points out as the right one; the other does not care how his neighbor gets there, so he himself is allowed to go in his own way. The one will not smile when he is happy; the other will not smile at any other time. The one would look sternly, and ask you what you meant by calling him a gentleman; the other would be angry if you called him any thing else. The one will destroy the character of his adversary by cruel defamation, or by insidious speech, but he will not fight his enemy; not from a lack of courage, but upon principle; the other is loth to insult a gentleman by words, but he is ever ready to take "or give satisfaction" for an insult. The one is scrupulously observant of all the external forms of piety; the other, if he has any religion in his heart, does not care to make a display of it before the world. The one is prudent, cautious, and calculating; the other inclined to be reckless, rash, and improvident. Each is great in his own way, each is capable of achieving glorious results, each is brave, each can worthily fulfil a high destiny, but in different fields, and upon diverging lines. What God in his wisdom and in the exercise of his inscrutable will has put asunder, let none attempt to join together. The New England Puritan fled from the home of his fathers in order to enjoy unrestricted freedom of religion upon the barren rock of Plymouth, but he whipped the Baptists who followed after him, for non-conformity, and drove them away into the deeper depths of the great forest. He made bondmen and bondwomen from the heathen round about him, and bought and sold them like cattle in the market, "for the glory of God and the spread of his holy word;" but his descendant would to-day, if he were allowed to follow the bent of his inclinations, adjust the rope around the neck of the Southern slaveholder, exhort him to repentance for the sin of holding his fellow-man in bondage, say a prayer, sing a psalm, let fall the drop, and after being assured that his victim no longer breathed, he would retire with the belief that he had acquiréd another claim to the joys of paradise.

These contrasts indicate the adverse principles, under the influence of which the public sentiment of the respective sections is developed or directed, in reference to all the affairs of life. Circumstances may and do modify, and no doubt in many instances change, these sectional or more properly speaking, national characteristics. The spirit of the cavalier has even made strong inroads upon the very soil, and in the very temples of the descendants of the roundheads, but the spirit of puritanism in its most strongly defined and most aggressive features, is, and always will be, the predominating power from whence the North will derive its inspirations, for if it were otherwise, New England would emigrate to another Plymouth rock, where her strong-minded men and women could enjoy, in undisturbed quiet, that liberty of conscience, and freedom of action, and supreme control, which they never concede to or share with any others of their fellow-men.

On the other hand, the puritan may emigrate into the South, and sometimes he adopts the tastes and habits of his new associates, and is lost by being merged into the mass by which he is surrounded; but as a general rule, he is and remains an exotic. The improvident prodigality of the Southerner is an ever present temptation for him to remain a little longer for the augmentation of his worldly stores, but ever his eyes wander back under the promptings of his heart to the land of wooden nutmegs, from whose soil he hopes to rise, when called to enter upon the realities of the other world.

Each ought to be, and would be all the happier for the separation, if the Northern people could but divest themselves of their insane ambition to govern the South. They once possessed all they should have desired, and might easily have retained their hold, but in mere folly or wantonness, they madly threw away from them forever the golden possession, as a child breaks its toy and casts it at its feet. For long and weary years, they have absorbed the lion's share of the profits of slave labor, while denouncing the South to the world as barbarians for the sin of holding slaves. They have grown rich upon the spoils wrung from the South by means of protective tariffs, while taunting them with their poverty. They have denounced them to mankind as a hideous reproach to the enlightened age in which we live, while they have proclaimed themselves to be at the head of the advancing columns of progress and civilization. If they believe to be true the smallest fractional part of what they have said, and have a proper self-respect, they should hail the separation as a deliverance, instead of fighting to bring them back. It is too late. The deed is past recall. The South can brave any danger, look death in the face without fear, and accept with reasonable composure any destiny which Providence may order, except that of entering again into a political union with those whose unkindness and injustice towards them when they were at peace, have only been exceeded by their atrocities in war—a war which they wantonly commenced, not because they believed they had right, but upon a calculation by arithmetical rules that they were the strongest; not because they had any hope by such means to restore the departed Union upon the terms previously existing, but as a mere gratification to their pride and ambition, and as a concession to the insidious counsels of foreigners, whose only claim upon their confidence was a common sentiment of hostility to the South.*

* In a preceding note I referred to the attitude of the extreme abolition element of England, in regard to affairs in the United States, at a period when it seemed doubtful whether the North would attempt the subjugation of the seceded States. The extent of this influence

No! The chain of the old Union is broken, and the links are cast into a bottomless sea where no line can ever reach them.

---

in turning the scales in favor of war, cannot, of course, be estimated with accuracy, but Southerners, at that time in Europe, believed that it would be very great. This belief was strengthened by the fact that anti-slavery men in England were in constant correspondence with leading abolitionists in America, and they announced with confidence, that the North would neither compromise with the South, nor permit it to withdraw from the Union. The following extracts from private letters, received by me from highly intelligent sources, may not be without interest. The two first are from an Englishman, and the third from an Italian, resident for many years in England:

LONDON, March, 1861.

My Dear Sir:—I have been in London almost ever since I last saw you, which is now nearly five months ago. You remember that we discussed the probable influence of the then pending election for the Presidency of the United States. You and I, of course, differed in our estimate of the institution of slavery, for you were a Southerner and I an Englishman. But I little thought that your apprehensions of a collision at arms between the North and the South, was so near at hand as it now appears to be. Such a conflict would be a public calamity, but I am satisfied from what I see and hear, that there will be war. Europe does not even yet credit the possibility of such an event; but I am confident that nothing but the prompt submission of the South can avert it. Why? Look for an instant into the facts. The North has, in the election of the President, Mr. Lincoln, entered into a moral compact with the enemies of slavery every where, to root out that evil from the United States. The anti-slavery party proper of Europe do not know or care whether this result is to be accomplished in one year or fifty; in truth, the latter period would suit the views of England much better than the former. But it does not matter about time or circumstance; the North is pledged to the deed. The abolitionists of the Exeter Hall school reason this way. The secession of the slave States is the perpetuation of slavery for ever; a

As distinct nations the North and the South may, by respecting each other's rights, learn to appreciate each other's virtues—for both possess qualities

---

compromise to keep them in the Union, would give a new lease to slavery indefinite in duration.

These are facts, and be assured that they are being employed upon America, from this side of the water with a force which will be irresistible. The truth is, I cannot see how the North can, in the face of its implied pledges, do any thing else but resist both secession and compromise, if they have been right in that which they have already done. At any rate, I do not believe they can resist the taunts which will be thrown upon them from this side of the water, if they show a disposition to abandon in a single moment the fruits of twenty years of labor, at the very time, too, when they have every thing their own way. I wish there may not be war; but I have lost hope unless the South surrenders. . . . . .

Yours, truly, * * *

PARIS, March 20, 1861.

My Dear Sir:—I arrived here yesterday. . . . . . Be assured I was right in my conclusion that there would be war between the North and the South, although the impression seems to be gaining ground, that all will end in smoke. The anti-slavery leaders are divided in opinion as to the proper policy of the North; but they are agreed in one thing, that the South can be brought to terms by a display of determination, without mnch bloodshed, and the most rabid amongst them, are those who, by their activity, will be likely to have the greater influence on the other side of the water.

I confess that my sympathies run with the Southerners, although my prejudices are rather against slavery. It is clear to my mind that the leading spirits of the North only desire to keep you all for their own picking. . . . . . Don't neglect or disregard what I say, if you have any arrangements to make which would depend upon such a contingency. *Submission on your part, or war*, is before you. . . . . . I hope to see you in London on your return voyage to the dis-United States. . . . . .

Yours sincerely, * * *

worthy of admiration—to respect each other's strong convictions; to smile at each other's foibles, and to

---

LONDON, March 20, 1861.

My Dear Sir: . . . . Well, the die is cast and you are going to have a civil war. I have thought so from the moment it was announced that the anti-slavery party had chosen their President. In fact I may say that I have thought such would be the upshot of the abolition movement ever since my visit to America. I have myself suffered for liberty's sake, but I detest that maudlin sympathy for the African, which makes men forget that millions of their own race might be benefitted by their efforts if properly directed. But still you have to fight, and I cannot help but wish you success. They say in Europe that the war will prove the insufficiency of democratic institutions for a stable government—a most absurd assumption; for I cannot see how democracy or monarchy is effected by the question at issue. Now I will give you reasons why I say you will have war. First, the Northerners would be ashamed to admit to the world that they had no right under the Constitution to interfere with slavery. Second, the anti-slavery people everywhere would look with contempt upon the North if they were to allow the slave States to secede, and thus establish in permanancy the very thing which they have agreed to destroy. Thirdly, the general impression is, that the Southerners although quick to anger, have not the stamina to stand up against the cool courage of the Northmen, and that one action, short and sharp would decide the campaign. I was never further South than Washington, but I am convinced that this is a great mistake—however the mistake will cost you a war, or rather it will turn the scales in favor of war. Now, sir, write home and tell your Southern friends not to allow any more Fort Sumters to fall into the hands of those who in one month from to-day will be at war with them. Let me give you a little advice gained by experience. If you are going to make up an issue with an adversary, the first thing to do is to make yourself master of the position, and then negotiate. If you *can* take forts take them, and you can make a merit of giving them back if you make peace. In your case the guns of every fort in the South, which you leave in possession of the United States, will be loaded with shot and shell, and turned against you. . . .

Yours truly, * *

thank Heaven mentally, from the depths of their hearts, that they do not resemble each other! They could only be held together hereafter, under the same Government, by the bonds of a common despotism. No true lover of liberty can desire that such should be the fate of either. In order that nations should be free and happy, whether they be monarchical or democratic, there must be homogeneity amongst their respective subjects. Where this bond of union exists, they are almost always virtually free and contented, whatever may be the form of government under which they live. The world abuses Austria, composed of its dozen different nationalities, speaking as many different languages, for not conferring upon her subjects the rights, and privileges, and guarantees of the English Constitution; whereas, if they wish to establish their point, they should first condemn Austria for being an empire at all. There are periods in the history of weak nations, when it is better they should be held together by the ligaments of a common government, in order, by their joint strength, to be able to repel exernal enemies, and thus avoid falling victims, in detail, to an unscrupulous and ambitious foe—just as the North and the South have been united, during their infancy and weakness—a period which both have long since passed. But whenever, and only, when a country is united together by the bonds of a common sentiment, a common sympathy, a common interest, a common language, and a common history, the people may look forward, without apprehension, to a common destiny. If ambitious men should refuse to render, or, afterwards, should rob them of their liberties, the people have but to bide the proper time, and, if they are worthy to possess them, day by day, year by year, or generation by generation, they will recover, or take possession of them, as the English people have done; or they will seize upon them suddenly, as did our forefathers, and once more enter quietly and smoothly upon the fulfilment of their destiny.

It is not only not necessary that nations should be very great, or very powerful, in order to be free and happy; but it is always to be apprehended that the possession of great strength will create a disposition to employ it, by invading the liberty of others; which event is very naturally followed by the loss of their own. If a people is strong enough to offer a successful resistance against external enemies, even though they may not have the physical strength to make successful aggressions upon the liberties of others, they have all the force necessary to maintain a government which will secure their own happiness, and the respect of mankind.

Such is precisely the attitude occupied by the Confederate States of America at this very moment. Never yet, in the history of any other people, was there so glorious a prospect of a bright and a happy and a great future. The mind becomes dazzled by a contemplation of the magnificent domain which is all our own. We could receive half of Europe into our embraces, and have more to spare. We have a productive soil, and strong hands and arms to work it. We have the Government of our choice, and stout and willing hearts to maintain it; and, with the approval of Heaven, we will maintain it at all hazards, and at whatever cost of blood, or treasure, or present comfort. The property and the lives of our citizens have been offered up upon the altar of their country, as freely as they would bestow a draft of cold water from the sparkling fountain upon the thirsty traveller on the way-side. If they do not themselves live to enjoy the ripe fruits of their labors, they know that they will live forever in the hearts of a grateful posterity; and whatever may be now the public sentiment of their fellow-men, who have been misled by the misrepresentations of their enemies, as sure as the sun shines, mankind will one day do justice to their motives and applaud their deeds.

In this connection may be noted one of the agreeable results which will immediately follow the complete establishment of the Confederate States Government. There exists among the people of all civilized nations a very natural desire to secure the respect of their fellow-men. The South has hitherto, from her unfortunate political associations, been constantly and grossly misrepresented by those who professed to be fellow-countrymen. Whatever prejudices may have been excited abroad against the people or the Government of the United States, whatever insult offered by the Northern press which foreigners might wish to resent, they had the ever present retort of the horrors of American slavery, as reported by those who were themselves American citizens. Thus has the South been a target for the shafts of the world, without having any means of defence. So in regard to suggested aggressions upon the territory of our neighbors. Cuba—rich, fertile, ever-blooming Cuba—was spread out invitingly before our eyes. Northern cupidity would have clutched the tempting prize, and the South would have taken in the bait of an augmentation of its political power, if Spain could have been induced to sell. But there was no Southerner of intelligence so blind as not to perceive that the acquisition, however valuable to the North, would have resulted in a heavy pecuniary loss to the South, because we could not have competed with her successfully in productions common to both. The South, like a drowning man, was willing to grasp at any straw, which would, by adding to her political power in the Government, have enabled her to make a few more feeble struggles to maintain herself against that storm of sectionalism and fanaticism by which she was at last overtaken; but it was well known that the only beneficiary would be the North.

These causes of irritation to European powers, have all been charged as the "aggressions of the slave power;" whereas, if the Southern States had been left to themselves, and had been free from constraint, while they would have been perfectly indifferent to any acquisitions which Spain might choose to make among the barbarous inhabitants of the American islands, who have shown their utter incapacity to govern themselves, the Island of Cuba, however desirable as an acquisition of political power, would have been one of the last possessions they would have coveted. Now, that we are and will remain free, sovereign, and independent upon our own soil, each of us will be judged by mankind by our own acts, and not by the interested and malicious representations of the other. The world will be surprised to find how egregiously it has been misled in regard to the characteristics and qualities of the people of the South.

Nevertheless, in the prosecution of the war in which the people of the South are now engaged, however gratifying it might be to have the sympathies of good men everywhere, we neither seek, nor desire, nor expect any foreign aid from any quarter of the globe. If we cannot win our own liberties by our own unaided efforts, we could not maintain them if they were bestowed upon us as a free gift. If other nations choose to recognize our just claim to independence, we will give them the right hand of friendship; but we do not desire them to fight our battles. If they should think proper to withhold that recognition, it will not occasion us the loss of a man nor a single element of success which we now hold, and we will prove to them by the result that we are capable of maintaining ourselves, single-handed and alone, now and in all time against all our enemies.*

No people have ever had more unmistakable evidences that they were guided and directed by an overruling Providence, which smiled upon their undertaking, than have the people of the South since the commencement of their great struggle. To crown all, we have been blessed with the most bountiful crops that have ever before been garnered in recompense for the toils of the husbandman. While our free citizens have shouldered their muskets and have gone forth to fight the battles of their country, the African is contentedly working in the fields. Our usual crops of cotton, and tobacco, and rice will be ready in due time for any purchaser who will come and take them, or who will bring to us in exchange the manufactures which we require. If none are so bold as thus to dare the frowns of the North, we can readily convert our

*The great powers of Europe are already committed to the recognition of the Southern Confederacy by their action in regard to the secession of Belgium from the mild and beneficent Government of the Netherlands. In this case, the principle that a nation had an undeniable right to create, and live under a government which they believed would promote their own happiness and interests, was conceded by all Europe, and Belgium was permitted to withdraw from Holland by the very same Great Powers which united them together, on the ground of a political European necessity. One of the most distinguished and able diplomatists of Holland stated to me that the party which had been most opposed to the severance of the kingdom, was now fully satisfied that the separation was an act of wisdom, and had undeniably added to the prosperity of both, while no European interest had thereby suffered detriment.

cotton plantations into grain fields, and divert a portion of the labor hitherto employed in planting, to the development of our great manufacturing resources. Under the stimulant of a present necessity, we can produce every thing within ourselves, which is important to our happiness, our daily wants, and even our luxuries. When the war is over all things will flow back into their old channel, or continue in the direction which they shall have received under the impulse of necessity.

The freemen of the South have entered upon their great struggle with a unity of feeling and purpose, which has struck terror into the hearts of their enemies, and amazed even their friends; but their glorious work is not yet finished. The clouds are over our heads, my fellow-countrymen, and the storm is still raging around us, and many a heart may yet mourn the loss of dear ones, and many a tear of bitter anguish may fall, as the eye wanders over the desolated track of the ruthless invader; but behind the clouds we can see the dawning of the bright and glorious sunlight, and above the roarings of the storm of battle we can hear the glad shouts of victory! And our soldiers will come back again to make joyous the homes which have been made solitary by their absence, and the tears of grief will be changed to tokens of rejoicings, and throughout our borders will ring forth the joyous cry of the people, "WE HAVE FOUGHT, WE HAVE CONQUERED, WE ARE FREE."

www.ingramcontent.com/pod-product-compliance
Lightning Source LLC
LaVergne TN
LVHW020221110826
845151LV00003B/785

* 9 7 8 1 4 2 5 5 3 2 0 0 0 *